Medium or Message?
Language and Faith in Ethnic Churches

LINGUISTIC DIVERSITY AND LANGUAGE RIGHTS
Series Editor: Dr Tove Skutnabb-Kangas, *Roskilde University, Denmark*

Consulting Advisory Board
Josef Attila, Szeged University, Hungary
François Grin, *Université de Genève, Switzerland*
Kathleen Heugh, *University of Cape Town, South Africa*
Miklós Kontra, *Linguistics Institute, Hungarian Academy of Sciences, Budapest*
Masaki Oda, *Tamagawa University, Japan*

The series seeks to promote multilingualism as a resource, the maintenance of linguistic diversity, and development of and respect for linguistic human rights worldwide through the dissemination of theoretical and empirical research. The series encourages interdisciplinary approaches to language policy, drawing on sociolinguistics, education, sociology, economics, human rights law, political science, as well as anthropology, psychology and applied language studies.

Other Books of Interest
Beyond Boundaries: Language and Identity in Contemporary Europe
  Paul Gubbins and Mike Holt (eds)
Bilingualism: Beyond Basic Principles
  Jean-Marc Dewaele, Alex Housen and Li Wei (eds)
Can Threatened Languages be Saved?
  Joshua Fishman (ed.)
English in Africa: After the Cold War
  Alamin M. Mazrui
Identity, Insecurity and Image: France and Language
  Dennis Ager
Ideology and Image: Britain and Language
  Dennis Ager
Language and Society in a Changing Italy
  Tosi
Language Attitudes in Sub-Saharan Africa
  Efurosibina Adegbija
Language, Ethnicity and Education
  Peter Broeder and Guus Extra
Linguistic Minorities in Central and Eastern Europe
  Christina Bratt Paulston and Donald Peckham (eds)
Motivation in Language Planning and Language Policy
  Dennis Ager
Negotiating of Identities in Multilingual Contexts
  Aneta Pavlenko and Adrian Blackledge (eds)
The Other Languages of Europe
  Guus Extra and Durk Gorter (eds)
Where East Looks West: Success in English in Goa and on the Konkan Coast
  Dennis Kurzon
Understanding Deaf Culture: In Search of Deafhood
  Paddy Ladd

Please contact us for the latest book information:
Multilingual Matters, Frankfurt Lodge, Clevedon Hall,
Victoria Road, Clevedon, BS21 7HH, England
http://www.multilingual-matters.com

LANGUAGE DIVERSITY AND LANGUAGE RIGHTS 1
Series Editor: Tove Skutnabb-Kangas, *Roskilde University, Denmark*

Medium or Message?
Language and Faith in Ethnic Churches

Anya Woods

MULTILINGUAL MATTERS LTD
Clevedon • Buffalo • Toronto • Sydney

Library of Congress Cataloging in Publication Data
Woods, Anya
Medium or Message? Language and Faith in Ethnic Churches/Anya Woods, 1st ed.
Linguistic Diversity and Language Rights: 1
Includes bibliographical references and index.
1. Linguistic minorities–Religious life–Australia–Melbourne (Vic.). 2. Melbourne
(Vic.)–Languages–Religious aspects–Christianity. 3. Immigrants–Religious
life–Australia–Melbourne (Vic.) 4. Language and languages–Religious
aspects–Christianity. 5. Melbourne (Vic.)–Church history. I. Title. II. Series.
BR1485.M4W66 2004
279.45'1083–dc22   2003024052

British Library Cataloguing in Publication Data
A catalogue entry for this book is available from the British Library.

ISBN 1-85359-723-6 (hbk)
ISBN 1-85359-736-8 (pbk)

Multilingual Matters Ltd
UK: Frankfurt Lodge, Clevedon Hall, Victoria Road, Clevedon BS21 7HH.
USA: UTP, 2250 Military Road, Tonawanda, NY 14150, USA.
Canada: UTP, 5201 Dufferin Street, North York, Ontario M3H 5T8, Canada.
Australia: Footprint Books, PO Box 418, Church Point, NSW 2103, Australia.

Typeset by Archetype-IT Ltd (http://www.archetype-it.com).
Printed and bound in Great Britain by the Cromwell Press Ltd.

Contents

List of Tables and Figures

List of Tables

List of Figures

Series Editor's Foreword

This is the first book in the series *Linguistic Diversity and Language Rights*. The series seeks to promote multilingualism as a resource, the maintenance of linguistic diversity and the development of and respect for linguistic human rights worldwide through the dissemination of theoretical and empirical research (see aims and scope of the series). *Medium or Message?* by Anya Woods touches on most of the aims in the series in discussing a topic that very few sociolinguists have approached: the relationship between language and religion in a situation where people have left their countries of origin. Does the maintenance of one presuppose and/or support the maintenance of the other? Or do you have to choose to maintain one at the expense of the other? Do you have to sacrifice the old language in order to maintain the young generation within the church? Or is there no relationship? Can you be (your type of) Christian equally well in English as in Latvian? As Anya Woods shows, there are almost as many answers to these questions as there are denominations and people in her study. The importance of the work is that some of the questions are being asked and the complexity of the issues highlighted.

All the denominations described in the book are Christian. Still, the diversity of both the many variants of Christianity and the languages, cultures and ethnicities of the various congregations represent more linguistic, cultural and religious diversity than what many Christians themselves in many countries might imagine when they envisage for themselves what Christianity 'is'.

Many other great religions have one (main) sacred language only, Sanskrit for Hinduism, Hebrew for Judaism and Arabic for Islam. In addition to the religion itself, the sacred language may in some ways unite many of the believers, regardless of which languages they use in their everyday life. This is certainly true for Muslims. It may also be easier to maintain the language of worship in the diaspora if it is the same all over the world. By contrast, Christianity does not have a sacred language. The message(s) can come through the medium of many languages, as this book shows. Does this mean that it is the content that is the most important issue in

Christianity (as well as in other religions?)? Does it mean that the language in which the Christian content comes is of no or only minor importance? Or is the medium part of the message, also for Christians? Or are Christians less prone than, for instance, Muslims, to maintain the language of their faith? Do they assimilate linguistically more easily than others? If they do – and there is some evidence to support this hypothesis – can we assume that it might be more difficult for Christians to understand the importance of other peoples' languages for these people? Are languages more, or less, often cultural core values for Christians than for people from other faith communities? And is religion less or more often a cultural core value for them than for people from religions with one main sacred language only? We have no answers for these questions yet and even the way they are asked here oversimplifies them – consciously.

What we know, though, is that there seems to be more interest today than a decade or two ago in the big questions that various faiths try to answer, each in their own ways. The uncertainties created by corporate globalisation and the concomitant speed of change force people to look into other sources of trust. The role of language in creating and maintaining the old sources at the same time as these are renewed is a vital issue for the maintenance or killing of other types of diversities too. *Medium or Message?* asks questions of global importance.

Tove Skutnabb-Kangas

Preface

Medium or Message? constitutes, in my estimation, a very significant contribution to the study of language and religion in a multicultural context, for
Anya Woods shows that relation to be two-way. Not only is religion an
important factor in the maintenance of minority languages. Not only do the
intertwining of language and religion of cultural core values provide a
context and an ideological motivation for language maintenance. Language
also plays a dynamic role in ethnic churches, both as a unifier and a divider.
It can facilitate the message or obscure and alienate people from it.
Moreover, not only do the ethnic cultures have their core values, which
may include language and religion. Different religious groups have
language–religion ideologies, determined by their theological orientation,
with a weaker or stronger link between language and religion and a more
intimate everyday language or a special language for communication with
God. Demonstrating this is Anya Woods's greatest contribution to the
field. Anya carefully documents the language–religion ideology and the
language situation in 16 ethnic churches across seven Christian denominations in the multicultural/multilingual city of Melbourne through
interviews with clergy and questionnaires with parishioners, with qualitative data from two in-depth studies, of an older established European
Lutheran group and a recently arrived Asian Uniting Church group. The
studies are preceded with concise background on the history of each
denomination and migrant group in Australia. Worship style, purism in
language and practical strategies for bilingual worship and communication across generations are discussed.

This vividly written monograph will excite the sociolinguist and the
sociologist of religion, fascinate the general lay-reader and provoke the
cleric.

Michael Clyne

Acknowledgements

My thanks are due, first, and foremost to the 16 members of clergy who so kindly participated in the research upon which this book is based and to the members of the two case-study churches who were also willing to be involved. It is with the warmest sincerity that I offer my gratitude to them for their preparedness to share their experiences with me.

Numerous others provided me with expertise and new perspectives as the research was being conducted: Gary Bouma, Robert Gribben, Joshua Fishman, Heather Bowe, Jim Houston, Steve Rhodes, Edgars Petrevics and Christos Galiotos each deserve thanks for sharing valuable insights at various stages. My thanks also go to George Smolicz, Penny Jamieson, Tope Omoniyi and Kathleen Heugh for their constructive comments and for providing me with the benefit of a breadth of experience and understanding. I am grateful to Philip Hughes and Sandra Kipp for their expert assistance with census data; and to E. Aminudin Aziz, my grandfather Valdemars Krauja and my mother Ingrid Lloyd-Smith, who each served as invaluable translation assistants. For important sources of encouragement and laughter, I thank my husband Tim and my daughter Emily.

I am indebted to Michael Clyne for his sustained provision of expertise, advice and inspiration. My thanks also go to Tove Skutnabb-Kangas for detailed and helpful comments, for her vision in heading up this series on Linguistic Diversity and Language Rights and being so keen for this work to be a part of it. It is indeed exciting that this is the first to appear in this series with Multilingual Matters – my thanks go particularly to Mike Grover and to Marjukka Grover for their enthusiasm for this project.

> After this I looked and there before me was a great multitude
> that no one could count, from every nation, tribe, people and language,
> standing before the throne and in front of the Lamb. (Revelation 7:9)

Chapter 1
Establishing the Context of the Study

Introduction

The processes of immigration and refugee resettlement have brought to Australia a great diversity of peoples and with them many cultures, languages and faiths. Figures from the 2001 Census revealed that of the 68% of Australians who identify with the Christian religion (12.7 million), 1,746,452 – or 13.7% – speak a language other than English at home; thus a significant percentage of the population are likely to experience first hand the tensions that may exist where culture, language and faith intersect.

Many of these tensions are the result of having to find a place both within the Australian *social* culture as well as the Australian *religious* culture when these facets of the migrant's life are firmly bound in the experience of life beyond Australian shores. Whether the Christian migrant adopted the faith in Australia or in the home country, there lies the inevitable question of how this faith may be lived out in the Australian cultural context.

While the nature of the cultures from which migrants come varies enormously, so too do the circumstances under which they leave their homes to seek a new life. Many leave war-torn lands where lives were constantly at risk, where persecution was a daily reality, where freedoms were few and where escape was a dangerous and heart-wrenching ordeal. In fleeing, many leave behind not only their homes and belongings but family members and friends. There are many, too, who come without these acute pressures but for whom the prospect of life in a new country still holds great promise.

There are those for whom life has always been lived as a member of a minority group, with the associated struggles being all too familiar. In this process, some develop a degree of resilience and determination to preserve and maintain their culture at all costs. Similarly, the struggle may be for religious maintenance, where the individual may be part of the cultural and social majority but the religious minority.

The place of language in all of these scenarios differs accordingly. Many

1

people come from bilingual and multilingual societies where different languages play different roles in the varying domains of life – such as work, school, home and religion – and where multilingualism is the norm and not the exception. Australia is extolled as a 'multicultural' society but the degree of multilingualism that it allows for is, in some senses, limited. Those from non-English-speaking backgrounds who come as monolinguals soon find that English is the language expected in almost every public domain. Under such circumstances English often extends to become the norm in the private domain as well.

While the religious expression of the Christian involves corporate worship and fellowship, part of the uniqueness of Christianity lies in the belief that one can enjoy a personal relationship with God, with 'one-on-one' communication. A Christian's language resources for use in the religious domain are, therefore, great because God is perceived as most Holy and most intimate all at once. The variety of language or languages a Christian uses in religious expression is a reflection of this and often of which aspect of the relationship the Christian feels is to be emphasised. In general terms, some may choose to use as a mark of veneration a language or variety of language which they deem to have a higher status and, in doing so, accord God the highest possible status. In contrast, a more colloquial type of language may be used – the variety used with close friends and family – as an expression of the intimacy of this relationship with God. And, of course, the Christian community, made up of a number of individuals each in relationship with God, reflects these language choices on a macro scale.

In the present work, the language needs, habits and preferences of Christian migrants will be explored as they are realised in 16 ethnic congregations in Melbourne, in order to move towards a more thoroughly documented response to the question of *what is the role of language in ethnic churches?*

The congregations involved in this study were selected for their ability to represent the heterogeneity of migrant communities in Melbourne. While some congregations were chosen because their members were part of the largest and most influential ethnic communities in Melbourne (such as Greek and Italian), others were chosen because of their relative 'obscurity' in Melbourne's cultural landscape (Oromo, for example). Importantly, they each represent different periods of Australia's migration history, as well as different languages, cultural backgrounds and religious orientations.

In some cases, the congregation chosen is both part of the ethnic community most commonly associated with a particular denomination *and* part of the denomination most commonly associated with their culture (such as Greeks in the Orthodox Church). In other cases, the congregation chosen may be part of a denomination which is not the dominant Christian grouping of their culture (such as Arabic speakers in the Baptist Church, when the majority of Arabic-speaking Christians are members of the Maronite, Melkite and Orthodox Churches).

In selecting the congregations for this study, it was determined that they should be members of, or closely affiliated with, the larger 'mainstream' denominations, i.e. not members of independent, unaffiliated churches. This was largely done to facilitate the collection of supporting material and to enable comparison between the experiences of different ethnic groups within the same denomination.

The 16 congregations which are the focus of this research are, therefore, from the Anglican Church of Australia – Chinese (Hakka) and Persian; from the Baptist Church – Arabic and Spanish; from the Lutheran Church of Australia – German, Latvian and Slovak; from the Reformed Churches of Australia – English (of Dutch heritage) and Chinese (Mandarin); from the Uniting Church in Australia – Indonesian, Oromo and Tamil; from the Catholic Church – Croatian and Italian; and from the Orthodox Church – Greek and Russian.

Two of these congregations – the Latvian Lutheran and the Indonesian Uniting – form case studies, enabling this research to illuminate the experiences of ethnic churches at both the macro and micro level.

The research is presented in four main sections. In order to establish the *context of the study*, a review of literature on multiculturalism and the Christian Church, relevant theories of language maintenance and a discussion of the role of language in the religious domain are provided in the remainder of the present chapter. This is further enhanced by a discussion of Australia's migration history and the Christian denominations which were brought with, developed by or integrated into the particular ethnic communities which form part of this research.

In Chapter 2 the *notion of language–religion ideology* is introduced and discussed as it applies to the denominations in this research.

The *findings of this research* are presented in Chapters 3–6. In the first of these chapters, the findings for the congregations are presented at a macro level. The diversity of experience of ethnic churches in Melbourne is then brought to life by descriptions of the two case studies in Chapters 4 and 5. In Chapter 6, results from all congregations are compared and discussed.

The final section of this study (Chapter 7) looks at various models of ethnic churches which have been proposed by other researchers and presents a *revised model* of language attitudes and practices which incorporates the notion of language–religion ideology. Conclusions are made and implications are discussed for ethnic churches and the denominations of which they are a part. Applications of this research to ethnic churches in other parts of the world are suggested, together with directions for further research.

As a major comparative study in a relatively under-researched field, it is hoped that the findings will add significantly to the understanding of community languages in the context of religious expression and might go some way towards clarifying the present state of and future directions for the vast number and variety of ethnic churches.

A note on terminology

The term 'community language' (CL) – rather than 'minority', 'foreign', 'migrant' or 'ethnic' language – has become the accepted term for a language other than English or an Aboriginal language which is present in Australian society (see discussion in Clyne 1991: 3) and is thus used throughout this work. It is similar to the Canadian term 'heritage language' in that it encompasses the fact that these languages are present as a result of immigration but are not merely used by first-generation immigrants. The term 'minority language', whilst acknowledging the place of these languages vis-à-vis a 'majority language', ignores the use of these languages by other ethnic groups within the community.

The term 'ethnic church' is widely used in Australia to refer to a church which is associated with a particular (minority) ethnic community: it may or may not use the community language. Ethnic churches are thus defined more on the basis of cultural affiliation than simply by the particular language used. Whilst acknowledging that 'ethnic' used in this sense is problematic in that it implies the existence of 'non-ethnic' churches (as if those of English-speaking background are ethnically 'neutral'), a more suitable term is not obvious. Other terms are occasionally found in use by individual churches, such as 'NESB (non-English-speaking background) congregation'; however, this is not widespread. It also does not take into account the fact that many of the members of the congregation may be second and third generation and may have English as a first language.

As a general rule, the term 'congregation' is used rather than 'church' to refer to specific groups involved in the research: some congregations were the sole occupants of their church building and could, therefore, be called a 'church', while other congregations shared church facilities and considered themselves one of many congregations making up a church. The terms are, to an extent, interchangeable.

Theoretical Framework

The body of literature on multiculturalism and the Christian Church, together with theories of language maintenance and the role of language in the religious domain, will be reviewed in order to establish the context of this research.

Multiculturalism and the Christian Church

Australian multiculturalism has been explored primarily through the fields of anthropology, sociology, sociolinguistics, education, history and politics but the literature concerning the relationship between religion and Australia's multicultural reality is still scanty.

In a Federal Government document entitled the *National Agenda for a Multicultural Australia: Sharing our Future* (1989: iv), the term 'multiculturalism' is defined in a number of statements:

In a descriptive sense 'multicultural' is simply a term which describes the cultural and ethnic diversity of contemporary Australia. We are, and will remain, a multicultural society.

As a public policy, multiculturalism encompasses government measures designed to respond to that diversity. It plays no part in migrant selection. It is a policy for managing the consequences of cultural diversity in the interests of the individual and society as a whole.

The Commonwealth Government has identified three dimensions of multicultural policy:

- cultural identity: the right of all Australians, within carefully defined limits, to express and share their individual cultural heritage, including their language and religion;
- social justice: the right of all Australians to equality of treatment and opportunity, and the removal of barriers of race, ethnicity, culture, religion, language, gender or place of birth; and
- economic efficiency: the need to maintain, develop and utilise effectively the skills and talents of all Australians, regardless of background.

These dimensions of policy are also based upon the premise that:

- all Australians should have an overriding and unifying commitment to Australia, to its interests and future first and foremost;
- all Australians are required to accept the basic structures of and principles of Australian society – the Constitution and the rule of law, tolerance and equality, Parliamentary democracy, freedom of speech and religion, English as the national language and equality of the sexes; and
- the right to express one's own culture and beliefs involves a reciprocal responsibility to accept the right of others to express their views and values.

Recent updates to this (Federal Government of Australia, 1999a, b) take multi-culturalism in a different direction, emphasising that refugees and migrants have as many obligations as rights and calling attention to the need to maximise the economic benefits of multiculturalism.

English is still the language used in most Australian churches but the need to embrace variety in the Church is being called for more strongly today than ever before. The former Primate of the Anglican Church of Australia, the Reverend Dr Keith Rayner, called for the Anglican Church to 'face the challenge of becoming less English and more Australian' (Anglican General Synod Multicultural Committee, 1996). While this challenge is directed towards the most Anglo-centric of Australian churches, it needs to be addressed by all Christian churches in responding appropriately to Australian society.

However, as Houston (1986: xv) points out, 'multiculturalism is far more than mere tolerance, or simply living side by side competing for the same limited resources. It is neither the old American melting pot, nor a series of monocultural ghettos. Christians need to be clear why multiculturalism is superior to these historic options . . . '.

Likewise, Conn, in his introduction to Ortiz's book *One New People: Models for Developing a Multiethnic Church* (1996: 10–11), writes:

> multiculturalism in the church is not a quick fix marked by simple tolerance for one another or by some idealistic retreat into politically correct language. Repentance for racism or ethnocentrism requires intolerance for sin; changed language is a reflection of transforming grace displayed in more than only a courtroom or public arena. Opening the doors of a church or a theological seminary to embrace cultural diversity will not be accomplished by ecclesiastical busing. It is a struggle to live out truth and justice and compassion as a fellow member of the body of Christ.

Clearly, multiculturalism in the Australian Church is a great challenge, not because it goes against the tenets of the Christian faith – in fact, exactly the opposite – but because of the ethno-centric and essentially monocultural walls which the Christian Church in Australia has, in the past, built around itself.

As *A Garden of Many Colours: The Report of the Archbishop's Commission on Multicultural Ministry and Mission* (Anglican Diocese of Melbourne, 1985:35) states:

> one may say that the central Christian doctrine of God, the Trinity, itself enshrines the principle behind true multiculturalism: unity in diversity, diversity in unity. Each 'Person' of the Trinity presents God genuinely to us, yet does not exhaust all that God is. In a similar

manner, even though in a manner finite and flawed, each culture presents an authentic humanity but does not contain all that is human. Again, the members of the Triune Godhead each have their own identity in their inter-relationships, but are entirely open to each other. Likewise, the fullness of being human includes both a security in one's own identity and an openness to others. True multiculturalism has the best credentials.

If the Church is to be multicultural, there are implications for what this means in the daily practice of faith. For when it comes to the working out of how migrant Christians are to worship in the Australian context, the issues are many, the responses as varied as the groups themselves. These responses typically fall between two extremes – with Christians gathering in isolated, homeland-looking churches of the community group on the one hand, or, on the other, assimilating into a sea of largely English-speaking Christians in the mainstream Anglo-centric churches.

Finding the place between these two extremes from which a community will seek to develop its religious identity is not an easy task. As Ortiz (1996: 37) points out:

> there is one set of cross-cultural dynamics that is operative when bringing together various groups that all speak English [or any other language]. There is a different set of dynamics working when numerous languages are represented. Within these sets of differences we also find cross-generational differences, first generation immigrants being much more protective of the traditions and customs of their homeland.

Ortiz's statement hints at some of the issues which become a reality when multiculturalism meets the Church and the difficulty ethnic churches have in balancing priorities: among the many issues faced is the question of whether getting the message across is more or less important than being a vehicle for cultural and language maintenance.

Language, religion and core value theory

Previous research examining the role of the Saturday School[1] in Latvian language maintenance in Melbourne (Lloyd-Smith, 1996; Woods, 1999) found that the Latvian language is considered most vital for the survival of the Latvian community in Australia, thereby making it a 'core value' of the culture, to use terminology first devised by Smolicz (1981). If the community's survival depends on the sustained existence of the language, the language's survival depends, in turn, on the existence of domains in which it may be used. Apart from the Saturday School, the Church is perhaps the most influential public domain for ethnic communities.

The term 'core value' is used by Smolicz to refer to 'those values that are regarded as forming the most fundamental components or heartland of a group's culture' and which 'act as identifying values which are symbolic of the group and its membership' (Smolicz & Secombe, 1985: 11; see also Smolicz, 1981). Smolicz's core value theory further postulates that community members who reject these values are endangering their group membership and that unanimous rejection will result ultimately in its 'dis-integration as a community that can perpetuate itself as an authentic entity across generations' (Smolicz & Secombe, 1989: 479).

Smolicz argues that groups who are language-centred, i.e. those for whom language is a core value, are more likely to maintain their language in minority situations. Smolicz and Lean (1979: 235) suggest that there is

> a basic division . . . between language-centred cultures, that is to say cultures for which the native tongue constitutes a core value, and other cultures, which are based upon family, religion or some other ideals, be they political, historical or structural (Smolicz, 1976). The majority of European cultures appear to be language-centred and here we single out for example, Polish, French and Greek cultures. In these cultures language has become equated with affiliation to the group. Such close ties between ethnicity and language can have various origins and in the Polish case, these are partly historical and relate to the persecution of the language during most of the nineteenth century by the occupying powers, which pursued the policy of enforced cultural assimilation.

Over the years, Smolicz and others have carried out research within different ethnic communities in order to determine their 'core values'. The Dutch language has not been shown to be a core value of the Dutch culture, hence providing an explanation for the high rate of language shift within the Dutch community. Studies conducted in the Latvian and Greek communities (Smolicz & Secombe 1985: 11–38), the Croatian community (Smolicz & Secombe, 1989: 478–511) and the Chinese and Tamil communities (Smolicz *et al.*, 1990: 229–46) have found all but the latter to consider its respective mother tongue as a core value. In fact, amongst the Tamil community, the Tamil language is considered a vital aspect of the culture only by those who are also devout Hindus. One Christian participant in this particular study commented:

> Language is important for culture, but is does not bother me as I am a Christian who lives according to what is said in the Bible. The religious

differences between Hinduism and Christianity are quite marked. My Christian values therefore separate me from the Indian culture because the culture is part and parcel of the religion. The fact that I do not know my ethnic language does not affect me personally and I am not affected by it as the language serves an insignificant function when you do not identify with the various Hindu traditions and social customs. (Smolicz *et al.*, 1990: 39)

The difference found between the core values of Tamil Christians and Tamil Hindus points to some difficulties which have been raised concerning Smolicz's theory: multiple group membership and problems in group definition (see Clyne, 1991; Kipp *et al.*, 1995). As mentioned earlier, ethnic churches are associated with the use of a particular language other than English which is common to the majority of those who attend. But where this language is a pluricentric language, such as German or Spanish, the situation is more complex. For example, speakers of Spanish may come from any number of countries – European, African or Latin American – where it is an official language. On the one hand, Spanish speakers are members of the same speech community at a global level, and on the other hand, they have different cultural experiences and expectations conditioned not only by their country of birth but in addition by their political and religious affiliations, their migration vintage and a host of other associated factors. As a community within Australia, therefore, Spanish-speakers do not have a single, definable 'Spanish' ethnicity: while members of such a speech community are united under the 'umbrella' of their church, 'they cannot and do not have a single cultural value system' (Kipp *et al.*, 1995: 129).

The issue of multiple group membership follows on from this: a speaker of Spanish in Australia identifies not just with the Spanish-speaking community but with subgroups within it (for example, identifying not just with the Latin American community but specifically with the Chilean community). Furthermore, members of ethnic churches not only contend with cultural and language community membership, but membership of a denomination and a religion at local, national and international levels. A Spanish speaker born in Chile who is Catholic thus identifies not just with other Chile-born Catholics but with Catholics worldwide. These overlapping ethnic and religious identities can result in competing loyalties, with implications for both language maintenance and language shift on an individual and community level, thus helping to explain why some ethnic communities tend towards greater community language use in their churches than others.

Before proceeding with an exposition of the relationship between

Table 1.1 Home-language use (2001 Census)

	CL use in the home, total Melbourne	*CL use in the home, total Australia*	*City with largest concentration of CL speakers*
Arabic (incl. Lebanese)	45,736	209,388	Sydney (Melbourne second)
Chinese (Hakka)	4,438	7,451	Melbourne
Chinese (Mandarin)	37,994	139,288	Sydney (Melbourne second)
Chinese (nfd)	4,321	14,561	Sydney (Melbourne second)
Croatian	21,690	69,850	Melbourne
Dutch	7,705	40,187	Melbourne
German	16,357	76,444	Melbourne
Greek	118,755	263,718	Melbourne
Indonesian	8,713	38,724	Sydney (Melbourne second)
Italian	134,657	353,606	Melbourne
Latvian	1,624	5,353	Melbourne
Oromo	465	545	Melbourne
Persian	5,725	25,237	Sydney (Melbourne second)
Russian	13,406	34,790	Melbourne
Slovak	1,664	4,695	Melbourne
Spanish	21,852	93,595	Sydney (Melbourne second)
Tamil	7,765	24,076	Sydney (Melbourne second)

language and religion, it is necessary to look at the actual maintenance of community languages specific to the present research.

The numbers of community language speakers according to the 2001 census are listed in Table 1.1. Although Mandarin and Hakka are the two Chinese varieties relevant to this research, figures for 'Chinese' are also provided with the recognition that some speakers did not differentiate between varieties when completing the census.

Information from the Australian censuses concerning the maintenance and shift of community languages in Australia is gleaned from answers to the question 'Does the person speak a language other than English at home?' (in which respondents are asked to give the name of the language). Language shift is calculated as the proportion of people born in a particular country who currently speak only English at home and therefore, birth-place – rather than language – is the starting point. Table 1.2 gives rates of

Table 1.2 Language shift in the first generation, (2001 Census)

Birthplace	Percentage using only English at home
Iraq	3.6
Taiwan	3.8
China (excluding Special Administrative Regions and Taiwan Province)	4.3
Lebanon	6.2
Greece	7.1
Hong Kong (SAR of China)	10.3
Chile	12.2
Russian Federation	13.3
Ethiopia	14.9
Italy	15.9
Indonesia	16.4
Other South America	18.4
Egypt	21.7
Spain	25.1
Malaysia	35.9
Latvia	38.2
Sri Lanka	40.4
Switzerland	44.6
India	47.6
Singapore	48.9
Germany	54.0
Austria	54.4
The Netherlands	62.6

language shift for those born in countries where the community languages involved in the present research are spoken. Because many of these community languages are pluricentric languages, multiple birthplaces are given. Data for Persian, Slovak and Croatian were unavailable.

As Table 1.2 illustrates, language shift rates may be difficult to calculate for pluricentric languages. For example, Chile-born Spanish speakers shift to English less than the Spain-born (see also Clyne & Kipp, 1999: 400); thus, it is difficult to generalise for 'Spanish' as a whole. Language shift may also

Table 1.3 Language-shift categories

Low language shift	Greek, Arabic, Chinese, (Persian?)
Medium language shift	Spanish, Russian, Oromo, Italian, Indonesian, (Croatian?, Slovak?)
Higher language shift	Latvian, Tamil, German
Very high language shift	Dutch

be hard to determine for a language which is only one of a number spoken in the home country, as is the case for Egypt.

In the light of such difficulties, the value of predictive theories of language maintenance is clear. Clyne and Kipp (1997: 459) refer to the significance of cultural distance in determining language maintenance:

> Those from predominantly Islamic or Eastern Orthodox cultures (Greek, Lebanese, Macedonian, Turkish) are more likely to maintain their languages at home than other groups from Europe. Groups from northern, central and western Europe tend to shift to English the most. Those from Asian countries, especially Chinese-speaking ones, tend to display a low or fairly low language shift.

Acknowledging these facts, the community languages featuring in this research may be broadly categorised according to the degree to which they are maintained. Without accurate census data, it is impossible to more than tentatively categorise Slovak and Croatian as medium-shift languages and Persian as a slightly lower shift.

As Table 1.3 shows, Arabic, Chinese and Greek are low-shift languages. At the other extreme is Dutch, whose speakers typically shift to English rapidly. German also experiences a high rate of shift, as does Tamil and, to a lesser extent, Latvian. All other languages experience moderate shift.

Language in the religious domain

There is no doubt that language can be indissolubly linked to religious expression. Boyd (1985: 163) sums up the potential strength of the relationship between language and religion by the following description:

> Decisions by church authorities to change the language used for religious activities have often been met by strong reactions on the part of the believers. Some prefer to leave the church rather than change the language they have been accustomed to use there, even though church officials motivate the change in terms of the members' lack of skill in the religious language. Even if the language is not established by

dogma as sacred, it takes on a sacred value by being used for many years in religious contexts. Usually, this sacred value is not shared by any other language or variety of language for the believer.

Language can indeed take on a distinct spiritual dimension. Hebrew, Greek and Arabic, as the language of sacred scriptures, have taken on particularly 'sacred' value for Jews, Christians and Muslims (Fishman, 1991: 360). Clyne and Kipp (1999: 328–9) point out that this sacred character is extended to the colloquial variety, as well as the ecclesiastical variety, firmly fixing the language as the only authentic one to use for religious expression.

Research – such as that by Katsikis (1993: 50–3) – illustrates the sacred value which Greek has assumed for members of Greek Orthodox churches.

> I do not understand [the liturgy], but I have a book with a translation. If I take it along with me, I understand, but if I don't, it doesn't matter, because it is a mystery – we are not meant to know and understand everything; that is the way of the church, of religion. [Subject D1]

> I pray in Greek because I'm an Orthodox. It feels as if I'm truly praying when I do it in Greek. If I say it in English it's like I'm saying it to somebody else, I don't feel as if I'm talking to God . . . [Subject A2]

The belief that religion is not 'pure' without the 'right' language has surfaced in many churches connected with revolutionary theological reform. Lehmann (1981: 30), discussing German Lutherans in South Australia in the late 19th century, refers to the conviction that 'God had revealed the true meaning of the Bible to Luther in the German language and it was their special obligation to preserve this precious gift'. Many held the view that there could be 'no genuine Lutheran faith without the German language' (p. 33).

Language plays an important role in religious expression whether the believer is monolingual or multilingual. When the individual is bilingual or multilingual, they have access to an even greater number of linguistic resources. The ways in which these resources become present in church life vary, clearly determined in part by the church of which the individual is a member. Are there policies at the top end of the denominational structure which stipulate which language may be used when in the church? Are there policies at parish or congregational level? Or are there simply long-held and largely unquestioned traditions at work determining the monopoly of one culture and language over all others?

On another level, language might be considered to be quite independent of religion. Smolicz (1994: 38) – speaking particularly about multilingualism in the Catholic setting – contrasts the additive nature of language, with the exclusive nature of religious faith:

> In the case of language, individuals can be bilingual, trilingual or mul-tilingual, but they cannot claim to be bi-religious or multi-religious in faith and doctrine. This is simply to say that one cannot be a practising Catholic and a pious Muslim at one and the same time. The strength and unity of the Catholic Church demands undivided commitment. In contrast, the use of diverse languages in the Church by the faithful does not hinder unity, but openly enhances it. The priest who says one Mass in English and another in Italian on the same Sunday, openly demon-strates that bilingualism, by being internalised in the same individual, causes no division, no conflict, but rather bears witness to the univer-sality of the Church.

The complex relationship between language and religion will be further examined in the following discussion on aspects of religious life.

Language and liturgy

Increasingly the language of liturgy has found its way into the spotlight, attracting strong debate from theological and social perspectives. Within English liturgies, the once controversial question of how to address God ('thou' *versus* 'you') has been replaced by other issues. While gender-inclusive terms for human reference are becoming more widely accepted and adopted, there has been much greater resistance to such terms being used for reference to God, whether in the place of or alongside the usual masculine term. 'God the Father and Mother' may be heard frequently in feminist liberal circles but the lack of a clear and sustained theological basis means that this concept is likely to face continued impassioned opposition.

These issues dominate discussions of language and liturgy but there has, of late, been a strong push for a more comprehensive review of church liturgy, focusing on the use of 'plain English' wherever possible, without sacrificing the poetic character of liturgical materials. This has been partic-ularly highlighted by the Anglican Church. As Clyne (1989: 5) writes in *Church Scene*, the former national weekly magazine of the Anglican Church in Australia, 'Anglican services still require a high level of literacy and may alienate working class people'. In his commentary to *The Lambeth 1988 Statement on Liturgy*, Buchanan (1989: 15) points out that the call for a simpler style of liturgical language 'reflects an awareness of a changed sociology of Anglicanism'. The Anglican Church in Australia is consider-ably more ethnically diverse than ever before, underscoring the need to re-evaluate Anglo-centric traditions and assumptions.

Recommendation 31 of *A Garden of Many Colours*, the report of the

Anglican Archbishop of Melbourne's Commission on Multicultural Ministry and Mission (Anglican Diocese of Melbourne, 1985), advises that 'the Diocesan Liturgical Commission make the provision of the Eucharist and Pastoral Offices available in multilingual form'. At that time only a few sections of the Anglican Church's *An Australian Prayer Book* [AAPB] were available in community languages. As Clyne (1989: 6) points out, such a recommendation raises the important issue of whether the liturgy should thus be 'imported' from the country of origin for use in Australia or whether an Australian version (in the case of the Anglican Church, based on *AAPB* or, more recently, the *APBA*[2]) should be translated into the appropriate community language.

It also needs to be noted that the appropriate community language for liturgical use may not be the language or variety used daily by that community to communicate with one another. Many migrants living in Australia come from diglossic communities where two distinct languages or varieties are used in complementary domains – the High (H) variety being used for religious functions (Ferguson, 1959). In other communities, God must be addressed or referred to in the variety which carries the greatest respect and reverence, while other aspects of the same religious meeting may be carried out in Low (L) variety. In Javanese society, for example, Alip (1993: 27–8) points out that during religious services (Christian or Muslim), 'prayers, being addressed to God, are in the "high" level, but the leader's address to the congregation is in the "low" level, which is responded [to] in the "high level"'.

The language of liturgy takes on a sacred character because of the environment in which it is used: changes even to style of language used can cause great controversy. After talking about the impact of Vatican II on the Catholic Church (see later in this chapter and Chapter 2), Crystal (1990: 122) reports:

> A similar impact, but on a smaller scale, was felt when the Series III texts were introduced into the liturgy of the Church of England. The main result of these changes was to alter the perceived distinctiveness of liturgical language. Regardless of whether one welcomed or objected to the new genres, there was a widespread claim – which is still to be heard – that there was no longer any distinctiveness about liturgical language. The language of the new liturgy was called 'everyday', 'mundane' and 'lacking in variety' (to take just three comments made by various correspondents to a religious newspaper). For some, this was a good thing. For others, it was a disaster.

These comments are pertinent to Australia's experience of liturgical change, representing the widely held viewpoint that liturgy should reflect the 'other-worldliness' of the spiritual realm.

Further examples from Katsikis' (1993: 51–2) research illustrate the tension between religious and cultural traditions in the Greek Orthodox community:

> If the liturgy was in English, it would be different, it would not be as if I was attending church. It would be like going to listen to a talk. (A3)

> I think they should say the liturgy in the original language, but then do a Modern Greek translation, which everybody understands. But, if they think that saying it in English will make the young people go, that is not going to make them go more, in my opinion. (A3)

> If the liturgy was in English, I would not go to church more. With the English translation you lose something from the liturgy; the melody is lost. There is no place for English at church. However, I can understand why they would include English – so they can attract the youth to church. (B1)

The importance of formal liturgy in helping to maintain the mother tongue in ethnic churches has been examined by Hofman (1966). According to his research among German Lutheran parishes in the United States and Canada, 'ritual reinforcement' – the use of the same (or similar) language in liturgy as for sermons – is a key factor in ensuring language maintenance in the church. (A second key factor is the immigrational recency of the group.) In Greek Orthodox churches, for example, Greek – and not English – continues to be the language of the Church because of the reinforcement provided by an Ecclesiastical Greek liturgy.

As Varcoe (1997: 63) points out, different churches have their own liturgical cultures. The Catholic and most of the Anglican Church use a 'fixed text with various degrees of outdated language', while the Uniting Church and parts of the Anglican Church have a 'normative text but liberty to vary or abandon it'. A third group, Varcoe says, 'has no texts but a recognisable and stable structure where music and preaching (but notably not the reading of scripture) dominate'.

When ethnic background is added to this equation of church and liturgical cultures, the situation becomes more complex, as 'the encounter between Christianity and culture involves the meeting of two symbolic processes, *both already heavily influenced by the other*' (Varcoe, 1997: 64; emphasis hers).

The style of the liturgy itself is also culturally bound. Certain discourse styles are more familiar to some communities than to others and are, thus,

more appropriate for use. Some communities prefer more congregational
participation than others. Concepts of God as 'Lord', 'Creator' and 'King'
may be more culturally relevant than understanding God as a 'friend' and
these affect the orientation of the liturgical flow. This inter-relationship
between culture and worship is known as 'inculturation'. According to
Atta-Bafoe and Tovey (1990: 14), inculturation may be defined as

> the incarnation of the Christian life and message in a particular cultural
> context in such a way that not only do local Christians find expression
> for their faith through elements proper to their culture but also that
> faith and worship animate, direct and unify the culture. Inculturation
> in this sense is the dialogue of gospel and culture.

Language and music

The relationship between language and music is linked to the relationship between language and liturgy, not least because in some traditions, all
or part of the liturgy is set to music. After all, liturgy may simply be defined
as the way a service is ordered (Robert Gribben, pers. comm. 21 January
2000) and, therefore, includes other elements such as music, prayer,
Scripture and sermons (see following sections).

The connection between music and liturgy has been described in the
following way:

> At the heart of the matter lies the idea that the liturgy must contain an
> element of mystery; that is, that which cannot be expressed precisely in
> verbal prose but not, of course, that which we cannot comprehend at
> all. This is one of many aspects of the close connection between musical
> and liturgical thinking. (Another is the problem of having to reject or
> renew a great inherited tradition.) For music is indeed a mystery in this
> sense, but this does not mean that it is incomprehensible. (Warren,
> 1990: 196)

Hymns, like liturgy, may preserve a particular form of a language, with its
characteristic lexicon and syntax, for centuries until revitalisation or
reform is sought. However, radical changes to styles of music used in a
church are often accompanied by a change in style of language used. For
example, the modern worship songs used in some Protestant churches are
often written with God as the addressee, using intimate vocabulary which
can cause discomfort for churchgoers used to traditional hymn-singing. In
contrast, where change is sought, 'often a musical accompaniment remains
intact while the new language is adjusted to it' (Dillistone, 1990: 6). This is
not only the case for styles of the one language but also for different
languages as well. Many ethnic churches may, in fact, be singing the same

hymns translated into their own language (German in one church, Latvian in another and English in yet another), or within the same church the one sung may be sung simultaneously in different languages as an inclusive strategy.

Language and prayer

The relationship between language and prayer is complex. On the one hand, prayer is always a part of Christian liturgy, often by means of a formulaic corporate prayer such as the Lord's Prayer. Prayer, on the other hand, is a personal dialogue with God. The language used in prayer is thus a reflection of this relationship. In discussing the use of different levels of Javanese, as well as Indonesian in religious contexts (both Christian and Muslim) in Indonesia, Alip (1993: 177–9) writes:

> Surprisingly, very few respondents use Javanese in praying . . . Christians show a higher percentage of the use of Bahasa Indonesia in personal prayers than Moslems . . . The use of Bahasa Indonesia in personal prayers also indicates that the respondents are more comfortable [praying] in Bahasa Indonesia than in Javanese. The ease of praying in Bahasa Indonesia indicates that Bahasa Indonesia is already internalised by the respondents and is felt more like a mother tongue than a second language. Because many of them find that their Basa Javanese, the deferential speech level in talking to God, does not meet their own expected standard, they avoid using Javanese and thus choose Bahasa Indonesia, which unlike Ngoko Javanese does not imply the absence of deference. For praying, Bahasa Indonesia has another advantage over Javanese because one can feel close to God. Basa Javanese makes them feel respectful to God but they might feel less intimate.

As this illustrates, the language of prayer is dictated by the a person's relationship with God, as well as being a function of external factors such as habit, familiarity and ability, and theological and social convention.

An interesting issue regarding the relationship between language and prayer in the Church is that of *glossolalia*, the practice of speaking in a state different from normally intelligible patterns ('speaking in tongues'). Glossolalia is found frequently in Pentecostal churches and ones with a charismatic influence. Such churches also tend to be, on the whole, non-liturgical and quite informal. Glossolalia remains an under-researched area.

Language and the Bible

One of the most significant features of the 16th-century Reformation was the great enthusiasm which arose for 'expressing the new consciousness of national identity and destiny in the vernacular' (Dillistone, 1990: 20). This included translating the Bible into the language of the people. Present-day organisations such as Wycliffe Bible Translators attest to the value of Bible translation work:

> Motivated by the pressing need for all peoples to have access to the Word of God in a language that speaks to their hearts, and reaffirming our historic values and our trust in God to accomplish the impossible, we embrace the vision that by the year 2025 a Bible translation project will be in progress for every people group that needs it. (Wycliffe Bible Translators, 1999)

This vision was inspired by the experience of the Wycliffe's founder, William Cameron Townsend, who, when trying to sell Spanish Bibles in Guatemala in 1918, was confronted by the penetrating question: 'If your God is so great, why can't he speak Cakchiquel?' As a result, Townsend resolved that every person should be able to read the Bible in his or her own language. Wycliffe Bible Translators are currently involved in 1023 language projects, having completed or help to complete a translation of the New Testament in over 530 languages.

The work of Bible translation organisations such as Wycliffe represents the belief in the centrality of the Gospel message for individual salvation and stands in contrast to the view that interpretation of the Scriptures is not for the ordinary person but only the trained and ordained. This latter view hinges on the sacred nature of the Scriptures: the view of the Bible as being 'God's Word' means that the language used to convey these words will take on a degree of sacredness.

It is interesting to consider that English is the language in which there exists the greatest number of modern-day 'versions' and 'revisions' of Scripture. Other languages/cultures are less able or less willing to allow the changing nature of language and society to render one version of Scripture in the vernacular obsolete.

Language and sermons

Sermons, or homilies, form an element of a Christian service in which the language use of the priest is considerably more flexible. While the liturgy may be in an ancient language or style of language, the hymns the same ones sung for hundreds of years and the prayers all formulaic, the sermon's function is to illuminate the meaning and significance of Biblical texts or themes in a way relevant to the present day. The sermon helps the listener to apply to daily life the aspects of worship which make up the rest of the service. The language used is, therefore, more likely to be that which is most easily understood by the congregation.

Hofman (1966: 133) suggests that the language used in sermons is an appropriate index of language maintenance in ethnic parishes, as the sermon is 'probably most sensitive to the linguistic needs and preferences of the congregation as a whole'. The sermon is, therefore, one of the parts of a church service which is most likely to show flexibility in its use of language, being adapted to suit its audience. It has also been suggested that the increasing heterogeneity of an ethnic church tends to result in a shift to use of English in sermons (Hofman, 1966: 136–7), as a result of the need to find a language common to all when language proficiency may vary (see later).

Language and worship style

The way language is used in a church is greatly influenced by the style of worship and *vice versa*. Worship style, of course, determines and is determined by all the components of a service already mentioned – liturgy, music, Scripture, prayer, sermon (elements which, to an extent, already overlap). Worship style also refers to the overriding character of a service – its level of formality or informality, the type and degree of congregational participation and adherence to traditions of the past or the replacement of these with contemporary forms. A formal worship style with a strong commitment to the traditions which have been passed down through generations of churchgoers may well be partnered by hesitancy in the area of language change.

Language and the clergy

The minister of a church frequently becomes the 'mediator of language transition in the ethnic parish' (Hofman 1966: 138). Overberg (1981: 27), in discussing the Dutch in Victoria between the years 1947–80, refers to the 'cultural tight-rope the ministers walked' in trying to satisfy the needs and preferences of their congregations. Making their job all the more difficult is that, over time, these needs and preferences are subject to change.

Time also sees a change in the clergy themselves. As Hofman (1966: 138) so clearly puts it for the American situation:

> Foreign-born and same-ethnic pastors are replaced by American-born and non-ethnic (or other-ethnic) pastors – not only to reinforce the Americanizing policy of the church and not only to gratify the more marginally ethnic second and third generation membership, but also because international political and cultural developments block the supply of foreign pastors or render them truly 'foreign' even to first-generation members of ethnic parishes in the United States.

This has weighty implications for language maintenance. A member of the clergy who speaks a more recent variety of the community language may not be viewed as being a proper 'role model' for the church by its older, more conservative members who may then become more staunchly inflexible about language issues. An Australian-born member of the clergy with a preference for English may steer the church towards greater use of English in place of the community language. The view of clergy as linguistic role models clearly places them at risk of criticism by those for whom notions of language 'purity' and the sanctity of religious practice are strongly linked.

The theological training of clergy also affects the role of language in the religious domain within a new country, depending on the language of study, the type of institution, the structure and policies of the Church of which they are a part (particularly its relationship in the homeland vis-à-vis the State), and the way in which overseas training is accepted within the new country. The theological, political and linguistic environment in which clergy receive their training may influence these same elements of the church in which they serve.

Language and the congregation

As outlined earlier, Hofman (1966) found through his research in the United States that the more heterogeneous the congregation, the greater the use of English. This heterogeneity may be along ethnic lines or may refer to (the often vast) generational differences. Other factors were found to be more ambivalent in their effect on congregational make-up and, therefore, language maintenance: the heterogeneity of the surrounding population and the size and growth rate of the church.

Communities which are not experiencing any further migration – and so cannot depend on an influx of migrants to boost church numbers – are particularly reliant on their youth for future growth.

The youth of a church community are vital for its future growth. Barriers created by language have been found to be one factor which can hinder youth involvement. Many ethnic churches have experienced this and have shifted towards English in public church life. Imberger (1979: 51), in an investigation of language maintenance among the Templars (a Palestinian–Swabian sect), found that the extensive replacement of German with English was justified by 'the attitude that the German language is impeding efforts to maintain the interest of the young in the Society's religious life'.

Hofman's (1966: 130) findings are similar: 'what is natural, traditional, and habitual for adults of the first generation is frequently far from being such for their second- and third-generation children and grandchildren'. His research indicated that, in some cases, 'the presence of older members in a parish may have prolonged the retention of "German-only" beyond the point of usefulness with younger members. Then, since the parish was too weak to try a bilingual solution, a switch to 'English-only' became inevitable' (p. 146–7).

Other research in the Orthodox context has suggested that a switch to English for the benefit of the youth is not enough in itself to attract younger members to the church:

> In an attempt to motivate more of the second generation to attend church, some of the priests have included English as part of their services. They believe that this will be sufficient to increase their attendance rates and make the youth return back to the church. The participants in this study, however, said that by including English translations during the ceremony would not make them attend church more . . . (Katsikis, 1993: 50)

Another process leading to increased heterogeneity in ethnic churches and, therefore, potentially also to language shift is out-marriage. According to Hofman (1966: 136):

> the influx of other-ethnics through marriage may be more powerful in its effects on language maintenance than the general expansion of membership. A new member-by-marriage may, in many cases, move right into the social nucleus of the parish and exert direct influence on opinion leaders and their families. (Fichter, 1951)

Those in mixed marriages, therefore, have much in common with youth, as potential agents of change in ethnic churches.

Methodology

Sixteen congregations from seven Christian denominations in Melbourne provide the data for this research. Grouped according to denominational affiliation or membership, they are:

I. Anglican Church	1. Chinese – Hakka
	2. Persian
II. Baptist Church	3. Arabic
	4. Spanish
III. Catholic Church	5. Croatian
	6. Italian
IV. Lutheran Church	7. German
	8. Latvian
	9. Slovak
V. Orthodox Church	10. Greek
	11. Russian

VI. Reformed Church	12. Chinese – Mandarin
	13. English of Dutch origin
VII. Uniting Church	14. Indonesian
	15. Oromo
	16. Tamil

The selection of these particular congregations, as outlined earlier, was based on a desire to represent different periods of Australia's migration history, as well as a broad range of languages, cultural backgrounds and religious orientations.

Data were collected by means of an interview with the minister, pastor or priest of each congregation listed here. In the case of the Latvian Lutheran congregation and the Indonesian congregation of the Uniting Church, additional forms of data collection were used in order to provide a more detailed picture of the language needs, habits and preferences of those attending ethnic churches. These two congregations formed case studies and, as such, saw the participation of church members via a questionnaire. Participants in this research, therefore, consisted of the 16 leaders of the churches and congregations involved, as well as those who attended the two case-study churches on one particular Sunday.

Interviews with church leaders were conducted using a detailed interview schedule which included questions covering four main areas:

(1) the ethnic backgrounds, language habits and abilities of the church leader and members of the congregation;
(2) details of the services conducted, including numbers attending, language(s) used during services and other areas of church life;
(3) attitudes towards particular languages in the church – the leader's own, as well as perceptions of the congregation's and the denomination's attitudes; and
(4) any language-related problems encountered.

The questionnaire which was used with members of the two case-study churches was constructed in a similar fashion to the interview schedule described earlier, with questions covering

(1) participant's own ethnic background, language habits and abilities;
(2) details about the services which they attended and why;
(3) attitudes towards particular languages in the church; and
(4) any language-related problems they encountered or perceived.

Some of the questions had to be rephrased or redesigned according to their suitability for the particular congregation. For example, allowances had to be made – in the structure of certain questions and their potential answers – for the fact that members of the Indonesian congregation would be very likely to speak a regional language of Indonesia in many situations, rather than the national language, Bahasa Indonesia, or English. The questionnaires and accompanying explanatory statements were provided in bilingual format, with English followed by either Latvian or Indonesian.

Church leaders were contacted by phone as a result of recommendation by contacts in the relevant denomination or by pre-established acquaintance with them. The leaders of the Latvian and Indonesian churches were met with individually to discuss the possibility of members of the congregations also being involved. A written description of the project was provided to all participants in plain English and, where necessary, in the relevant community language as well. Church leaders were interviewed individually, except where a spouse was invited by the participant to contribute or where the presence of another person was arranged to aid the participant's understanding if they were not confident of their English language skills. All interviews were conducted in English and all except two were tape-recorded: one of these was the result of technical difficulties, while the other interview was not taped at the request of the minister. In these instances, detailed notes were taken during the course of the interviews and summaries were made immediately after the interview in order to record as accurately as possible the information provided by the participant. The tapes of the interviews were transcribed and then summarised. This information was then collated; the reader is referred to the Appendix for a detailed presentation of these results.

Questionnaires were given to participants at the conclusion of services at the Indonesian and Latvian churches on a particular Sunday morning. Advance notice of the intention to do so was given via an announcement during the previous week's services and/or in the church newsletter. Non-members of the church who were attending on the particular day were also encouraged to complete a questionnaire. Participants were able to complete the questionnaire at their own leisure and return it in the stamped addressed envelopes which were provided.

All data were collected between 1997 and 1999.

'Religious Settlement' and Some Christian Churches in Australia

The aim of this section is to 'set the scene' by providing descriptions of the backgrounds of the congregations involved in this research. These descriptions will begin with a look at the history of the denominations with which they are affiliated, using Bouma's (1997) concept of 'religious settlement' as the starting point for this discussion. The focus will then be

Table 1.4 Population by religious identification, (2001 Census)

Denomination	Percentage Australian population	Percentage Melbourne population
Catholic	26.7	29.4
Anglican	20.7	13.7
Uniting	6.7	4.6
Presbyterian & Reformed	3.4	2.7
Orthodox	2.8	6.2
Baptist	1.7	1.5
Lutheran	1.3	0.7
Total all Christians	68.0	62.8

directed to the presence of speakers of particular community languages in those denominations.

Table 1.4 shows the breakdown of the Australian population according to religious affiliation, listing those denominations which are relevant to this research. Note that Reformed Christians are enumerated along with Presbyterians in census figures.

Catholics and Anglicans represent the numerically largest denominations in Australia, though there are regional differences. Immediately following the Second World War, there were twice as many Anglicans as Catholics in the population. However, by the early 1980s, Catholics were able to claim the greatest number of affiliates (Hughes, 1993). As Table 1.4 shows, there is some difference between the rankings for some denominations when totals for Melbourne and Australia are compared; members of Orthodox churches dramatically outnumber members of Uniting and Presbyterian and Reformed churches in Melbourne, a situation which is reversed for the Australian population as a whole. This difference reflects the overwhelming concentration of Greek speakers in Melbourne, as evidenced in Table 1.1.

The concept of 'religious settlement' as a means of describing 'the ways in which a religion becomes part of a society and culture' was developed by Bouma (1997). More explicitly, this concept focuses on the processes by which a religion, or religious group, becomes part of a society and culture, either by 'migrating' along with migrants or being brought by missionaries (who may or may not be 'migrants' but for whom spreading the religion is the purpose of arrival). As Bouma (1997: 1) states:

The shape of Australia's religious profile is primarily a function of its migration history and only secondarily a function of conversion or changing religious identification. Many forms of Christianity, Islam, Buddhism, Hinduism are found in Australia because people of these religious traditions have migrated to Australia and have worked to establish religious organisations to enable religious practices not previously found here.

This is supported by Hughes (1993: 68), in summing up a discussion of the place of religion in society based on 1991 census figures: 'Immigration patterns more than any other single factor have shaped the religious life of Australia.' Six of the seven denominations which are represented in this research – Anglican, Baptist, Catholic, Lutheran, Orthodox and (the antecedent denominations of) the Uniting Church (Congregational, Methodist and Presbyterian) – were all firmly established in Australian society within the first hundred years of its colonial history (with the Reformed Churches arising out of – and other churches being strengthened by – 20th-century migration). Each was established by migrants who, prior to arrival in Australia, were familiar with a particular kind of religious practice which they wished to continue in the new country.

The Anglican Church

When the 16th-century English Church declared itself independent of Rome, the monarch replaced the Pope as the Head of the Church. As the State Church, it spread through the British Empire and – via missionary activity – into other parts of the world. As contradictory as it might sound, the Anglican Church is both catholic and reformed – in heritage and in practice. Anglicanism has developed several (overlapping) streams. First, there is a continuum between Evangelicalism and Anglo-Catholicism within the Church, one end holding strongly to Evangelical theology (emphasising personal salvation through faith in the death of Jesus Christ and the teaching and authority of the Scriptures, over that of the Church), the other following Anglo-Catholic traditions (reflecting the historical links with the Catholic Church). Second, there is a continuum of tradition from conservative to liberal. The Evangelical/Anglo-Catholic and conservative/liberal continua intersect so that, in fact, there are several factions within Anglicanism. While each of these schools of thought are represented and are influential within the Australian Church, the majority of Anglicans in Australia follow moderate forms of these traditions.

Anglicanism was established in Australia in the earliest days of colonial history. The road to complete autonomy and independence from the Church in England, as well as the development of an Australian Anglican identity, has been long and, of course, still continues. Only since 1981 has the Church been known as the Anglican Church of Australia (rather than the Church of England). Though its autonomy is complete, it is part of the worldwide Anglican communion whose symbolic – but not legal or formal – head is the Archbishop of Canterbury.

The strongly Anglo-centric heritage of the Church is still evident. Figures from the 2001 Census show that 97% of Anglicans speak only English at home. The dilemma facing the Anglican Church has been aptly stated by the former Primate, the Reverend Dr Keith Rayner, in a four-page brochure distributed to all Anglican clergy (Anglican General Synod Multicultural Committee, 1996):

> We [the Anglican church] began our life in this country as the church of English migrants. The danger for us is that we simply remain the ethnic church of the English. If that occurs the influence of our church will steadily diminish as the Anglo-Saxon component of our population diminishes. We shall then find that we are not ministering to the Australia that is, but to an Australia that was – many years ago.

Within the English-dominated Anglican Church, the number of ethnic congregations is quite small, although multicultural ministry was, for a time, experiencing a period of growth. In different parts of Australia, Anglicans worship in Swahili, Vietnamese, Chinese, Arabic, Persian, Tamil, Spanish as well as Aboriginal languages. However, the Church as a whole is still 'heavily Anglo-Celtic, middle-class and oriented to the literate' (Anglican Diocese of Melbourne, 1985: 25). Despite revision, *An Australian Prayer Book* (published in 1978 as a supplement to the *Book of Common Prayer*; see Chapter 2) is still clearly 'dominated by its roots in English culture, language and assumptions'; only some sections are available in community languages.

Chinese speakers in the Anglican Church

The Chinese varieties if taken together would constitute the most widely used community language group in Australia. Sydney has the highest concentration of speakers of Chinese varieties collectively (Melbourne second) but Melbourne has the highest concentration of some *fangyan* (varieties) such as Hakka and Hokkien. Chinese migration to Australia flourished in the mid 19th century with the gold rush but the Immigration Restriction Act of 1901 all but ended migration of Chinese speakers. The abolition of discriminatory immigration laws and the advent of the Australian Government policy of multiculturalism – both features of the 1970s – have resulted in a great wave of Chinese migration from China, Singapore, Hong Kong, Malaysia and, more recently, Taiwan. Due to the geographical, political, cultural and linguistic diversity within the Chinese community in Australia, internal divisions have at times arisen. Clyne and Kipp (1999) found that linguistic diversity within the Chinese community caused some difficulty in religious settings, with separate congregations often being established for those more comfortable with Cantonese, Mandarin, another *fangyan* or even English.

Chinese Christians belong to a number of different denominations, with most attending independent congregations. Within the Anglican Church, Chinese speakers come mainly from the former British colonies of Singapore, Malaysia and Hong Kong; however, within the congregation which took part in the present research, there is also a large group of East Timorese refugees. This particular congregation, in fact, began as an initiative of the late Archbishop, Dr David Penman, as a ministry to refugees of Chinese origin from Vietnam and Timor. After an initial five years, two lay evangelists from the Diocese of Singapore were recruited to assist with the ministry, which subsequently began to attract migrants and overseas students from Singapore, Hong Kong and Malaysia. This congregation has been described as 'the strongest ethnic one in Melbourne' (Houston, 1993: 91).

Persian speakers in the Anglican Church

Melbourne is home to the second-largest concentration of Persian speakers in Australia, after Sydney. Several waves of migration from Iran have occurred, principally around the time of the 1979 Revolution and the Iran–Iraq war. While most Iranian Christians in Australia converted to Christianity after migrating, some worshipped within the greatly persecuted Christian community in Iran. Interestingly, Christians form a much larger component of the Iranian community in Australia than they do in Iran. The Anglican Church there forms the Diocese of Iran, of the Episcopal Church of Jerusalem and the Middle East. There is currently one Persian Anglican congregation in Melbourne.

The Baptist Church

The Baptist Church began out of one of the many reform movements of the 16th and 17th centuries. It thus holds to evangelical theology but gives sole authority to Scripture for all beliefs, practices and patterns of church organisation. No authority is given to tradition or to creeds (on the basis that creeds are not mentioned in Scripture in any form other than to 'accept Jesus Christ as Lord and Saviour'). The belief is also held that a person should only be baptised where a personal profession of faith has been made (thus infant baptism is not practised) and that every baptised member is able, with the aid of the Holy Spirit, to interpret the Scriptures for themselves.

Baptist migrants, largely from the United Kingdom, settled in Australia during the 19th century, often gathering for worship in private homes or together with other non-conformists in Churches of Christ or Congregational Churches. Some divisions of theology initially hindered their organisation but by the 1890s, a Baptist Union was established in each of the states. In 1926 they joined to form the Baptist Union of Australia.

After the Second World War, immigration boosted the numbers of Baptists, particularly through further immigration from the UK. The arrival of Baptist migrants from other non-English-speaking countries saw the beginning of language-specific congregations in the Baptist Church. Congregations using the same language formed 'National Language Associations' and, in 1968, the ethnic churches of the Baptist Union established the 'New Settlers' Baptist Association of Victoria', which aimed to promote communication between the various congregations and to encourage evangelism amongst migrants (Hughes, 1996: 34). A national association was established in 1974. At present there are 32 congregations worshipping in languages other than English in Melbourne. As Hughes (1993: 68) reports, '[Baptists] have been more successful than most other denominations with an English background amongst people with non-English-speaking backgrounds.'

Arabic speakers in the Baptist Church

Arabic is the fourth most widely used community language in Australia, with Melbourne having the second highest concentration of speakers, after Sydney. Arabic speakers in Australia have tended to come from Lebanon or Egypt and the majority are Christians (Eastern Rite Catholics, Coptic Orthodox and Greek Orthodox) (Clyne & Kipp, 1999).

Within the Baptist Church in Melbourne, there are currently two congregations consisting of Arabic Christians from a number of different Arabic-speaking countries. While there are Baptist churches throughout the Middle East, there is also a range of other theologically similar churches. The pastor of the Arabic congregation involved in the present research ministered within a 'Holiness Movement Church' in Egypt (brought by American missionaries). After coming to Australia and being sought by Arabic Christians in need of a pastor, the Baptist Union was approached for support.

Spanish speakers in the Baptist Church

Melbourne is home to the second-largest concentration of Spanish speakers in Australia, after Sydney. Spanish, as a pluricentric language, is the official language of no less than 21 countries (Clyne & Kipp, 1999: 63). Immigration to Australia began in the 1940s, both for political and economic reasons, and from Latin American countries immigration was most significant in the 1970s. While most Spanish-speaking countries are Catholic, the strong missionary activity of the Baptists has resulted in the presence of Baptist churches in many parts of the Spanish-speaking world, particularly in Latin America. Upon migrating to Australia, attachment to the Baptist Church was a natural course of action. There are currently two Baptist congregations of Spanish speakers in Melbourne. The congregation involved in the present research is led by a Spain-born pastor, while members of the congregation are almost exclusively from Latin America.

The Catholic Church

The beliefs of the Catholic Church are those central to mainstream Christian denominations. The main differences concern the role of the Pope as the supreme and infallible leader of the Church, the place of the teaching of the Popes, bishops and Church councils through history, the power of the Pope to proclaim saints, and the veneration of Mary as pre-eminent among the saints. Other distinguishing practices and beliefs include the emphasis on (seven) sacraments, belief in the inerrancy of Scripture, belief that the Christian community includes all faithful followers of Jesus, living or dead, and belief in the practice of prayer to and for the dead.

Catholics form the largest branch of the Christian Church in Australia today. The first Catholics arrived in Australia during its early colonial days, with even the first priests arriving as convicts.[3] In 1820 the first two chaplains appointed by the Government in London arrived – an event which is considered to mark the formal establishment of the Catholic Church in Australia. Catholicism was, for a long time, equated with Irishism: as Dixon (1996: 2) states: 'Many Irish priests, and most of the bishops as well, saw their task in Australia as nurturing the growth of an offshoot of the Irish Church, one that would preserve the characteristics they had known at home.' Despite the fact that Irish priests were regarded as less suitable than the Australian-born priests by the end of the 19th century, it was not until the 1930s that Australian-born priests outnumbered the Irish.

The 1960s and 1970s saw enormous social change in Australia, with a large post-war influx of non-English-speaking migrants from places such as Italy, Malta, The Netherlands, Germany, Poland, Croatia and Hungary. The controversial decision of the Second Vatican Council in 1962–65 to allow mass in the vernacular thus came at a significant time for Australia: it provided opportunity for the new Catholic migrants to have their spiritual needs met in their own language. The Church in Australia responded by obtaining priests from the main countries of origin.

Recent figures show that around 22,000 people in the Archdiocese of

Melbourne attend Masses celebrated in a total of 29 languages other than English each week. However, 'after 50 years of significant immigration from non-English-speaking countries, Catholic immigrants and their chaplains find that they are expected to fit into a Church still largely shaped by an Irish mould' (Dixon, 1996).

Croatian speakers in the Catholic Church
    With the growing number of Catholic migrants from Croatia arriving during the 1960s, a church was established in 1962 in an inner-city suburb of Melbourne, and pastored for 30 years by the Reverend Josip Kašić. It was here in 1964 that the first Catholic service in Croatian was held. The church continues to have a strong connection with the Catholic Church in Croatia – all the priests have been sent from Croatia to Australia. Tkalcevic (1988: 89) reports that in the early years the Croatian Catholic Centre catered not just for the spiritual needs of migrants but also for their welfare and cultural needs, offering emergency accommodation, financial support and assistance finding employment. Tkalcevic continues: 'To this day, the Croatian Catholic Centre . . . continues to be an important religious, social educational and cultural centre for the Croatian migrants in Melbourne' (p. 91).

Italian speakers in the Catholic Church
    In the 1950s and 1960s, large waves of migrants came to Australia from Italy and in doing so 'bolstered the Catholic Church, bringing new dimensions to the denomination which was previously strongly Irish in ethnicity' (Hughes, 1993: 68). Amongst the Italian community in Australia, the Scalabrinians, an Italian order founded especially to work with immigrants, have been active since 1952. For the purposes of the present research, the senior Italian priest in Melbourne was interviewed. This priest is a member of the Scalabrinian order, and as well as looking after the needs of the Italian community (though not through attachment to any one church), oversees the work of the other Catholic migrant chaplains.

The Lutheran Church
    The Lutheran Church began out of the 16th-century movement led by Martin Luther, which sought the reform of the western Christian church. Lutheran Churches prospered mainly where the State Church was Lutheran, under the reign of Lutheran princes. Thus it flourished in Germany, Scandinavia and other parts of Europe: this political and geographical diversity meant that despite relative doctrinal uniformity Lutheran Churches reflected some cultural and practical differences. The authority of the Scriptures is emphasised within the Lutheran Church, with Christ the final authority and His grace considered the only means for salvation.

The Lutheran Church has been in Australia for around 170 years. In the 1830s, small groups of Lutherans who believed they were prevented from practising the true Lutheran faith in their German-speaking homeland migrated, settling mainly in rural areas of South Australia (and later in other states). Lutheranism in Australia, however, became divided in its early history. After the end of the First World War, there existed two Lutheran synods in Australia. One, the United Evangelical Lutheran Church in Australia (UELCA), perceived a strong link between 'true' Lutheranism and the German language, while the other, the Evangelical Lutheran Church in Australia (ELCA), was less committed to German as the only language of true Lutherans and dissolved its ties with the homeland prior to the First World War (Kipp, 1999; Lehmann, 1981; Clyne, 1991: 134). In the time surrounding both World Wars, the German roots and character of the Lutheran Church was perceived as problematic, with consequences ranging from the closure of many Lutheran parish schools to the banning of the German language in the Lutheran press and the cessation of German language services in the church. After the Second World War, Lutherans from a number of other European countries arrived in Australia, many as displaced persons. They began to establish their own churches, thus contributing to the greater cultural diversity of the Lutheran Church. The ELCA and the UELCA merged in 1967 to form the Lutheran Church of Australia. There also exist in Melbourne some Lutheran churches which are not part of the Lutheran Church of Australia: among these are the congregations of the Evangelische Kirche Deutschlands (German Protestant Church) and the Swedish Church.

German speakers in the Lutheran Church
German immigration to Australia began most prominently in the 1830s, coming, as mentioned earlier, as a result of the suppression of Old Lutheranism in eastern Germany. The migrants tended to settle in rural areas, particularly of South Australia, Queensland and Victoria. Kipp *et al.* (1995: 136) report that by the latter part of the 19th century, the German-speaking community was the largest non-British ethnic group in Australia. During the 1930s, German speakers came as refugees of National Socialism and after the Second World War, many came as displaced persons. By far the largest group came as part of the post-war immigration programme.

Kipp *et al.* (1995: 139) report that while there are several denominations (Catholic, Baptist, Lutheran) which have a specific German ministry, 'the vast majority of German-speaking churchgoers in Melbourne are absorbed within English-speaking parishes'. The Lutheran congregation which took part in the present research was established in 1960 by immigrants from Germany, Switzerland and Austria, who settled in Australia to work in the nearby factories. It is in 'altar and pulpit fellowship' with the Lutheran Churches of Australia.

Latvian speakers in the Lutheran Church

Latvian migration to Australia occurred almost entirely between the post-war years of 1947–50, with the arrival of around 20,000 displaced persons (Putniņš, 1981: 16). With Lutheranism being the predominant religion in Latvia, the Latvians who came to Australia were quick to establish their own churches according to the Latvian model: 'Martin Luther's thesis that everyone had the right to listen to God's Word in his mother language was used as an argument for establishing separate Latvian congregations' (Silkalns, 1988: 170). The Latvian community in Melbourne is the largest in Australia and is served by three Lutheran con-gregations. Only two of the three are members of the Lutheran Church of Australia, the other acting as a fully independent church body. The Latvian congregation which is involved in the present research is the largest of the three. Though it is a part of the Latvian Church Outside of Latvia (formerly, the Latvian Church in Exile), the congregation has been a full member of the Lutheran Church of Australia since 1972.

Slovak speakers in the Lutheran Church

After the Reformation of the 16th century, Lutheranism spread through-out Slovakia. When Slovakia came under the Austro-Hungarian Empire, the majority of Protestants fled as Catholicism took hold. A small group of Slovaks fled to what was later to become Yugoslavia, and there were able to preserve their language, culture and customs. Today, the Slovak Republic is mostly Catholic, while Slovaks in other parts of the world are generally Lutheran. Although Slovak-speaking migrants came to Australia as early as the 1920s, migration began in earnest in the 1950s. In particular, the late 1950s brought thousands of Slovaks from the northern Yugoslav provinces. The Slovak Lutheran church involved in this research is the only Lutheran ministry to Slovaks in Australia and its congregation is made up of Slovaks from the former Yugoslavia. It is pastored by a Slovak from the Slovak Republic but as the pastor's wife is a Yugoslav Slovak the political tensions which may otherwise have arisen are greatly lessened.

The Orthodox Church

The Great Schism of 1054 resulted in the division between the 'Western' Church and the 'Eastern' Church. Orthodox Churches became the national Churches in many parts of the world, however in the 20th century, political changes resulted in some cases in the separation of Church and State. For example, in Russia the atheistic stance of communism removed the

Orthodox Church from its privileged position. Political differences have also resulted in the formation of many non-canonical Orthodox Churches: jurisdictional problems such as these characterise many of the Orthodox Churches found in Australia. All canonical Orthodox Churches are theologically identical, differing only in the cultural context in which they are practised. The central beliefs of the Eastern Orthodox Church are that God has revealed himself in Jesus Christ, as well as through the Church and the Holy Tradition. All teaching and even interpretation of the Scriptures must be measured against Tradition; this Tradition includes the liturgy, creeds and sacraments of the Church, the dogmatic decisions of the historical Councils, the writings of the Church Fathers, the lives of the saints, the Holy Icons, as well as the Scriptures. The Orthodox Church believes itself to be practising the true and complete faith passed down through the centuries, beginning with Christ and continuing from the apostles without deviation through to the present-day Church.

While migrants with Orthodox backgrounds have been present in Australia since the late 19th century, Eastern Orthodoxy has really only become a significant part of the religious scene since the Second World War, when large numbers of Orthodox faithful migrated to Australia from countries such as Greece. It was clear that the Church was the centre of stability and unity for the new migrants:

> Even today, to belong to a particular Orthodox church means more than just accepting a set of beliefs; it may also define a national, social and cultural identity . . . The ancient Orthodox Church has had to confront the complex issues to be found in modern, pluralistic societies while maintaining its faithfulness to its traditional beliefs and teaching. In this new, migrant situation, the church has, once again, become a focus for social and cultural identity in multicultural situations, especially if the people come from a country where Orthodoxy is the majority or, indeed, the official religion. (Godley & Hughes 1996:3–4)

The establishment of the various Orthodox Churches in Australia was strengthened in 1979 when an official body was created which could link the Churches in a formal sense, adding to the theological unity already existing. Through this body, known as the Standing Conference of Canonical Orthodox Churches in Australia (SCCOCA), the Orthodox Churches have the opportunity to speak with a common voice in dialogue with the rest of Australian society. The very presence of this body implies the existence of non-canonical churches which are outside of it and this is the case particularly within the Russian and, to a lesser extent, the Greek communities.

An important step in ensuring the continual growth of the Orthodox

Churches independent of overseas assistance was the founding of St Andrew's Greek Orthodox Theological College in Sydney in 1986. Through this college theological training is provided for candidates for the priesthood in the Greek Orthodox Church and, more recently, for other Orthodox Churches as well.

Greek speakers in the Orthodox Church
As previously mentioned, some Orthodox Christians were present in Australian society during the later part of the 19th century, Greek speakers among them. The early Greek Orthodox communities were primarily the initiative of lay people. In the early years, clergy arrived at the insistence of Orthodox immigrants already in Australia who were anxious to once again be part of a community centred around Orthodoxy. By the end of the 19th century, there was a sufficient number of Greek migrants to establish Greek parishes in Melbourne. Initially, the Greek Orthodox in Australia were looked after by the Greek Orthodox Patriarchate of Jerusalem, which supplied priests (who could speak both Greek and Arabic and could, therefore, also look after the small community of Lebanese Christians and Syrian Orthodox) and church resources until 1902. The Church was under the administration of the Holy Synod of the Church of Greece between 1902 and 1924, when the Ecumenical Patriarch of Constantinople assumed jurisdiction over the Diaspora. Soon after, the Greek Orthodox Archdiocese of Australia and New Zealand was established. The Church began to grow with vigour when Greek migration saw a dramatic increase in the 1950s and, more particularly, in the 1960s. Today there are dozens of Greek Orthodox churches in Melbourne alone but of these, only one is known to regularly conduct the Divine Liturgy exclusively in English. The church which is involved in the present research is one of the many which see no pressing need to turn to the use of an English liturgy.

Russian speakers in the Orthodox Church
The presence of Russian Orthodoxy in Australia is more recent. Two of the more distinct waves of Russian migration came through China: in the 1920s a small number of Russians migrated to Australia from Manchuria, China, and following Mao Tse Tung's rise to power, a larger influx of Russian Orthodox refugees came from China in the early and mid 1940s. The first Russian Orthodox parish began in 1922. Today the Russian Orthodox situation in Australia is complex. Most of the Russian migrants worship within what is known as the Russian Orthodox Church Outside Russia, or the Russian Orthodox Church Abroad, which was established by a 'group of bishops opposed to the Soviet regime who refused to recognise the Patriarchate of Moscow' (Garner, 1988). Within the Australian diocese

there is a convent, a monastery as well as numerous parishes. However, as these communities are not in communion with the Russian Orthodox Church (Moscow Patriarchate), they are therefore considered to be non-canonical. There are only two canonical Russian Orthodox Churches in Melbourne, under the jurisdiction of the Ecumenical Patriarchate and the Moscow Patriarchate respectively. Interviewed for the present research was a parish priest within the Russian Orthodox Church Abroad, who also acts as Dean of the southern Australian parishes. The church which he pastors is attended by migrants from Manchuria and China from the 1960s.

The Reformed Church

The Reformed Church arose out of the teachings of the 16th-century Protestant reformers Huldreich Zwingli and John Calvin. Calvinist theology centres on belief in the complete sovereignty of God – that salvation is the result solely of God's choosing and is limited to those He has pre-ordained (the 'elect').

Any description of the establishment of the Reformed Church in Australia is difficult to separate altogether from the history of Dutch migration in Australia for, as Bouma (1995: 78) puts it, 'for some, being Reformed is the same as being Dutch'.

Religiously-based organisations in The Netherlands during the period immediately following the Second World War were active in recruiting potential migrants from amongst their members and virtually 'defined the migration experience' (Overberg, 1981: 18). The support provided by such organisations continued throughout the migration process, including the presence of their own chaplains on the journey over as well as assistance in settling on arrival. Around 30% of Dutch migrants to Australia were from the Reformed denominations (Bouma, 1995: 77).

The first Reformed ministers who migrated to Australia became the founding fathers of the Reformed Churches in Australia. They were said to be 'saddened by the repeated disruptions and schisms of the past in The Netherlands . . . and tried hard to bring together all those who were of the Reformed family, be they Reformed (GKN), Christian Reformed (CGK), Dutch Reformed (NHK) or Free Reformed (GKV)' (Vanderbom, 1991: 19).

The majority of Protestant Dutch migrants were from the Hervormde Kerk (NHK) and the Gereformeerde Kerk (GKN), the former being advised to join the Presbyterian Church of Australia (PCA), while the latter, due to the perceived theological liberalism of the PCA, turned towards the Free Church (Presbyterian Church of Eastern Australia, PCEA). Members of the Free Reformed Church in Holland (GKV) also joined the Free Church on arrival in Australia.

While NHK members were welcomed readily into the PCA, the relationship between the Free Church and the GKN deteriorated over differences in church worship and customs and it became clear that the two could not worship together in unity. In 1952, the decision was made to establish a denomination independent of any other in Australia or The Netherlands. This became the Reformed Churches of Australia (renamed the Christian Reformed Churches of Australia[4] in 2000).

Despite the fact that the exclusive use of the Dutch language dwindled long ago (see Chapter 2), the 'ethnic' image of the Christian Reformed Churches of Australia continues to a certain extent today. Overberg (1981: 30) states that, 'paradoxically, for all the group's insistence on being an Australian community, it exhibits strong tendencies towards preserving group distinctiveness'. The presence of other ethnicities within the Reformed churches has tended to come via marriage or because of transference of membership from other non-Dutch Reformed churches overseas, such as in Indonesia, South Africa and Sri Lanka.

Chinese (Mandarin) speakers in the Reformed Church
The presence of Chinese members within the Christian Reformed Churches of Australia is the result of increased migration from a number of Chinese-speaking countries in the early 1990s, not all of whom have had previous contact with the Reformed tradition in their homelands. The Chinese-speaking congregation in the present research is led by a minister (of ethnic Chinese descent) born in Taiwan. After completing his theological training in the Reformed seminary in Australia, the pastor felt called to begin a ministry to the Chinese community. Cantonese was originally used for services but it was later decided that Mandarin was a better choice to facilitate communication within the diverse Chinese community.

Dutch speakers in the Reformed Church
Dutch migration to Australia began in earnest in the late 1940s, continuing into the major part of the 1950s. The decision to migrate seems to have been the outcome of a number of factors, including previous experience of life outside The Netherlands (such as the experience of Dutch servicemen in Indonesia), dissatisfaction with life in The Netherlands and the desire for change (Van Zetten & Deenick, 1991: 21). Australia was simultaneously encouraging British and European migration and through opening its doors to the Dutch ushered in the beginnings of the Reformed Church. There are now a number of Reformed churches in Melbourne but Dutch services are infrequently conducted in any of these. The Reformed church which took part in the present research is pastored by a minister of Sri Lankan Burgher heritage. It is well attended by many of Sri Lankan background as well as by those of Dutch heritage. As Aldridge (1991: 156–7,161)

points out, Sri Lankans have made a significant contribution to the life of the Reformed Churches in Australia. In the 1950s, a relationship was established with the Dutch Reformed Church of Ceylon (Sri Lanka). The Dutch Reformed Burgher community in Sri Lanka extended financial support to the new Church in Australia, and the nature of the relationship between the Churches in the two countries has since enabled ministers and members to transfer from one to the other easily. As a result of political changes in the 1960s, a large number of Sri Lankans migrated to Australia. The many who came from the Dutch Reformed Church of Sri Lanka were naturally drawn to the sister Church in the new country.

The Uniting Church

The Uniting Church in Australia is unique among the denominations in the present study as it is the product of the union of three separate denominations – the Methodist Church of Australasia, (most of) the Congregational Union of Australia and (parts of) the Presbyterian Church in Australia – each having been brought to Australia during its early colonial history and maintained for a significant period as distinct entities. Congregationalism began in Australia through missionary efforts and grew essentially as a result of migration from England. The Methodists came predominantly from England and Wales, while the Presbyterians were largely of Scottish background. With their union in 1977, a 'new' 'Australian' Church was created. The beliefs and practices of the Uniting Church in Australia (UCA) reflect its origins. It does not view itself as being the sole 'true' Church but rather as part of a whole and, thus, values ecumenical relations. While the Uniting Church believes the Scriptures to be an authoritative guide for church and individual life, it does not believe the Scriptures to be inerrant or to be taken literally.

The union of the three Churches came after more than 20 years of negotiation and faced obstacles not least because of the greater numerical strength of the Methodists (59%) and Presbyterians (36%) than Congregationalists (5%). As Bentley and Hughes (1996: 7) point out, there were also differences to be reconciled concerning the 'major traditions within each group, their quite different church structures, and the differences in the practices of worship and ways of fostering spiritual life'.

While the antecedent denominations of the Uniting Church came predominantly from the United Kingdom, the 'new' Church's identity has been emerging as one characterised by openness to the presence and influence of all cultures. In 1985, the UCA's Fourth Assembly proclaimed itself to be a 'multicultural church', stating 'the fact that our membership comprises people of many races, cultures and languages, is a reminder that the Church is both product and agent of mission' (Statement adopted by the fourth Assembly of the Uniting Church in Australia, 1985). The result of Methodist missionary efforts in places such as Fiji, for example, meant that Fijian Christian migrants to Australia comfortably moved towards the Methodist Church and, subsequently, the Uniting Church. The implications of the proclamation of the Church's multicultural nature include the encouragement of congregations to worship together in their community languages.

Indonesian speakers in the Uniting Church

Melbourne is home to the second-largest concentration of Indonesian speakers in Australia, after Sydney. Immigration from Indonesia began in the 1960s and, in recent years, large numbers of overseas students have also come, attracted by Australian universities. A great majority of Indonesian migrants are of Chinese descent and this ethnic composition is reflected in the Indonesian congregation studied in the present research. Within this congregation of the Uniting Church, a variety of Indonesian denominational backgrounds are represented, at home with the UCA's tolerance for theological diversity. Indonesian congregations in Melbourne number around a dozen, and are affiliated with the Catholic, Baptist and Reformed denominations, in addition to the UCA.

Oromo speakers in the Uniting Church

Melbourne has the highest concentration of Oromo speakers in Australia, with 85% of the total of just 545 speakers (2001 Census figures). Oromo speakers are part of a recently established (1990s) but rapidly growing community[5] in Australia, when compared to the other ethnic groups taking part in this research. Many have come from Ethiopia as refugees. The Oromo people practise Islam, Christianity or the traditional Oromo religion. Among Oromo Christians, most are Catholic or Protestant, the Ethiopian Orthodox Church (linked to the Coptic Church) being associated with the Ethiopian colonisers. Devotion to Islam and non-Orthodox Christianity has been said to have enabled the Oromo to assert their identity vis-à-vis the Ethiopians. A group of Oromo Christians from a variety of denominational backgrounds – primarily charismatic – meets for worship under the wing of the Uniting Church, although they have not been accepted as full members of the UCA as yet.

Tamil speakers in the Uniting Church

Melbourne is home to the second-largest concentration of Tamil speakers in Australia, after Sydney. Most Tamil speakers have come to Australia as refugees of the civil war in Sri Lanka which began in 1983. The first Tamil congregation in Melbourne was formed in the mid 1980s by an

Anglican priest seeking to minister to the Tamil community. A Tamil priest travelled to Melbourne from regional Victoria on a monthly basis to conduct Tamil services but was eventually unable to continue. Some members of the congregation were dissatisfied with the absence of the Tamil language in services and the lack of a Tamil-speaking minister, and began worshipping independently in a Uniting Church building. In the late 1990s, this congregation was accepted as a full member of the UCA. The congregation has strong links with the Church of South India and uses its liturgical resources in addition to those of the UCA. A Tamil congregation still exists in the Anglican Church, with whom the UCA Tamil congregation enjoy a close relationship.

Closing Remarks

This chapter has presented the theoretical, methodological and historical context of the research. Smolicz's 'core value theory' was discussed and found to be helpful in illuminating the underlying values of an ethnic community, particularly with respect to language. The role of language in various aspects of the religious domain was examined, followed by a discussion of the 'religious settlement' of the seven denominations – and the 16 constituent congregations – involved in the research. The following chapter ties these threads together, and by introducing the notion of 'language–religion ideology', will begin to examine the findings.

Notes

1. Community-run, ethnic supplementary schools held on Saturdays, primarily teaching language and culture.
2. In 1995, the Anglican Church of Australia produced *A Prayer Book for Australia* [APBA] (see Chapter 2).
3. The first Catholic mass was taken by the convict priest Fr James Dixon, who had been granted restricted permission by the Governor to perform certain religious duties. Dixon had been charged on suspicion of having taken part in the 1798 Wexford Rebellion against the English and, though initially being sentenced to death, received a commuted sentence of transportation to New South Wales.
4. A CRCA congregation newsletter (http://www.pastornet.net.au/yangebup/newsletter.htm) states that reasons for the name change included the desire to clarify the Church's standing in opposition to groups outside of orthodox Christianity using the title 'Church'; and to reflect the generally closer links to overseas Churches with the name 'Christian Reformed' rather than simply 'Reformed'.
5. Note that the total of number of Oromo speakers in Australia has more than doubled since the 1996 Census total of 269 speakers.

Chapter 2

'Language-Religion Ideology' in an Ethnic Church Context

Introduction

Smolicz's theory of core values, which was examined in Chapter 1, helps explain why language is more central to one culture than another. A similar construct is needed to explain why language is more central to one branch of Christianity than another. For this purpose, the notion of 'language–religion ideology' (LRI)[1] is helpful.

Each denomination has its own ideology about the role of language in religion: each considers that language enhances the spiritual experience but in different ways. The formation of the language ideology of a denomination has much to do with its theological orientation. At one extreme, God may be viewed as so special that only a special language or variety of language (such as Cultivated Australian English[2] within some parts of the Anglican Church) may be used to communicate with or about God. At the other extreme, the emphasis on having a personal relationship with God results in the promotion of the vernacular as appropriate for worship. In other words, churches which feel that God needs to be directly accessible might consider 'ordinary language' appropriate, while churches which hold a view of God which places Him at greater distance may consider that only a 'sacred' language admits them into His presence. The LRI of a denomination thus describes the nature of the link between language and religion. This notion may be illustrated by Figure 2.1.

The role which language is deemed to play within a denomination influences many aspects of its character, creating traditions and patterns of doing things which are particular only to that denomination. The term 'language–religion ideology' therefore appropriately describes a denomination's actions, attitudes, traditions and official/unofficial policies which pertain to language. (It should be noted that as much as ethnic communities have subgroups within them, so too do denominations – these subgroups

Figure 2.1 The LRI continuum

(or 'subcultures') may represent spiritual orientations such as the charismatic movement or evangelicalism and may span denominations. Where these complexities bear some influence, discussion concerning them has been included; however, as this research is denominationally based, denominations will, for the time being, be treated as cohesive units.)

The LRI of a denomination affects its view not only of language *per se* but of *specific* languages and *varieties* of languages and, in this sense, some contradictions may be evident. Even denominations which see the 'ordinary language' as acceptable for worship may accept the 'ordinary language' of only one group of people. What place does such a denomination give, within the context of the church, to any other languages of its parishioners? This is particularly relevant in the Australian context, where speakers of languages from all over the world have played an important part in the developing identity of the nation. How do the different LRIs of the denominations affect the placement of community languages within them? Are these 'foreign' languages accepted and acceptable in denominations which may be historically and dogmatically associated with one specific 'church' language?

This leads us to ask questions such as the following: Can a Lutheran service be equally Lutheran if held in Arabic? Can a Catholic mass be equally reverent if said in Hakka? Can an Orthodox divine liturgy convey the same sense of mystery if said in English? Can you have an 'Australian Orthodox Church'?

The LRI of a denomination is further affected by the role which language plays in particular ethnic communities (which is where Smolicz's core value theory is particularly helpful). A community which has strong oral traditions may easily fit within a denomination which is strongly liturgical, well able to handle recitation of long liturgical passages. Communities in which there is diglossia may be more attracted to a tradition which uses a special language or register for liturgy: some groups, however, may have difficulties in denominations whose traditions require high degrees of literacy in the religious language. An ethnic community which places a high value on transmission of the community language through the generations may view the church as being another vehicle for language maintenance and, therefore, may insist on the use of the community language in church activities. Such a community may have difficulties in a denomination which prioritises the transmission of faith over the transmission of language, where the two are at odds.

In the following section, the LRI of each denomination involved in this research is discussed in order to shed light on the role that the Church plays in language maintenance for ethnic communities in Melbourne.

The LRI of the Anglican Church

One of the many consequences of the Protestant Reformation was the dissemination of the view that there is no difference between the language used between people and that which is appropriate to use with or about God (see later). The Anglican Church began with a similar premise – that the ordinary language of the people, their vernacular, was suitable for church and for communicating with God. However, after the publication in 1662 of *The Book of Common Prayer*, the language used in church, ironically, became crystallised. Suddenly church language had become sacred again and the English of the Church became the standard against which English in all other domains was measured. Having become 'sacred', it could no longer be altered and so ideas of appropriateness and authenticity again became a part of the Church.

Anglicanism in Australia has clearly developed out of this heritage. The Anglican Church has been slow to adopt new forms of English. *An Australian Prayer Book* was published in 1978 as a supplement to the *Book of Common Prayer*. It offered the services of the *Book of Common Prayer* in contemporary English, as well as alternative forms representing more radical reform. *A Prayer Book for Australia* was published in 1995 and 'represents liturgical evolution rather than revolution' (p. vii). The relatively small number of ethnic congregations in existence in the Diocese of Melbourne may in part be due to the difficulty with which community languages are incorporated into the Anglican liturgical experience.

The LRI of the Baptist Church

The Baptists may be characterised by their primary emphasis on having a one-to-one relationship with God and a secondary emphasis on organisational structures and liturgy (Hughes, 1996:2). The Baptist movement has grown since its inception in the 17th century, due in part to the appeal of its informality of worship and the language used. The strong missionary activity of the Baptists resulted in Baptist churches in many parts of the world and the massive immigration to Australia of the 20th century brought many non-English-speaking Baptists. The Baptist Church in Australia has also been strongly influenced by the charismatic movement of the late 20th century.

The LRI of the Baptist churches may be one reason why Hughes (1993) rates the Baptists as so successful amongst migrants from non-English-speaking countries: worshipping as Baptists is not dependent upon the translation of liturgy or creed, though personal interpretation of the Scriptures (and, therefore, some proficiency in the language of the Scriptures used) are of paramount importance. The emphasis on a personal relationship with God and the lack of authority given to the traditions of the Church (including liturgy) has ensured the continual renewal of language in Baptist churches: no single language has become irrevocably linked to private or public worship through its preservation in liturgy, thus preventing Baptist theology from becoming the property of any one ethnic group.

The LRI of the Catholic Church

Any discussion of the LRI of the Catholic Church today cannot but view the Second Vatican Council of 1962–65 as formative. Prior to Vatican II, Latin had been the only language considered sacred enough for use in the Catholic Church, because of its use in the Vulgate. Reform movements in the western Church from the 14th to the 16th centuries demanded liturgies in the vernacular, however, when this was put to the Council of Trent (1545–63), the Council 'confirmed the Latin Vulgate and the Latin order of the Mass as official church documents against either Scripture or litanies in local languages' (Noll, 1997: 207). The Latin language united linguistically disparate peoples throughout the world in the one 'universal church' (Lewins, 1978). The outcomes of Vatican II were thus nothing short of revolutionary: 'No imposed linguistic change has ever affected so many people at once as when Latin was replaced by the vernacular in Roman Catholic Christianity' (Crystal, 1990: 122).

As outlined earlier, the Catholic Church in Australia was, until the post-war immigration boom, particularly Irish in flavour. With the radical changes heralded by Vatican II coming at the same time, the Catholic Church was faced with the prospect of having to accommodate thousands of non-English-speaking faithful within its fold. Most of these non-English speakers had only ever celebrated the Catholic mass in Latin in their home countries; in effect, the Vatican II rulings simultaneously changed the LRI of the 'universal' Catholic Church. The introduction of the vernacular mass paved the way for cultural diversity which had been suppressed both through the universal use of Latin and because of the Australian Government's (and, for that matter, the Church's) policy of assimilation during the first 70 years of the 20th century. However, masses held in community languages are so common today, that while 'Irish' and 'Catholic' may be still coterminous in Australia, so too are 'Italian' and 'Catholic', and 'Polish' and 'Catholic' to name just a few indivisible pairs.

While the Vatican II ruling on mass in the vernacular provided new opportunities to Latin Rite Catholics, one group of Catholics had already been celebrating mass in the vernacular for centuries. As mentioned earlier, the majority of Arabic-speaking migrants to Australia are Christians and, of these, a great many are part of the Catholic Church according to its Eastern Rite. The three largest Eastern Rite churches in Melbourne are the Maronite, Melkite and Ukrainian, the first being of the Antiochene tradition and the latter two being of the Byzantine tradition. Dixon (1996: 49) reports that there is a conviction within the Eastern Rite churches 'that language and culture are the keys to the continued existence of each Church: if the language and culture are maintained – a difficult task – then the Church will continue'. Dixon (1996: 50) pinpoints the crux of the problem when he states: 'Many young people, however, even if they speak the language of their parents, do not know the frequently more ancient liturgical languages used by their Churches, despite efforts by the different Churches to offer programs aimed at maintaining their liturgical languages and the language of their cultural background.' In this sense, the LRI of the Eastern Rite Catholics is akin to that of the Orthodox churches (see later).

The LRI of the Lutheran Church

In discussing the LRI of the Lutheran Church, the position of Luther is clearly fundamental. Luther believed that having a personal relationship with God required an individual to examine the Scriptures personally and, thus, Scriptures in the vernacular were needed. In discussing his view of the language best suited to the Scriptures, he wrote:

> We do not have to ask about the literal Latin or how we are to speak German – as these asses do [the Papists]. Rather we must ask the mother in the home, the children on the street, the common person in the market about this. We must be guided by their tongue, the manner of their speech, and do our translating accordingly. Then they will understand it and recognise that we are speaking German to them. (Luther, 1530)

Luther's translation of the Bible was instrumental in giving shape to a standard German language and, to many Lutherans, the German language took on a certain kind of authenticity.

The two synods of the Lutheran Church which existed in Australia until 1967 meant that (at least) two quite different LRIs based on different theological interpretations coexisted. At the beginning of the 20th century, the United Evangelical Lutheran Church in Australia (UELCA) attached to the German language a degree of sacredness:

> [the UELCA felt that] God had revealed the true meaning of the Bible to Luther in the German language and it was their special obligation to preserve this precious gift. If they wanted to remain in possession of God's true word, they argued, then they had to hold the language of Luther in the highest respect. (Lehmann, 1981: 30)

In this respect, English or any other language was considered a threat to the true faith. The Evangelical Lutheran Church in Australia (ELCA), in contrast, felt that 'the word of God had never been and should not be tied to any one language' (Lehmann, 1981: 35). They acknowledged the exclusive use of German as a barrier to English-speaking friends and family and encouraged flexibility. The forced assimilation of the First and Second World Wars, particularly for the UELCA, changed the LRI of Lutherans in Australia. After the Second World War the influx of migrants from other Lutheran countries added to the growing understanding that if the Church was to survive, it could not stay a German Church. However, many of these newly migrated Lutherans, such as the Latvians, were strongly nationalistic and so the Lutheran Church retained its ethnic character – not as a German Church, but as a stronghold of particular immigrant cultures (such as Latvian) and perhaps more generally as the Church of 'Europeans'. In more recent years, as many of these immigrant groups are into the third or later generations with little new migration to boost numbers, the LRI of the Church is again changing.

The LRI of the Orthodox Church

The LRI of Orthodox Christianity is fully influenced by its view of the role of 'Tradition': by contributing to the continuity of the faith, the liturgical life of the Church is considered a vital element of this Tradition. 'Although these Orthodox churches are themselves often divided by political, religious and ethnic antagonisms, certain features of Orthodoxy remain strikingly similar to the church . . . in 1054. The liturgy remains the heart of Orthodox life and theology' (Noll, 1997: 145). The liturgy used most often by Orthodox Churches is that of St John Chrysostom, 325AD.

The continuity afforded by the use of such an ancient rite in close-to-original form renders dramatic change – such as translation into modern vernaculars – almost unthinkable.

The use of ecclesiastical Greek (incorporating Koine, Attic and Alexandrian Greek; Christos Galiotos, pers. comm. 10 December 1998) in the liturgy of the Greek Orthodox Church is considered vital to the mystical experience of worship, as well as to its authenticity (by using the language of the New Testament).[3] The Russian Orthodox Church view the 10th century Slavonic translation of the Byzantine liturgy as similarly integral to the genuine and full expression of faith. Fishman (1996: 11) puts it this way: 'Such lack of understandability may even be interpreted favourably, in terms of the mysterious nature of sanctity as a whole, being above and beyond mere human understanding and, indeed, as reflecting, underscoring and even adding to the very aura and mystery of sanctity per se.' Despite – or perhaps because of – holding similar views about the role of language in worship, 'the various jurisdictions have tended to emphasize their own customs and language to the exclusion of all others', including other Orthodox (Garner, 1988: 62–3).

In the immigrant context, the separation of ethnicity and Orthodoxy, and the impact upon the faithful of the incomprehensibility of the liturgical language, has not yet been fully explored, 'even though it is supposed to be a principle of Orthodoxy that the language of the country should be used in church services' (Waddams, 1964: 111). Moves towards English in the Orthodox Church are happening more rapidly in the United States, where its incorporation into the liturgy is testing whether Orthodoxy 'can exist outside the ethnically confined boundaries that have traditionally structured Orthodox life' (Noll, 1997: 147). This is an issue which is of increasing importance for second and later generations of Orthodox migrants, who in Australia are often more familiar with English than the community language and whose estrangement from ancient liturgical languages is even greater.[4]

The LRI of the Reformed Church

While the beginnings of the Reformed Church in Australia were fraught with internal divisions carried over from The Netherlands, attitudes towards language were remarkably uniform within the orthodox Protestant groups which eventually united to form the Christian Reformed Churches of Australia (CRCA). While the Catholics and the liberal Protestants (Hervormde Kerk) sought assimilation into existing structures, the orthodox Protestant groups (Gereformeerde Kerk) moved towards separatism in the form of a new denomination, not for the sake of cultural preservation, but due to irreconcilable theological differences (Overberg, 1981: 28). Once within this context of separatism and theological integrity, came the desire to assimilate culturally:

> Let us try to become English in every way as quickly as possible. Surely being in Australia we should earnestly seek to master the language and show outsiders that we are not just foreign churches. We should put away all those things that brand us as foreign, providing that we do not sacrifice scriptural principles. (Reformed Churches of Australia, 1962: 114–15, quoted in Overberg, 1981: 29).

Until that time services were held in Dutch, and psalms and hymns used by the Gereformeerde Kerk were still used by the CRCA. But by the end of the 1960s, with decreasing Dutch migration, questions were being raised about the 'acceptability' of the denomination in the new environment. Language, as well as particular Dutch customs within the Church, were considered a barrier to both assimilation and evangelism, and efforts were made to remove these. The *Protocol of the Establishment of the Reformed Church of Melbourne* (1951) (cited in Van Zetten, 1991: 40) stated: 'By adopting more and more the English language in public worship we will endeavour to become a *real* Australian church as soon as possible' (italics mine). This directive was echoed by church members, in sentiments such as those found in letters to the editor of *Trowel and Sword* (1957, reported in Warren, 1990):

> I am afraid that too many people are of the mind-set: How long can I hang on to the Dutch language? rather than, How quickly can I get rid of it?

> It is our duty before God to do away completely with the use of the Dutch language in the public life of the Church. The 50–50 system (half-English, half-Dutch) is wrong, terribly wrong.

Clyne (1991:136) states that the '"de-ethnicization" of the Reformed Church is intended to make its (characteristically Dutch Calvinist) doctrine accessible to all Australians and to ensure that the second and third generations are not lost to the church for linguistic reasons'.

Immigration to Australia of members of Reformed denominations in other parts of the world has broadened the ethnic base of the CRCA. Yet what is particularly interesting is the continuing Dutch character of the Reformed Church, despite the presence of other ethnicities and the lack of intentional Dutch language maintenance (and in fact despite even intentional language shift). Bouma (1989: 42) puts it this way:

while the Reformed Church of Australia was definitely not founded in order to promote the development of Dutch ethnic identity or the preservation of Dutch culture, it has become and is likely to remain the single most effective agency for the expression and celebration of Dutch ethnicity in Australia. In this case, the strength of an ethnic community is likely to increase into the future rather than decrease with length of time in the host country. This is a very ironic twist for both the church which had no intention of becoming an ethnic church and the one ethnic community which was considered to be the most likely to assimilate rapidly and disappear into the fabric of Australian society.

Despite the widespread replacement of the Dutch language with English in the Church, this retention of Dutch ethnicity – largely via retention of particular religious traditions and styles of worship – may act in the long term as a barrier to the full incorporation of other community languages and cultures.

The LRI of the Uniting Church

The LRI of the Uniting Church is essentially a product of the language attitudes and practices of its antecedent denominations: Congregationalism, Methodism and Presbyterianism. It is, therefore, affected by the views on language in the religious context which were evident in Calvinist, Reformed and evangelical theology. It is significant that the Presbyterian churches which joined the Uniting Church in Australia were those which held to a more liberal Reformed theology. While the first members of these denominations in Australia were immigrants from England, Wales and Scotland, missionary activity (particularly of the Methodists in the Pacific region) and theological affinity (of the Dutch Reformed migrants with the Presbyterian Church) have resulted in the presence of other ethnicities. After Union in 1977, the UCA allowed the constituent churches to continue using their own orders of service but by 1988, the UCA's Commission on Liturgy had published a resource book entitled *Uniting in Worship*. 'The Uniting Church actively encourages the use of formal liturgy, but ministers and members are not bound to follow a particular liturgical formulation in the approved services or to use the services and resources provided in [*Uniting in Worship*]' (Bentley & Hughes, 1996: 17). Similarly, the Uniting Church has encouraged its ethnic congregations to use the liturgical resources with which they are most comfortable, thus increasing the Church's appeal to a wider range of ethnic communities. The Uniting Church's flexible attitude towards the use of particular languages in worship is matched by the openness of its attitude towards the reform of

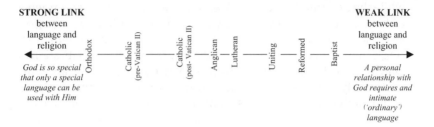

Figure 2.2 Application of the LRI continuum

language in a more general sense, such as the adoption of inclusive language.

Closing Remarks

Having examined the LRIs of the various denominations involved in this research, they can now be placed on the LRI continuum according to the nature of the relationship between language and religion which they exhibit (see Figure 2.2).

The Orthodox and Baptist denominations represent the two extremes of the continuum. Catholicism, prior to Vatican II, exhibited an LRI closer to that of the Orthodox, valuing Latin as the sacred language linking the 'universal' (worldwide) church. Since Vatican II, the introduction of the vernacular has seen Catholic Christianity loosen its emphasis on distinguishing between the language of everyday life and the language of spiritual matters. Anglicanism is in a similar place on the continuum. Having rejected Latin as the language of the Church (at the same time as the rejection of papal authority) in favour of the vernacular, a particular literary form of English became fossilised for the ensuing centuries (and may be witnessed today by the use of a Cultivated Australian English by some Anglican priests). Luther sought to change the emphasis upon particular languages as being more authentic than others but for followers of Luther, the German language took on a certain kind of authenticity as the language of the 'true' faith. The Uniting Church has been particularly influenced by liberal reformed theology and by Methodism which, as an offshoot of Anglicanism, exhibits a similar LRI but with a reduced emphasis on formal worship. The emerging identity of the Uniting Church has a stronger social justice emphasis and the accompanying interest in migrants and refugees has brought an openness to a multicultural ministry and the incorporation of community languages in worship. The Reformed Church, with its Calvinist theology, rejected the need for liturgy and a distinctive language for worship and, in the Australian context, has further loosened the link between language and its expression of religious faith.

At the 'weak' end of the continuum, the emphasis on having an individual relationship with Jesus (and on personal salvation) means that individuals have a responsibility to understand for themselves the Gospel message. The Gospel must, therefore, be communicated in a language which the individual can understand and will vary between groups of individuals. At the 'strong' end of the continuum, the priest is the mediator between man and God, and has the responsibility for learning the 'language of God' – the sacred, ecclesiastical variety. Faith is seen as a *community experience* which is led by the clergy and, therefore, the individual does not need to know the language of God to participate. The reservation of instruction in the ecclesiastical variety for the seminary serves to increase the divide between the ordinary person and the priest who is able to communicate directly with God. This is another reason why Vatican II was significant – in allowing ordinary Catholics to read and interpret the Scriptures by themselves, the LRI of the Catholic Church was changed.

In this chapter, the complex link between language and religion has been discussed in some detail, with particular reference to the seven denominations which are involved in this research. Using the notion of 'language–religion ideology', the ways in which language is used in particular religious traditions was investigated. This concept forms the basis of the present research and will enable an examination of the degrees to which ethnic churches exhibit the LRIs of their 'parent' denominations.

Notes

1. This concept was originally referred to as 'language–culture'. My thanks are due to Michael Clyne, whose thoughts were fundamental to its formulation, and to Tove Skutnabb-Kangas, for suggesting a more transparent term.
2. After Mitchell and Dellbridge (1965): The pronunciation of vowels, in particular, approximates British Received Pronunciation.
3. Fishman (1991: 360) refers to Hebrew, Greek, Arabic and Aramaic/Syriac as the 'religious classicals', the first three being the language of sacred scriptures and the latter being the language spoken by Jesus.
4. It is interesting then, to note that the only Russian Orthodox Church of the Moscow Patriarchate in Melbourne, is English-speaking, though it is led by a recently migrated Russian priest. Its congregation is made up of second and third-generation Russian speakers, as well as Orthodox from other jurisdictions and converts to Orthodoxy (Robert Gribben, pers. comm., 21 January 2000).

Chapter 3

Views from the Pulpit

Introduction

This chapter will present the results of interviews – conducted between 1997 and 1999 – with all 16 church leaders involved in this research. Chapters 4 and 5 will elaborate on the interviews with the Latvian and Indonesian ministers, complementing them with questionnaire data from church members. The reader is also referred to the Appendix for a tabulated presentation of these results.

Summary of Church Findings

Anglican: Chinese (Hakka)

The Malaysian-born Chinese minister interviewed for this research completed his theological training in Australia and became the first full-time incumbent of his congregation. The weekly service at the church is bilingual in that Hakka and English are officially used (Hakka proceedings are translated sentence-by-sentence into English) but because the backgrounds of the 80-member congregation are so varied, small groups dotted around the church tend to translate among themselves into other Chinese varieties where required. At the time of the interview (1997), it had been decided that from 1998 the church would separate into a Chinese congregation and an English congregation. The Chinese-speaking church members mostly come from either southern China or as refugees from East Timor, while those who prefer English are the younger members, many of whom are young professionals from Malaysia, Singapore and Hong Kong. The minister sees the congregation as falling into two very distinct groups of people whose needs are often not met by worshipping together in the one congregation. The congregation as a whole is reported to be generally happy with the decision to separate into two but are concerned that the sense of community may be lost. It is planned that combined services will be held on special occasions. The congregation does not often follow the Anglican liturgy in its services because there is no existing complete translation of the prayer book into Chinese. This has resulted in 'in-house' translation efforts (related problems also exist due to the lack of other resources, such as Bibles, in Hakka). A second reason for infrequent use of a printed liturgy is the reasonably high rate of illiteracy, particularly amongst the East Timorese. Third, the church prefers a charismatic style of worship. No official links exist with overseas churches. While the minister sees language maintenance as important, he recognises that there are differences between the language skills and preferences of the young people in his congregation (depending largely on country of origin and migrational recency) and thus feels that English ('simplified' where necessary) is the best language to use with youth in communicating the Gospel. The minister's vision for the church is a 'multicongregational' church, with new separate congregations established as the need arises.

Anglican: Persian

The Iranian-born leader of the Persian congregation is also vicar of the English-speaking church of which it is a part.[1] He therefore conducts weekly (Sunday morning) services in English and monthly (Sunday evening) Persian services. He sees the Persian congregation as a vital outreach to Iranians and, therefore, to the wider Islamic community. Nevertheless, the minister wants to distance himself from the stereotype of ethnic churches as 'ghettos' and does not want his congregation to be perceived as one. As the 20–25 Iranians who attend the monthly service come from a very widespread area, the minister encourages them to attend their local 'Australian' churches every other week for spiritual growth. The minister sees the spiritual growth of his parishioners as being of paramount importance and thus discourages them from exclusive membership of a congregation that is only able to offer one service each month. This particularly applies to youth: the minister's first priority is to see the Persian youth grow in their Christian faith and he seeks to assure them that attending an English-speaking church will not jeopardise their Persian heritage. While all regular parishioners are reported to be able to speak some Persian and varying degrees of English, the minister recognises that the youth speak English better and, for this reason, he frequently and intentionally uses English in services in the form of sermon summaries for the benefit of the youth and non-Persian-speaking guests. Bilingual services have been held on special occasions. No Sunday School or official youth activities are attached to either the Persian or English services. Despite the openness to English, Persian language maintenance is considered important and the minister is actively involved in translating liturgy, songs and other resources. The services of the Persian congregation essentially follow the liturgy of the Anglican Church, using some pre-existing translations of older versions (some having been brought from Iran), while continuing to work on new translations of the more modern versions of liturgy. A Persian-language Good News Bible published by the Bible Society is currently being used, although a new paraphrase Bible has recently been published. Through the minister, who completed his theological training in the Anglican Church in India before serving for a time in the persecuted Church in Iran, the Persian congregation maintains strong connections with the homeland, as well as with Persian-speaking churches world-wide. The future of the congregation is seen as being dependent on further immigration and on the home country's political situation.

Baptist: Arabic

The Egypt-born-and-educated pastor of this Arabic Baptist congregation came to Australia in 1976 to visit his ailing mother, leaving his own family under the care of the 'Holiness Movement' church he pastored in Alexandria. During what was intended to be a three-month stay, he was approached by Arabic Christians in Melbourne in need of a pastor, a role he subsequently took up (his family being brought out a year later). The congregation today consists of Arabic-speakers not only from the Middle East (Egypt, Lebanon, Iraq, Syria) but from other Arabic speaking regions such as Sudan and Somalia. In this sense the congregation is already multicultural and multilingual. Arabic is the main language used in the congregation; however, English also has a prominent place. In the weekly Sunday morning service, before the Sunday School children and youth group begin their separate (English-medium) activities, both English and Arabic are used for songs, prayers, Bible readings and notices. After the young people leave, the remainder of the service is conducted in Arabic. Once a month a combined service is held in which the congregation stays together for the entire service. On these occasions a (non-Arabic) guest speaker is invited to preach and a sentence-by-sentence translation is given from English into Arabic by a lay member of the church.

The Bible used by the church is, according to the pastor, the only Arabic Bible available. The pastor describes it as being similar to the New King James Version, having been translated from the Greek and Hebrew into a 'very holy, very nice' Arabic. When the proliferation of English versions of the Bible began in the 1980s, some Arabic speakers began to call for a more modern version of the Arabic Bible, to no avail. The pastor's explanation for this inaction is that a 'new' version would cause the Islamic community to question the Christian community over which of the two Bibles is 'true' and which is 'false'. The young people in the Arabic Baptist church are content reading the English New King James Version, the pastor claims.

The pastor emphasises the importance of family in the Arabic culture as a reason for paying great attention to the linguistic needs of Arabic youth;

he feels that it is 'very important to give youth the impression that the church is not against their language, that it is not against them'. The pastor hopes that the young people will establish their own English-speaking congregation within the Arabic church, where they can bring non-Arabic friends but still remain within the Arabic community. While the pastor and his congregation warmly and genuinely welcome non-Arabic speakers, he feels a special attachment to the Arabic language and the Arabic people: 'I love everyone, but I love my language, I love my people'. He envisages that the congregation will continue to be an Arabic-focused ministry, as long as immigration doors remain open.

Baptist: Spanish

This congregation is already 'multicultural', as those who attend are Spanish speakers from a number of different backgrounds, Latin America in particular. The Spain-born-and-educated pastor is, in fact, the only speaker of 'Spanish Spanish'. Because migration from these countries still continues, Spanish proficiency tends to be high, while English skills are more variable. A number of services and activities are held each week but as the 200-strong congregation uses another church's facilities, these are either held at the owning church's convenience or in private homes. The church provides simultaneous translation into English through headphones during the Sunday afternoon service. English Sunday School classes are also held for adults as well as children. Despite the provision of these and other English-medium activities, the pastor perceives Spanish as the preferred language of the congregation overall and does not anticipate problems with a disparity between adults' and children's preferred languages for at least another generation. Due to the strong evangelical tradition in South America, there is no shortage of Spanish church resources. The future of the congregation as a Spanish one depends, to some extent, on continued immigration from Spanish-speaking countries. Language maintenance is very important to the pastor. While Spanish is still considered the most appropriate language for the congregation overall, and Spanish ministry is the current focus, it is the pastor's goal to bring to life a church model that he feels does not yet exist in Australia. This model involves ministry to other cultures, with services in large numbers of languages other than English: English services would also be held but on an equal footing with other services. Such a church model is what the pastor feels should be every church's goal.

Catholic: Croatian

This church was established in 1962 and is part of a Croatian community centre, where the boundaries between religious activities and other community activities are, to some extent, blurred. The current priest was appointed in 1992 after the death of the priest who founded the church. The church has a strong connection to the Catholic Church in Croatia, all its priests having been trained and sent out from the homeland. While Croatian language and cultural maintenance is important, the Croatian-born priest sees their loyalty as being to the Catholic Church. It is only the use of the Croatian language which the priest believes differentiates them from any other Catholic church. For this reason he finds inappropriate any description of his church as being 'Croatian Catholic', preferring it to be known as a 'Catholic church in the Croatian community'. The priest says he does not want to assimilate into the Australian Church but rather to integrate. However, the goal of the church is to exist for 'those from overseas who cannot understand English liturgy'. The 800-strong congregation is an aging one, with poor English skills. Young people with limited proficiency in Croatian are encouraged to attend English-speaking Catholic churches: many of these return to the Croatian church for weddings and baptisms and the priest will incorporate English elements into these services. The Bible used by the church is said to be a direct translation from the Greek and Hebrew, published in 1974.

Catholic: Italian

The Italian priest interviewed for this research is part of a religious order called the Scalabrinians, which was founded in 1887 to care for Italian migrants in North and South America. The ministry of Scalabrinians in Australia has moved from a focus on the Italian community to a more wide-reaching service to other migrant groups such as the Filipino community. The Italian-born priest undertook his theological training in the United States and, since migrating to Australia, has taken on many roles in the Catholic community: as the current director of the Catholic Italian Resource Centre and the main Italian chaplain in Melbourne, he is in constant pastoral contact with the Italian community. In addition, he acts as coordinator of all the other Catholic migrant chaplains. So while he is not currently 'attached' to a parish, he is in ministry to Catholic migrants – Italians in particular. The church where he frequently takes mass has a congregation of around 150 people, mainly first generation, over the age of 50. There are very few teenagers. The priest believes that this is a typical profile of Italian Catholic churches today. Within the Italian community, he sees the lack of a youth presence in church as being partly a language-related issue and partly reflective of the general lack of interest in Christianity and the Church found amongst all young people today, regardless of ethnic background. There are about 40 Italian masses spoken in Melbourne every Sunday. Some are celebrated by Italian priests, some by Maltese priests who know Italian, some by Australian priests who have studied in Rome and some others by Australian priests who have acquired the language 'along the way'. Some of these priests find it difficult to give a sermon in Italian but they may be able to read a text, so the mass is said in Italian and the homily is delivered in English. The priest believes that the change to mass in the vernacular after Vatican II was a change for the better, enabling priests to communicate with their parishioners better. According to this priest, the change to the vernacular, however, does not mean that a dialect such as Venetian could ever be considered appropriate for use in the Catholic Church. Italian is reported to be the preferred language of parishioners, with English being dispreferred not only due to a lack of English proficiency but due to a lack of proficiency in the English church register. The second generation are more familiar with English and often have bilingual wedding and baptism services. Funerals tend to be in Italian: very few funerals for members of the first generation are conducted in English. The priest believes that, at some point in the future, Italian Catholic churches in Australia will no longer find itself using Italian. However, while there are still a number of first generation migrants, there is a need for Italian ministry and pastoral care. The priest is adamant that ethno-specific congregations are not divisive but are merely an appropriate response to the reality of the social environment. He believes that ethno-specific ministries are preferable to multicultural ones in which the languages of several ethnic groups may be used 'because the purpose of Sunday worship is not to display multicultural diversity or unity, but to worship God'. He believes that the church plays an important role in language maintenance for the community but that language maintenance should always be subordinate to worship.

Lutheran: German

A total of 60–80 people attend the three German and two English services which are led by the German-born-and-trained pastor each month. This church is in 'altar and pulpit' fellowship with the Lutheran Church of Australia (LCA) and, in practice, their links are stronger to the LCA than to the Church in Germany from whom they receive some financial support. The liturgy used is said to be not specifically Lutheran but is an old German Protestant liturgy which has been used since the congregation began. For English services, a direct translation is used. The congregation are predominantly from Germany, although some members are Swiss or Austrian. Social motivation is strong for attending the church – it is seen as a place for the community to gather together. English is also used in the German service – through distributed English translations of the sermon and Bible readings and through hymns that may be sung in either language. Some strong opposition to the use of English has been expressed. According to the pastor, his parishioners tell him, 'I feel at home in the German service, not because of the quality of the service, but because of the tone of the language, the images the language creates in me'. The pastor feels that language-related issues were more prominent in the church in the past, such as when English was introduced into the Sunday School. The greatest opponents to this were the parents who spoke English at home – perhaps because they saw the church's role as providing the language instruction their children were not receiving at home. While the pastor feels that English is the best language to use with youth to communicate the Gospel, getting the message across is not so much a language-related issue as an issue of relevance in contemporary society. The pastor estimates that the majority of the congregation would want the church to be a 'German' church but acknowledges that there is a strong group who see a theological basis for a multicultural church. The pastor himself does not have a strong preference in either direction but he sees a need for the German language services to continue to enable many in his congregation to understand and to communicate effectively. 'I think that language and faith are something very intimate . . . Certain feelings, religious feelings, come only in the language of your mother.' While he sees language maintenance as important, he sees his vocation as serving his congregation and not as a call to serve a specific language or culture. Whether the church remains a German church is not important to him, as long as it remains a 'church of Christ'.

Lutheran: Latvian

This church was established by post-war 'displaced persons' from Latvia. 'Built for Latvians, by Latvians' (see Chapter 4), the church has always played an important role in language maintenance for the community. At the time of the interview (1997), one traditional Latvian Lutheran service was conducted weekly and a small contemporary-style service in English was conducted fortnightly, these being supplemented by a number of (mostly Latvian) Bible study groups and a range of social activities. However, moves to develop an English ministry in the church have been controversial. The inclusion of English-language activities is strongly supported by those who feel exclusive use of Latvian causes unnecessary alienation of family and friends, but is vehemently opposed by those who feel the use of English betrays the heritage of the church. The church has a clear language policy within its constitution regarding the circumstances in which English may be used in services and activities. Proposed changes to this constitution outline the limited circumstances in which non-Latvians may join the church. The American-born-and-trained Latvian pastor, who has been at the church since 1987, disagrees with aspects of these language-based policies, resulting in tensions within the church. While the pastor places a high priority on language maintenance, he sees an English ministry for those whose Latvian is poor or non-existent to be vital: the use of English in appropriate activities gives priority to the Gospel message rather than merely to 'Latvianism' and has the potential to keep the Latvian community together in the one church by seeking to meet the generations' disparate needs. (See Chapter 4 for detailed discussion of the Latvian Church.)

Lutheran: Slovak

While the pastor is from the Slovak Republic, the majority of his congregation are Slovaks from the former Yugoslavia, whose Slovak language is heavily influenced by languages such as Serbian. Until the present pastor was appointed, there had been no Slovak-speaking pastor from the Slovak Republic – the previous ones were from USA and Argentina – and thus the pastor sees himself as a role model for 'correct' Slovak. The English language skills of parishioners depend on migration vintage (and therefore education) rather than age. At the time of the interview (1997), a range of services and activities in both English and Slovak, as well as in different liturgical styles, are conducted each week. Translation through headphones of a printed English version of the sermon is provided during the main Sunday service. The introduction of contemporary-style English-language services (with a band) encountered great opposition from some in the church on the grounds of style (specifically the use of drums) rather than language. The congregation has no links with Slovak congregations of other denominations in Australia and links with the Slovak Church overseas are more with the Church in the former Yugoslavia rather than in the Slovak Republic because of the origins of the congregation. A Slovak Bible (1979) and hymnal (1994) produced in Slovakia are used in services. Previously the hymnal had been in Czech and included politically based texts such as 'O Lord save us from the Turks' (pastor's own translation). While some members of the congregation want membership to be restricted to Slovak-speaking people only, the congregation has been quite active in outreach amongst the community, setting up, amongst other things, a Christian bookshop.

Orthodox: Greek

This church is situated in the increasingly expensive inner-city area of South Melbourne; however, most of its members are elderly Greek speakers who moved into the area before its economic boom. The church may be considered trilingual in the sense that ecclesiastical Greek, modern Greek and English are regularly used in various components of the church's activities: English is used for Sunday School, for Scripture readings (after they have been read in ecclesiastical Greek), for an English rendition of the sermon (after it has been given in modern Greek) and for the recitation of the Creed and the Lord's Prayer (after they have been recited in modern Greek). While many who are not members of the parish choose it as a venue for weddings and baptisms because they know that the priest is willing to incorporate some English, there have been no moves to have the regular liturgy entirely in English. The emphasis on the 'mystery' of the Church sustains the use of what to most is an unintelligible language. The role of the Greek Orthodox Church is seen as being to serve those who regard themselves as Orthodox, particularly Orthodox of Greek background. The Australian-born priest – who undertook his theological training in Greece – does not see a need for an 'Australian' Orthodox Church (as opposed to having various jurisdictions, e.g. Greek, Russian), as he feels that those who want to hear an Orthodox liturgy in English are already sufficiently catered for by the small number of churches who offer it.

Orthodox: Russian

As mentioned in Chapter 1, the Russian Orthodox priest interviewed for the present research is a parish priest within the Russian Orthodox Church Abroad, a non-canonical Orthodox Church which broke away from the canonical Russian Church in the 1920s. Most Russian Orthodox churches in Melbourne are part of the non-canonical Church. The Serbian-born priest, who has looked after his parish for 20 years, has also acted as Dean of the southern Australian parishes for the last 11 years. His own parish is attended largely by Russian migrants from Manchuria and China who came during the 1960s. Russian is still the dominant language amongst his parishioners, who tend to represent first-generation migrants more than the second. To these post-war migrants, the church personified their lost homeland and was the centre of community life. Most families live within walking distance of the church, as well as the community centre, the Russian school and the retirement home.

In the Divine Liturgy, Old Church Slavonic is used, although the Gospel and Epistle are read in Slavonic and English and the sermon and notices are given in modern Russian. The priest is aided by an English-speaking non-Russian priest whose contribution (such as the Epistle reading) is always in English. There is an English-language liturgical book available at the entrance to the church, which is used by visitors and sometimes by the teenagers of the church. The priest feels that Russian/Slavonic is still the preference of the congregation as a whole and that the church has not reached the stage where English is necessary, except for youth groups and Bible study groups. Catechism is taught at the Russian Saturday School in

Russian. The priest says he does not know whether the youth of the church would prefer to have the liturgy in English, as he has 'not asked them'. However, he does not feel that an English liturgy would destroy the mysticism, as the mystery is found in other elements of the service as well (when he does the annual English-language service for school children on the day before Palm Sunday, he still says the secret prayers of the sanctuary in Slavonic). If a change in the language of liturgy occurred, the minister predicts it would be a change to English, not to modern Russian which he feels would seem crude compared to Old Church Slavonic. The priest believes that introducing English into the church for the sake of the youth would only bring tension within families. In time, he feels, the language issue will resolve itself.

Reformed: Chinese (Mandarin)

The pastor of this Reformed congregation is Taiwanese-born and founded the congregation at the end of the 1980s. The congregation numbers about 60, its members coming from China, Hong Kong, Singapore and Malaysia. Cantonese was originally used for services but as the congregation grew in number, it was clear that Mandarin was known by more of the congregation than Cantonese and would, thus, be a better choice to facilitate communication. Only one combined service has been held with the English-medium congregation of the church from which they are renting (see next section). It is unlikely that any further such services will be repeated, as it is the pastor's impression that most of his congregation are uncomfortable in that environment. Links with the Reformed Church are generally not strong, although the congregation is a member of the Christian Reformed Churches of Australia and the pastor undertook his theological training at the Reformed seminary in Australia. One formal service is held each week, as well as youth activities and Bible studies. When children are present at services, English is used in the service as well as Mandarin. The pastor feels that English is the best language to use with youth and that youth resist learning Chinese because they think it is too difficult. The pastor feels that a bilingual 'open-door' church is the best model to have.

Reformed: English (of Dutch origin)

This pastor is responsible for the main congregation of a Reformed Church in the eastern suburbs of Melbourne. (The Mandarin congregation described in the previous section is a 'tenant' of this 'landlord' English-medium congregation.) While 70% of the 500 or so in the congregation are of Dutch background, Dutch services were phased out approximately 20 years ago, a move which was noticeably 'traumatic for some'. The only regular Dutch-medium event is the annual Dutch Christmas service. The remaining members of the congregation are mostly of Sri Lankan Burgher background, as is the pastor, and, as such, have English as their first language. The pastor's Dutch language skills are negligible and very few parishioners now speak Dutch. The pastor, who undertook his theological training in Sri Lanka and the United States, wants to move away from what he considers the 'European model' of a church to an 'Australianised' church. This is causing some tensions with some of those of Dutch origin who, according to the pastor, still hold dear certain Dutch traditions and styles of worship (despite the cessation of Dutch-language services). Though he once considered having a separate congregation for the Sri Lankan members of the congregation, the pastor saw little point because of their high level of English language proficiency. He thus felt their needs could be met in the communal service. As the non-Dutch component of the congregation increases, the church will most likely continue to lose its particularly Dutch character.

Uniting: Indonesian

At the time of the interview (1997), this Indonesian congregation shared a church building with a separate English congregation. The Indonesian congregation is young, largely made up of students – thus the size of the church fluctuates according to the Australian university calendar – and some parishioners are in mixed marriages. Simultaneous translation into English is provided through headphones and a number of activities, particularly for youth, are conducted in English. Most of the congregation are of Chinese descent, with strong Javanese cultural influence. Most would, therefore, speak a number of languages including Javanese but would not necessarily be proficient enough in the appropriate speech level to discuss religious matters. The congregation comes from a variety of different denominational backgrounds and the UCA gives them flexibility to develop their own unique liturgy. The Indonesian-born-and-trained minister feels that the opportunity for a person to use his or her first language in the religious domain is important as it enables that person to 'feel very close to what they believe'. Non-Indonesian visitors to the church are welcomed by the minister, who has expressed his desire to have a 'multicultural church'. (See Chapter 5 for detailed discussion of the Indonesian congregation.)

Uniting: Oromo

The 40 or so who attend the weekly Oromo fellowship are mainly refugees from Ethiopia, with the longest period of residence in Australia being eight years. They come from different denominational backgrounds but generally with a charismatic leaning and as a congregation do not follow a liturgy. As the service must be held on a Saturday afternoon to fit in with the owner church's schedule, some Oromo who are opposed to activity on what they consider to be the Sabbath refuse to attend. The leader, who undertook theological training in Ethiopia, sees his role as reaching the Oromo people and teaching the Oromo language. Language maintenance is perceived as being very important, as spiritual matters are thought to be best understood with one's mother tongue. The Oromo language has undergone recent change, with a Latin script now being widely used. However, only the New Testament is available in the new script: a complete Oromo translation of the Bible only exists in the old Oromo script which many of the youth cannot read.

Uniting: Tamil

The first Tamil congregation in Melbourne was an Anglican one formed in the early 1980s. Once a month, a Tamil priest travelled to Melbourne from a town in regional Victoria to conduct Tamil services but was eventually unable to continue. Without a Tamil minister, services were conducted in English. The Tamil congregation felt a strong desire to worship in Tamil and eventually moved away from the Anglican Church to begin worshipping independently. After renting the facilities of a Uniting Church for some time, they were accepted as a congregation of the Uniting Church in Australia in 1996. Within this parish, there are five congregations: two English-speaking, one Tamil, one Cook Islander and one Oromo (see previous section), which is not yet a member. Three ministers share the responsibility for these five congregations and whenever there is a fifth Sunday in the month, a joint parish service is held – thus living up to the parish motto 'a parish for all nations'. At the time of the interview (1997), the Tamil congregation had two services a month[2] (at 5 pm) and had started another congregation in another suburb which also meets twice monthly. Almost all members of the congregation are involved in their local Uniting churches as well as with the Tamil congregation, enabling their children to attend Sunday School more regularly than the once-a-month English-medium Tamil classes. Religion is very important within the Tamil community and Tamil-speaking parents are concerned about the spiritual growth of their children. While they would like the youth to be proficient in Tamil, most young people are unable to read or write the Tamil script, thus, the minister feels, making it pointless to translate resources into Tamil. Of the two monthly Tamil services which are conducted, the first is bilingual (being run by and aimed at youth) and the second is exclusively in Tamil. All youth activities are conducted in English. The minister uses the liturgy of the Church of South India – in which he was trained – with some alterations, and has also translated some UCA prayers for use. The Tamil Bible has undergone many revisions and a new 'more pure' version has just been published: both the old and new versions are used in the service. Most of the congregation have come through the trauma of civil war in Sri Lanka and many have relatives and friends still there, thus heightening the sense of responsibility felt by the minister to care for the Tamil community and cater specifically for its needs. In response to public criticism over the perceived ethno-centricism of ethnic churches, the minister says that the Tamil people are well integrated in the work environment and local (English-speaking) churches but require Tamil fellowship because the community feels a need to preserve something of their culture: they do not wish to 'isolate themselves from others, but to have something to offer to multicultural Australia'.

Closing Remarks

As the preceding descriptions have illustrated, ethnic churches vary greatly in their precise circumstances but have in common certain difficulties which accompany the minority status of their languages. The most significant of these are the differences in community language proficiency between the first and subsequent generations, due in no small way to the effect of English-medium education and the influence of English-medium media and entertainment. In response to these and other pressures, three general reactions are apparent: some churches choose to shift completely to English in order to become 'more Australian' and 'less ethnic'; others make a range of concessions for the sake of youth and English-speaking church members, such as English-language translations during services or specific English-medium activities; still others prefer to persevere with their community language in all aspects of church life in order to pass on what is considered to be a sacred heritage to future generations.

In the following chapters, two of these 16 congregations will be looked at in greater depth. Differing in their social, historical and theological backgrounds and attitudes, they will provide additional insight into ways in which language and faith intersect.

Notes

1. This interview was conducted in 1997 and thus represents the situation at that time. In late 1998, the minister retired and the church building was sold to the Orthodox Church. After a period in which services were conducted in private homes, the congregation began meeting for monthly services in an Anglican church in the eastern suburbs of Melbourne. A suitable replacement for the minister has not been found and he thus continues to conduct the Persian services.
2. This interview reflects the situation in 1997. Weekly services were being conducted in Tamil by February 2000.

Chapter 4

Case Study 1: The Latvian Church

Introduction

In order to illuminate some of the issues faced by ethnic churches, an in-depth examination of two quite different congregations was undertaken. The results from one of these 'case-study' churches – a Latvian Lutheran church – are presented and discussed in this chapter.

The Latvian Church in Social, Historical and Theological Perspective

A group of Melbourne Latvians began gathering together for worship around 1950–51, soon after arriving as post-war 'displaced persons' in the years 1947–50. They met together in a Lutheran church building in East Melbourne until 1972, when a church of their own was built and dedicated.

Since its beginnings, the church's goal was not merely to meet for spiritual nourishment and fellowship with other Latvian Christians but to gather together a community of those wanting to preserve their cultural heritage and uphold the dream of a 'free Latvia' where this cultural inheritance could take its rightful place. The sense of nationalistic pride and patriotic fervour was strong: cultural and language maintenance in all domains of life became a way of showing support for a free Latvia. When the goal of independence was achieved in 1991, the original church members continued with still strong voices of patriotism: the goal had been attained but decades (in fact, centuries) of guarding against outside cultural and linguistic influence had made it into a way of life not easily changed. In the meantime, however, the sons and daughters of the original migrants had grown up and had themselves raised children: with each new generation, more and more Latvians were marrying those of other ethnicities. Mixed marriages created new family dynamics, with (a) Latvian-speaking grandparents, (b) parents who could speak either language but were more comfortable with English and (c) children who typically could speak only a little Latvian. This reflects the church's current situation.

The current pastor of the church arrived in Australia from the United States to begin ministry at the church in October 1987. He is the senior pastor, the sole full-time staff member. The church is a part of the Latvian Church outside Latvia (formerly, the Latvian Church in Exile) and have been full members of the Lutheran Church of Australia (LCA) since 1972.

There are currently two other Latvian Lutheran congregations (while one is a member of the LCA, the other is a fully independent church body) and one Latvian Catholic congregation in Melbourne. These two other Lutheran congregations are unable to meet weekly as they share the facilities of a German-language Lutheran Church. The Latvian church in the present research is the largest, with around 1000 members (though, as outlined later, the number of members in the Church records bears little resemblance to weekly attendance numbers).

Two services are regularly run: the 9 am English-language service and the 11 am Latvian-language service. The Latvian service is held weekly, with an accompanying Sunday School class held fortnightly. The English service is usually held only fortnightly, with an English-language Sunday School until recently being held once a month: it became no longer feasible to continue it due to declining numbers. English evening services have also been conducted in previous years, as well as a youth group. The average number of those who regularly attend services is typically around 10–15 for the English service and around 120 for the Latvian service. While the average age of those who attend the English-language service would be, based on observation, around 40, the average age of those who attend the Latvian service is recorded at 65. According to the pastor, those in the thirties age group who attend the Latvian service usually do so because they are making an effort to be involved, to actively maintain their language. Many of these send their children to the Latvian community-run Saturday School as well – of the ten or so children who attend the Latvian Sunday School most also attend the Saturday School. While the pastor takes regular Religious Education classes at the Saturday School, the School is not run by or officially connected with any of the Latvian churches.

The church has its own constitution, in which its aims are set out as follows:

> 4.1.   The aims of the Congregation are:
>
>> (a)   to proclaim and worship Jesus Christ as our Lord and Saviour;
>>
>> (b)   to hold and celebrate religious services, religious ceremonies, prayer sessions, Bible studies, Holy Communion, Christenings, Marriage ceremonies, Funeral services and other like activities;

(c) to hold confirmation lessons and confirm the youth of the Congregation, to teach and guide the youth in Christian Latvian Lutheran traditions and to hold Sunday School for the children;

(d) to provide for the spiritual care of the members of the Congregation, and within the means of the Congregation to materially support the needy members;

(e) to remain part of the Evangelical Lutheran Church of Latvia in Exile;

(f) to maintain a relationship with the Lutheran Church of Australia

(g) to inspire and support the Latvian cultural and social activities and to co-operate with and participate in (where appropriate) other Latvian Cultural and Community organisations;

(h) to publish the Congregation's periodical newsletter in the Latvian language (with an alternative English text provided, if the Committee so desires);

(i) the activities of the Congregation and its religious services shall be performed in the Latvian language, additional services and activities may also be provided in the English language for those who do not speak Latvian.

The last of these bylaws, which allows for the provision of 'additional services' in English where these are required, has been interpreted in various ways. One interpretation which is being strongly voiced is that 'additional' means 'not equal to', thus meaning that *weekly* English services are not permissible. This has been disappointing for those who regularly attend and enjoy these services, for these services do not only provide an alternative language for teaching and worship but an altogether different style. While the 11 am Latvian service is a traditional Lutheran service, the 9 am service is described by the pastor as 'contemporary liturgical'. The style is informal, with interaction between the pastor and the congregation being more frequent and less rigid. For example, the 'Greeting of Peace' is shared between members of the congregation, an activity which causes awkwardness and discomfort if used in the Latvian service. Congregational participation is also encouraged by inviting individuals to share aloud any personal needs for which they would like prayer and during times of prayer, some members of the congregation may 'pray in tongues': in the Latvian service, participation by the congregation is confined to set liturgical responses. For the English service, the pastor wears ordinary 'civilian' clothing and not the traditional vestments which are afterwards donned for the Latvian service. Songs include both hymns and modern choruses and are accompanied by keyboard and guitar, instead of the organ. The sermon is not given from the pulpit but from the chancel steps and while much of the sermon content is the same as for the Latvian service which follows it, there may be greater emphasis on topics which reflect a charismatic orientation.

The Interview

An interview was conducted with the pastor of this church in order to gain his perspective on the church's part in language maintenance and the role of language in any issues faced.

For the duration of the current pastor's term of ministry, language has been a factor in most of the problems encountered. In his early years, the pastor made efforts to use both English and Latvian in the one service, something which was received with great hostility by some church members. He refers to this as his 'biggest mistake' during that period. Over the years he has come to a change of position, seeing the only way forward as being the temporary separation of English and Latvian, by keeping the services and activities held in the two languages as separate as possible. He now restricts his use of English in a Latvian service to providing explanations of concepts referred to in the sermon which cannot be expressed equally well in Latvian. He is, at the same time, very anxious not to put a 'stumbling block' in the way of his parishioners who find the use of English objectionable. He bases this philosophy on a Biblical passage, Romans 14:13: 'Therefore let us stop passing judgement on one another. Instead, make up your mind not to put any stumbling block or obstacle in your brother's way.' If anything becomes a 'barrier to the Gospel', the pastor sees it as his role to remove that barrier. If he sees the use of a particular language as not aiding communication but impeding it, he will choose the language he considers more useful for the task.

This attitude is at times at odds with the 'Aims of the Congregation' (see previous section). While the present bylaws of the church constitution state that the *Latvian* Lutheran tradition and culture must be imparted in activities of the church, the pastor does not see this as a goal over and above imparting the Gospel. He thus holds Confirmation classes in English, partly because the materials used are from English sources – videos, course notes, etc. – and partly because he feels that this is the language in which the confirmants can most readily grasp the message of Christ. While weddings are increasingly conducted (partly or wholly) in English because of the growing number of mixed marriages, funerals are the more common service conducted by the pastor. On such occasions, he says, there are large numbers of family members and friends from other spheres of life who do not speak Latvian and so he switches freely between Latvian and English.

The fact that the bylaws state the necessity of imparting Latvian culture through the church is one of the points held up in objection to non-Latvians becoming part of the church – it is thought that people of other backgrounds would be unable to appreciate Latvian customs and traditions. Another fear of some church members is that if non-Latvians became part of the church community in increasing numbers, then the annual general meeting would have to be held in English. As a result, many of those of Latvian descent with no or poor Latvian skills feel they are seen as not 'valuing' Latvianness as it should be valued. Some of those from other ethnic backgrounds, who for various reasons wish to attend the church, feel they have not been welcomed.

The objection to an 'open door' style of church seems to be found amongst Latvian Lutherans not just in Melbourne, Australia. The pastor has met with leaders of Latvian churches in the United States who have had similar experiences. Some pastors are leaving the Latvian Church and are going into ministry in other churches out of frustration at being forced to make cultural maintenance their first priority over teaching the Christian faith (Edgars Petrevics, pers. comm., 28 July 1998, confirms this). A discussion between the LCA's district governor (of German background) and the Latvian pastor about the Latvians' 'closed door' attitude brought forth the following comment from the district governor: 'Well, that's the way *we* felt before the war'.

A set of 'proposed changes' to the church bylaws has recently been put forward by the church council, which directly addresses the question of who may become a member of the church. If a non-Latvian wishes to join the church, they are required to find two Latvian 'sponsors' who are already members. The sponsor cannot be their Latvian spouse (in the case of a mixed marriage).

The pastor is concerned about such proposed changes and questions whether it is the church's role to promote Latvianism – and whether, in fact, Latvianism has become the 'golden calf' of the people. While not rejecting the importance of Latvianness to one's identity, he rejects its imposition upon all. He is saddened by the church community's unwillingness to change, at least, to allow others to change.

The pastor's own language use at home provides an interesting contrast to the philosophy he supports at church. At home, together with his wife, he is enthusiastic and committed to passing on the Latvian language to their baby daughter and is vigilant in keeping his Latvian 'free' of English. At church, however, he is conscious of the fact that sharing the Gospel is his goal and will do so in whichever language is more easily understood and appropriate. Imparting the Gospel, not the language, is the goal he strives for there.

The Questionnaire

One hundred and twenty-three questionnaires were distributed to those attending the 9 am English-language service and 11 am Latvian-language service on a particular Sunday. These services happened to be confirmation services; therefore, many of those attending were friends and relatives of the confirmants and not members of the church (however, membership was not a prerequisite for completing a questionnaire). This may, however, have affected the return rate, with non-members possibly opting not to participate: a total of 46 of the 123 (37.4%) questionnaires distributed were completed and returned. It may also be that the rawness of some of the issues raised within the questionnaire in this particular church context caused some potential participants to withdraw. The process for returning questionnaires was facilitated and encouraged as much as possible by the distribution of stamped addressed envelopes and by giving reminders during subsequent services. The low return rate detracted from the value of undertaking any detailed statistical analysis of questionnaire responses; however, the qualitative data obtained from open-ended questions provided valuable insight into the Latvian situation, representing a wide range of viewpoints.

Thirty-three (71.7%) participants completed the questionnaire using English only, eight (17.4%) used Latvian only and five (10.9%) used different languages for different questions.

The participants

An even spread of the 46 participants eventuated with 50% being male and 50% being female. The majority of participants were over the age of 65, with the next greatest number being in the 45–54 age group, representing the second generation.

While all held Australian citizenship, ten participants (21.7%) indicated that they held dual citizenship (eight [17.4%] with Latvia and two [4.3%] with the USA). One participant (2.2%) held citizenship in Australia, Latvia as well as the United States.

Just over half of the participants were born outside Australia, with the greatest proportion of these being born in Latvia. Of the 25 overseas-born participants, nine (36%) were aged 12 or under, four (16%) were teenagers and the remaining 12 (48%) were between the ages of 24 and 48 when they arrived in Australia.

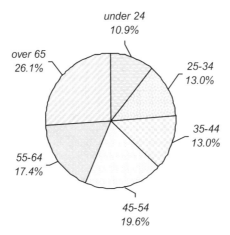

Figure 4.1 Age distribution of participants

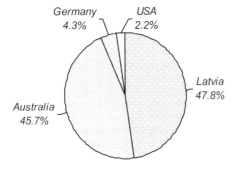

Figure 4.2 Distribution of participants by birthplace

As can be seen from Figures 4.3 and 4.4, the vast majority of participants were of Latvian ancestry. While most participants had at least one Latvian parent and could, therefore, claim Latvian heritage, three non-Latvians completed questionnaires. Two of these participants were married to a Latvian (see Figure 4.5); however, only one of these participants regularly attended the church. The third non-Latvian participant attended the English services of the church with their non-Latvian spouse. Mixed marriages made up only a small proportion of participants' parentage with two participants (4.3%) having a Latvian mother and Australian father and one participant (2.2%) having a British mother and Latvian father. Of the 37 participants (80.5%) who were themselves married, there were more mixed

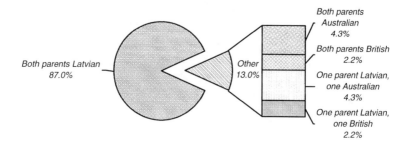

Figure 4.3 Distribution of participants by ethnic background, both parents Latvian

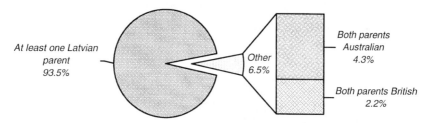

Figure 4.4 Distribution of participants by ethnic background, at least one parent Latvian

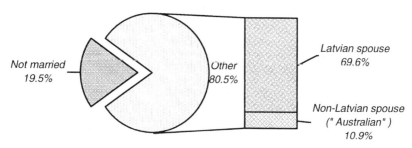

Figure 4.5 Distribution of participants by spouse ethnicity

marriages, thus confirming the expected tendency for mixed marriages to increase in the second and third generations.

Participants' language skills
    Self-assessments of language skills were made for speaking, under-standing, reading and writing on a scale which included the categories

'fluent', 'very well', 'moderately well', 'a bit' and 'not at all' (see Tables 4.1 and 4.2). Adding together the percentages for the 'fluently' and 'very well' categories to form a single 'good' category, the distribution of responses becomes more reliably representative. While a much greater proportion of participants considered themselves more highly proficient in English than in Latvian, only Latvian writing skills clearly trailed behind other skills in either language – 69.6% for 'good' Latvian writing compared to percentages in the eighties for other Latvian skills (speaking 80.5%, reading 80.4% and understanding 84.8%), and percentages in the nineties for all English language skills (speaking and writing both 91.3%, understanding 97.9% and reading 97.8%). This is likely to be due to the perceived difficulty of writing Latvian with its morphological complexities (which can be easy to mask in the spoken form).

Participants were asked to indicate whether or not they were familiar with any other language or dialect other than English or Latvian: Table 4.3 lists the languages which were mentioned by participants.

In total, 20 participants (43.5%) indicated that they were familiar with another language. Seventeen of these 20 indicated that this other language was German, while three of these participants indicated that they were familiar with Russian in addition. One participant was familiar with both Russian and French; one participant with French only; one participant with

Table 4.1 Participants' self-assessments of Latvian language skills

	Fluently	*Very well*	*Moderately well*	*A bit*	*Not at all*	*Missing*
Speak	20 (43.5%)	17 (37%)	2 (4.3%)	4 (8.7%)	3 (6.5%)	–
Understand	28 (60.9%)	11 (23.9%)	–	3 (6.5%)	3 (6.5%)	1 (2.2%)
Read	25 (54.3%)	12 (26.1%)	2 (4.3%)	3 (6.5%)	4 (8.7%)	–
Write	19 (41.3%)	13 (28.3%)	7 (15.2%)	–	7 (15.2%)	–

Table 4.2 Participants' self-assessments of current English language skills

	Fluently	*Very well*	*Moderately well*	*A bit*	*Not at all*	*Missing*
Speak	34 (73.9%)	8 (17.4%)	4 (8.7%)	–	–	–
Understand	36 (78.3%)	9 (19.6%)	1 (2.2%)	–	–	–
Read	37 (80.4%)	8 (17.4%)	1 (2.2%)	–	–	–
Write	32 (69.6%)	10 (21.7%)	4 (8.7%)	–	–	–

Table 4.3 Languages other than English or Latvian known by participants

Language	No. of speakers	Language	No. of speakers
German	17	French	4
Russian	4	Indonesian	2

Table 4.4 Participants' self-assessments of skills in known language(s) other than English or Latvian

	Fluently	Very well	Moderately well	A bit	Not at all	n/a
Speak	1 (2.2%)	4 (8.7%)	11 (23.9%)	10 (21.7%)	1 (2.2%)	26 (56.5%)
Understand	1 (2.2%)	5 (10.9%)	11 (23.9%)	9 (19.6%)	1 (2.2%)	26 (56.5%)
Read	1 (2.2%)	7 (15.2%)	4 (8.7%)	13 (28.3%)	2 (4.3%)	26 (56.5%)
Write	1 (2.2%)	5 (10.9%)	4 (8.7%)	14 (30.4%)	(3 (6.5%)	26 (56.5%)

Indonesian as well as German; and one Indonesian as well as French. Both of these latter two participants were under the age of 24, having learned (or currently still learning) these languages at school. None of the participants who were familiar with other language(s) indicated that they used this language during church-related activities.

Participants' self-assessments of proficiency in languages other than English or Latvian are given in Table 4.4. Overall proficiency in these languages was clearly lower than proficiency in English and Latvian. The only languages other than English and Latvian which participants claimed to know 'fluently' or 'very well' were German and, in one case, Russian also. All but one of these participants was over the age of 65, having come to Australia from Latvia as adults, thus having had some amount of pre-war education in German and/or Russian. Those who claimed lower proficiency tended to be younger, most having either been born in Australia or having come to Australia as infants.

Language use in the home

A 'home language' question was included to gauge the linguistic environment in which most participants lived: results of this section of the questionnaire are presented in Table 4.5. Six of the 46 participants (13%) lived alone and so the question was not applicable to this portion of the group. Overall, 29 out of the remaining 40 participants (72.3% or 63% of the total number) indicated that some Latvian was used in the home.

Table 4.5 Language use in the home (P = Participant)

	Spouse		Children		Mother		Father		Grandparents		Siblings		Friends	
	To P	By P	To P	By P	To P	By P	To P	By P	To P	By P	To P	By P	To P	By P
Latvian only	5	5	2	3	–	–	1	1	–	–	–	–	–	–
Latvian with English words	12	12	3	5	2	2	–	–	–	–	–	–	–	–
English only	5	7	5	5	5	5	1	1	1	1	1	1	1	1
English with Latvian words	4	3	2	1	3	3	3	3	–	–	–	–	–	–
Other language(s)	–	–	2	–	–	–	–	–	–	–	–	–	–	–
Depends on circumstances	3	3	1	1	–	–	–	–	–	–	–	–	–	–
No response/not applicable	17	16	31	31	36	36	41	41	45	45	45	45	45	45

Language used with spouse. While information was sought as to the language used with a range of possible occupants in a participant's home, the 'language used with spouse' category provided the most useful data, given the age of most participants (see earlier section). In this category, 30 participants indicated the language they used when speaking to their spouse, while 29 participants indicated the language in which their spouse spoke to them. It may be assumed from this that 30 out of a total of 46 participants (65.2%) live with their spouse (with one of these participants neglecting to provide information on both directions of the communication). As can be seen from Table 4.5, Latvian is the most commonly used language between participants and their spouses, although a very large number claim to incorporate some English into their communication.

Language used with children. Fifteen participants (32.6%) indicated that they lived with children. Overall, the language used between participants and their children was more variable than between participants and their spouses, with parents using slightly more Latvian to their children than their children use to them. The two participants who, in Table 4.5, indicated that their children used another language or combination of languages were referring to what they called 'baby talk'. The children of these participants were both infant girls aged 1.5 years and 9 months. The older girl was spoken to by her parent (the participant) in Latvian only, while the younger girl was spoken to in Latvian with some English words.

Language used with mother/father (or mother/father-in-law). It is interesting to note that interaction in both directions between participants and their parents is reported to happen in the same language or language combination; participants did not claim to use more English to their parents than their parents used to them (or *vice versa*; participants did not claim that their parents used more Latvian to them than they used to their parents). An English predominance is apparent in the interaction between participants (who tended to be younger) and their parents.

Language used with grandparents, siblings and friends. As Table 4.5 illustrates, only one person (2.2%) claimed to live with a grandparent, one (2.2%) with a sibling and one (2.2%) with a friend. Given these low percentages, it is impossible to generalise patterns of language use beyond these specific cases.

The participant who lived with a grandparent was a male under 24 of mixed Latvian ancestry living with a non-Latvian ('Australian') grandparent and, thus, English only was spoken between them.

The participant who lived with siblings also lived with their Latvian mother but English was the sole language of communication between them.

The only participant who lived with friends was a male under 24 of mixed Latvian/Australian ancestry who spoke English only with his friends. No information is supplied as to whether these friends are of Latvian ancestry.

Language use in church-related activities

Other language-use questions were also asked. The first of these related to the language(s) used in church-related activities: the results of this question are presented in Table 4.6. Again, the number of those involved in these activities was small and so raw figures only are provided in the table.

Language used during elders' meetings and church council meetings. Seven participants (15.2%) indicated that they were involved in elders' meetings, with three each claiming to use Latvian only or Latvian with some English words during these meetings. The only participant who claimed to exclusively use English was under 24, with minimal Latvian skills.

Four participants (8.7%) indicated that they were involved in church council meetings, with two each claiming to use Latvian only or Latvian with some English words during meetings. Both elders and church council meetings are attended by those given a certain degree of responsibility for the life of the church; it is therefore not surprising that Latvian predominates.

Table 4.6 Language use in church-related activities

	Elders' Meetings	Council Meetings	Sunday School		Bible study	Ladies Group	Music rehearsals	Youth activities	Other
			Lat	Eng					
Latvian only	3	2	–	–	6	5	3	–	–
Latvian with English words	3	2	2	–	3	1	2	–	–
English only	1	–	–	2	5	–	–	–	–
English with Latvian words	–	–	–	–	2	–	–	–	–
Other language(s)	–	–	–	–	–	–	–	–	–
Depends on circumstances	–	–	–	–	1	–	–	–	–
No response/ not applicable	39	42	44	44	29	40	41	46	46

Language used during Sunday School classes. Two participants (4.3%) indicated that they taught Latvian Sunday School classes and both indicated that they used Latvian with some English words. English only was used by the two participants who indicated that they were involved in teaching the English Sunday School, although it should be noted that this has now ceased to run.

Language used during small group/Bible study meetings. Seventeen participants (37%) indicated that they were involved in Bible studies. Around half a dozen Bible study groups exist at the Latvian church, with one in particular often being held in English. As Table 4.6 indicates, slightly more participants claimed to use Latvian than English.

Language used during 'Ladies Group' meetings. Six participants (13%) indicated that they were involved in Ladies Group meetings, with all but one using only Latvian during meetings. The remaining participant claimed to use Latvian with some English words.

Language used during choir/church band rehearsals. Five participants (10.9%) were involved in a choir or music group, three of these indicating that

Table 4.7 Language use in other aspects of the religious domain

	Talking after service	Discussing religion away from church	Informal private prayers	Formal private prayers	Lord's Prayer in questionnaire	Bible for personal use	Bible used in Bible study	Meeting Latvians in the workplace
Latvian only	15	8	19	31	20	13	5	1
Latvian with English words	9	6	4	–	–	–	–	5
English only	4	11	6	8	9	23	12	–
English with Latvian words	1	1	5	–	–	–	–	–
Other language(s)	–	–	1	–	–	–	–	1
Depends on circumstances	14	10	7	2	–	5	3	3
No response/ not applicable	3	10	4	5	17	5	26	36

they used Latvian only and two using Latvian with some English words during rehearsals.

Participants were also asked about the language(s) used during any youth activities – but it was reported that the youth group no longer existed. One participant (L24) indicated she had been part of the youth group when it had existed and that during youth group activities the members spoke Latvian with some English words. No participants indicated that they were involved in any activity other than the ones mentioned.

In summary, Latvian was reported to be the language predominantly used in all church-related activities, except those – such as the English Sunday School – which are intended to be English-specific. Those involved in elders' meetings, council meetings, Latvian Sunday School, music rehearsals and Ladies' Group meetings all claimed to speak 'Latvian only' or 'Latvian with some English words' with the exception of one young participant.

Questions were also asked of participants' language use in other activities related to the church or their individual faith: responses are given in Table 4.7.

Language used when talking after the service. As Table 4.7 illustrates, Latvian was clearly the language favoured by participants when talking with others after a service, although it was reported that English may also be used depending on the interlocutor.

Language used when discussing religion away from the church. Participants' responses indicated a greater variability in deciding which language to use when discussing language away from the church setting, the language chosen again being clearly influenced by the interlocutors or audience present. It is worth noting that of the ten participants in the 'no response/not applicable' category, seven indicated that they did not discuss religious matters outside of the church context.

Language used for informal private prayers (said away from the church). Table 4.7 illustrates a strong preference for informal prayers to be said in Latvian. Only one participant (the pastor) indicated that he used a language other than simply Latvian or English, referring to his practice of 'praying in tongues'. He characterised his prayer habits by saying ' I use a real mix, as the Spirit leads me'. Of the four participants in the 'no response/not applicable' category, one indicated that they did not pray other than in church.

Language used for formal private prayers (said away from the church). Table 4.7 shows a clear link by participants between the recitation of formal prayers and the Latvian language. When asked to write down the version of the Lord's Prayer which they would use the most, the majority wrote a Latvian version. Nearly as many, however, left the question blank.

Language of Bible for personal use and in Bible study meetings. It is interesting to note from Table 4.7 that English-language Bibles were used by most of the participants, whether in private use or in small group meetings. Three of the five participants who came under the 'no response/not applicable' category for personal use, indicated that they did not read the Bible except when at church. Eleven of the 26 participants in the 'no response/not applicable category' did not attend Bible study.

Versions of Bible for personal use. Participants were also asked to indicate the version of the Bible they used most for personal study/reading. The most commonly used versions are given in the following table (note that some participants named two different versions their answers):

Latvian Bibles are not available in as great an array of versions as English-language Bibles, many still being second-hand translations from the German and so this question resulted in a few nonsensical answers such as 'New International Testament' and *Dziesmu grāmata latviešiem tēvzemē un svešumā* [*Hymnal of the Evangelical Lutheran Church of Latvia and in Exile*].

Table 4.8 Versions of Bibles for personal use

Language	*Version*	*No. of participants*
English	Good News Bible	10
	New International Version	7
	New Revised Standard Version	3
	King James Version	2
	New King James Version	2
	New Living Bible	2
Latvian	Holy Bible – British and Foreign Bible Society 1965/6/7	5
	United Bible Society 1988	2
	New Testament – British and Foreign Bible Society 1954	1
Unknown/ Other	New Testament	2
	New International Testament	1
	Jaunā [The New]	1
	Bible Society	1
	Song Book	1
No Response/do not read the Bible		10

Other aspects of language use

Language use in the workplace. Language use in the place of work/study was also examined. Participants' occupations varied, though predictably there was a large percentage of pensioners among this group.

As indicated in Table 4.9, ten out of the 46 participants (21.7%) indicated that they came into contact with other Latvians in their place of work/ study (two of these were engaged in home duties who made reference to family members or friends who visit). One pensioner (L12) indicated that he used to come into contact with other Latvians in his workplace before his retirement and spoke Latvian in private conversations with them. Again, the use of Latvian with Latvian speakers was the most common choice, with the incorporation of varying degrees of English.

Code-switching. In order to gauge attitudes on a general level to notions of language purity, participants were asked about their code-switching behaviour.

Table 4.9 Participants' occupations

Occupation	No. of participants
Retired / pensioner	12 (26.1%)
Engineer / doctor / dentist / accountant	9 (19.6%)
Home duties	7 (15.2%)
Administration / management	5 (10.9%)
Other – kitchen hand / work with elderly / clerk / driver	5 (10.9%)
Other professional – army officer / sales / teacher	4 (8.7%)
Church work – pastor / church secretary	2 (4.3%)
Student	2 (4.3%)

Do you ever find you begin a sentence in one language and finish it in another? For example, do you begin a sentence in Latvian (or another language which you are able to speak) and finish it in English? Can you think of an example when this happened? Why do you think this happened?

Participants' responses:

Does code-switch (Yes)	Does not code-switch (No)	No response
26 (56.5%)	12 (26.1%)	8 (17.4%)

Most of the participants claimed that code-switching formed part of their daily speech behaviour, though some indicated strong disapproval of it:

> For ease of conversation languages do get mixed – although one does not approve of this kind of frivolity but to avoid possible long pauses whilst searching for the missing word in Latvian – a substitute is welcome. (L22)

> Yes – carelessness. I think in both languages and when I *do not* concentrate on what I am saying I mix Latvian and English, but only when speaking with Latvians – not the others. (L40)

> Yes sometimes this happens out of laziness, i.e. it is easier to finish in English rather than think about how to say it in Latvian. Sometimes this happens because I lack the vocabulary for that particular topic of discussion, e.g. technical language. In some instances there aren't the appropriate words in the Latvian language. (L21)

Many participants indicated that they code-switched particularly to enhance fluency when lacking the necessary vocabulary in one language:

> Yes, reasons: 1. Technical information more easily expressed in English. 2. At a loss for words in one or other language. 3. Each language has non-translatable subtleties. (L16)

> Yes, and if I speak to a Latvian who also speaks English I find that I get a point across better or I speak quicker mixing both languages. Whereas I cannot do this with someone who speaks English only or another language and does not understand Latvian. (L44)

> Yes! When speaking to friends who are also Latvian – basically undecided which language to use. Sometimes the languages drift from one to another. Sometimes if I need a word in English, e.g., *cute* or *swing tag* on a dress in a shop – then I continue in English. (L29)

Other participants, such as the pastor, indicated that code-switching helped reinforce a concept which might otherwise be difficult to express:

> In preaching it happens, sometimes planned for (I'll write down both language translations). I think it happens because I need to be clear about what I'm saying and I assume it might help some others as well. Latvian vocabulary is somewhat limited and English often expands understanding. On the other hand, sometimes I can't find right English word for a concept I have in my head in Latvian. (L20)

Other participants believed that they never code-switched:

> *Vēl nav tā noticis* (That has never yet happened.)[1] (L35)

Participants were also asked whether they recalled ever responding in English to questions asked of them in Latvian.

> *If a Latvian speaker says something to you in Latvian do you ever find you respond in English? Can you think of an example when this happened? Why do you think this happened?*

Participants' responses:

Does code-switch (Yes)	Does not code-switch (No)	No response
14 (30.4%)	25 (54.3%)	7 (15.2%)

Participants generally expressed disapproval of switching to English when addressed in Latvian by a Latvian speaker, particularly if the speaker was older:

> If I am speaking with an older Latvian I will always respond in Latvian but if it is a younger person, with whom I also speak English, I sometimes do respond in English (as it is easier for me to express myself in English). (L19)

> Definitely not. (L22)

> Not too often, unless I know the person pretty well (and *vice versa*). I would only do so if I really thought it would help communication. (L20 – the pastor)

A desire to maintain language purity was also evident from some participants' responses:

> No. I try very hard to use Latvian whenever and wherever possible in order to remember appropriate language / words. (L34)

> Try very hard not to. (L29)

Some participants claimed they initiated a code-switch to let their interlocutor know of their preferred language:

> Yes – I wanted to make them understand I predominantly speak English and wish to be spoken to in English. (L38)

The need to be understood was also given as a reason for initiating a switch:

> Yes. Again no examples, but generally if there are other people with me who don't understand or I feel may not understand what is being said in Latvian I'll respond in English. (L36)

Other participants indicated that they would code-switch for the sake of efficiency:

> Yes frequently. Unfortunately if I try and respond in Latvian it takes so long for me to think of all the words that they have usually walked away or changed the subject. Other times I have tried to answer in Latvian using vocab I'm not sure of and have either not been understood or been laughed at. (L37)

Two additional questions were asked to gauge participants' attitudes towards code-switching in the church. The first of these used a scale with antonymous adjectives at either end for participants to indicate how they feel when English words or phrases are used in the sermon or in other parts of the church service. This question was not answered well, particularly by the older Latvians, and would seem to indicate a problem with the design of this section of the questionnaire. For many of the adjectival scales no answer was given or, in some cases, the adjective itself was circled rather than a number on the scale.

The second question also used an adjectival scale instrument so that participants could indicate their assessment of the person who code-switched during a sermon or other part of a church service. The same problems as just outlined were again experienced. One difficulty associated with these two questions related to their bias in the direction of those who attend Latvian services: the wording of the questions makes reference to English words used and asks for participants' reactions to these and is thus not applicable where English is the language of the service. The results of these two questions are thus considered too inconclusive to warrant analysis.

Participants' attitudes towards code-switching – evident from responses to open-ended questions – make it clear that this is an area worth exploring further, being directly connected to notions of language purity and the appropriateness of language used in religious contexts.

Summary

Participants involved in the research carried out at this Latvian Lutheran church were typically of Latvian background, having at least one Latvian parent. Participants were typically first- or second-generation migrants with high language skills in both Latvian and English: all participants were able to speak/understand/read/write English 'moderately well' at worst, while a relatively small percentage claimed to only be able to speak/understand/read/write Latvian 'a bit' or 'not at all'. Participants typically lived with a spouse, with whom more Latvian was spoken than English.

Participants were involved in church activities of varying levels of formality, but typically 'Latvian only' or 'Latvian with some English words' was spoken during the course of these activities. The only activities in which English was the main language used were those which were specifically designed for those with poor or no Latvian language skills: the English Sunday School (which no longer exists but which used to run approximately once a month) and the meetings of some particular 'small groups' (Bible study groups) which are recognised as English-medium groups.

While Latvian is very clearly the language participants typically use for formal prayers when said away from the church, the majority of participants use an English Bible for their personal study/reading at home (if they do, in fact, read the Bible away from church). Of those who attend a Bible study, English-language Bibles are typically used (perhaps because it is those with stronger English language skills who typically attend the small groups). The most commonly used versions are the Good News and the New International Version. The language of informal personal prayers varies more, though still half of all participants use 'Latvian only' or 'Latvian with some English words'. 'Praying in tongues' adds a further dimension to the linguistic intricacies of prayer, although this was mentioned only by the pastor. Latvian was also commonly used when talking with others after the service or when discussing religion away from the church setting.

Just over a quarter (26.1%) of this group of participants was retired, with another significant occupation grouping being 'home duties' (19.6%). Those who worked outside the home typically worked in professional environments, with less than one-quarter of participants coming into contact with other Latvians regularly in the workplace. Where Latvians are encountered, at least some Latvian is used in communication.

Many of the participants claimed that code-switching formed part of their language behaviour, even though some expressed regret at doing so: notions of politeness as well as linguistic purity are strongly held.

Questionnaire findings

In this section, the responses of participants to the (remainder of the) open-ended questions included in the questionnaire are presented and discussed.

Reasons for church attendance

Thirty-eight (82.6%) of the 46 who completed questionnaires claimed to attend the church regularly, some saying they had been members since the church was built. Those who did not regularly attend indicated that they attended on special occasions such as Christmas and Easter and had attended that particular service – a confirmation service – because a friend / relative was one of the confirmants. Reasons given for regularly attending the church included for many the opportunity to be able to participate in services which are conducted in Latvian:

> *Uzņemt Dieva vārdus latviešu valodā.* (To receive God's word in the Latvian language.) (L11)

Some participants felt that Latvian was the easiest language for them to understand, while others felt that Latvian had a particular association with their religious beliefs that made it difficult to use any other language in religious activities:

> Because I find that to properly worship, pray and sing hymns I have to do it in Latvian. (L15)

> I prefer to continue to attend a Latvian service and belong to Latvian congregation, as Latvian was my first introduction to religion. (L39)

Many of those participants who regularly attended the church had been doing so for a considerable amount of time, with the presence of relatives and friends making church attendance a community activity:

> This has essentially been my church all my life and I have developed many relationships within it. It is also the church that my family/ extended family attends. Also I am trying to maintain my Latvian heritage in my family. (L21)

> Because it is our church. My husband helped to build it. We were married there and our children were christened there. The sermons are conducted in my mother's tongue. It is also very close to where we live. (L43)

In some cases, the social aspect of church attendance was clearly a stronger motivation for participants than the religious aspect:

> To attend with my spouse despite personally being an atheist. (L2)

For some, this activity had become a tradition – a ritual in itself:

> Because I always have and see no reason to change. (L36)

Some participants mentioned the significance of the denomination as well as the importance of the cultural/language function of the church, stating simply:

> Because it is Latvian Lutheran. (L44)

Among those who regularly attended the English services of the church came the following reasons for attending:

> Excellent minister and warm Christian fellowship. (L9)

> We were invited by Latvian friends and felt it was where God wanted us. (L6 – not of Latvian background)

> Because I enjoy the way that it is done and the way that it is so laid back. (L30)

Responses such as these point to the importance attributed to the style and atmosphere of the English service over and above the language in which it is conducted.

Table 4.10 Services regularly attended by participants

Latvian services only	Latvian services and occasional English service	English services only	English services and occasional Latvian service	Both Latvian and English regularly	No response – do not attend church regularly
21 (45.7%)	13 (28.3%)	3 (6.5%)	4 (8.7%)	4 (8.7%)	1 (2.2%)

Only five participants (10.9%) indicated that they attended the church alone, the vast majority attending with a family member also of Latvian ancestry. Thirty-two participants (69.6%) had children, with 18 of these 32 indicating that their children attended the Latvian services of the church and nine indicating that their children attended the English services of the church. Four of the 32 indicated that their children attended the Latvian Sunday School, while some indicated that their children attended when they were of the appropriate age. (At the time of the survey, the English Sunday School had ceased to run and, therefore, no participants indicated that their children attended.)

Six participants (13%) claimed to attend another church regularly, with one participant (2.2%) attending an English-speaking Anglican church because the English service at the Latvian church is held only fortnightly (L6). One participant (2.2%) attended an English-speaking Uniting church because it was more convenient geographically and one (2.2%) attended an English-speaking 'Presbyterian/Uniting' church because of social connections. A further one participant (2.2%; who has only lived in Melbourne for the last three years) claimed to regularly attend the 'Pentakostu Latviski Vasarsvētku' or 'Pentecostal Latvian Summer Church' which is held in English (and seemingly in New South Wales) because *'tajā laikā mums nebija latviešu mācītāja Sidnejā'* (at that time we didn't have a Latvian pastor in Sydney) (L8). Another participant (2.2%) also attended a local Assemblies of God church regularly, as this partici-pant lived in regional Victoria and was unable to attend the Latvian church every Sunday. Two school-age participants (4.3%) indicated that they regularly attended another Lutheran church – the daily chapel which was a compulsory part of the curriculum at a Lutheran school.

The clear majority of this group of participants claimed to attend the Latvian services. While one of the participants, who was not a regular member of the church (having attended the church on the morning the questionnaires were distributed because of the confirmation service), left the question blank, the remaining seven participants (total 17.4%) who were also not regular attenders still completed the question in relation to the services they occasionally attended at the church.

Have you ever attended the English services of this church?

Participants' responses:

No, never	No, but planning to	Yes, once	Yes, a few times	Yes, regularly	No response
12 (26.1%)	2 (4.3%)	7 (15.2%)	13 (28.3%)	11 (23.9%)	1 (2.2%)

Reasons given for preferring Latvian services included greater proficiency in Latvian:

> *Apmeklēju latviešu dievkalpojumus tādēl, ka tas varu labāki izprast.* (I attend the Latvian services because that's what I can best understand.) (L8)

For some parishioners, Latvian services aroused feelings of familiarity and comfort, as well as nostalgia:

> *Tikai latviešu valodā varu iejusties mācītāja runātajā. Angļu valodā tektais nedod to sajūtu.* (Only in the Latvian language can I feel at home with the preacher. Stories in the English language don't give me this feeling.) (L46)

> [I] like to hear service in my own language. (L4)

Not uncommon was the view that the use of Latvian was necessary to heighten the religious experience:

> I choose to attend only Latvian services because I feel closer to God when the Latvian language is spoken and sung. (L19)

> I attend Latvian services regularly as I consider Latvian my preferred language for religion. I have attended a few English services for special occasions only. (L39)

A preference for the ritual and style of Latvian services was expressed by some participants:

> Don't like the style used in English services. Prefer that my children learn Latvian. (L23)

> I can relate to Latvian language and church ritual as expressed in Latvian language better than English. (L34)

Sometimes, however, the much-loved tradition of the Latvian Lutheran service did not escape criticism:

> Latvian services are somewhat closer to the Lutheran tradition – but not close enough any more. (L45)

One participant, who identified himself as an atheist, claimed to attend Latvian services in order to 'accompany my spouse, to reaffirm in myself why I don't believe' (L2). This particular participant showed insight into the issues at play in the church, seemingly having a greater understanding of the tensions occurring between ethnicity and faith than many of the Christians who attended.

Participants who claimed to attend the English service regularly varied in age, with the majority being over 35. Many of these were proficient in Latvian but chose to attend English services for the benefit of a non-Latvian spouse or because the time of the service was more convenient. The style of the service also appealed to many.

Other participants saw the benefit in attending both Latvian and English services:

> I attend Latvian services because of the language and relationships with others who attend this service. I attend English services because I prefer the style of worship and structure of service at these services. (L21)

> I enjoy the informal English services for attending regularly and the formal Latvian services for the special occasions of Christmas and Easter. Also since my Latvian is not strong I can easily understand and get more out of the English services. (L37)

The pastor of the church provided the following comments:

> [I am the] pastor of both, but also fluent in both languages. I also appreciate the variety of spiritual experience (traditional and formal versus non-traditional and informal). (L20)

Views on language in the church – the 'appropriateness' of language

> *Do you feel that certain languages are more appropriate/proper than others for use in the church?*

Participants' responses:

Yes	No	No response
11 (23.9%)	28 (60.9%)	7 (15.2%)

Participants were predictably divided on this question. Amongst those who felt that certain languages *were* more appropriate for church use were those who linked the question to their own church experience and their evaluation of Latvian as the 'right' language for a 'Latvian' church:

> Yes – the church was established for Latvians by Latvians. (L42)

> It depends what your background and culture is. I am sure Chinese would prefer to worship in Chinese. (L43)

Those who felt that there was no single 'appropriate' language referred to the universal and transcendent nature of the Gospel message:

> For a true believer the language is irrelevant. The faith is more important, ie. God no.1, ethnicity no.2. (L2)

> God speaks all languages. (L6)

> No – Matthew 28:19 'Therefore go and make disciples of all nations'. (L26)

Some participants emphasised the importance of conveying this Gospel message, and the language as being merely a tool:

> I think that the message is the crucial thing and the language is the means used to deliver this message. The main language used will be that which the majority of people speak, however, this shouldn't exclude the use of another language (for some activities) for the minority of people who don't understand the dominant language. (L19)

> No – of primary concern is not the language, but that the message can be clearly and effectively communicated and people can experience a living relationship/experience of God. (L21)

The importance of acknowledging that different languages are needed to convey the Gospel message to different people was emphasised by one participant:

> At this stage both Latvian and English should be used. Latvian to cater particularly to the elderly and English for mixed marriages and the younger generation. (L9)

Views on language in the church – Latvian language only?

> *Should all activities of the church, including the services, be conducted in Latvian only?*

Participants' responses:

Yes	No	No response
8 (17.4%)	34 (73.9%)	4 (8.7%)

The vast majority (73.9%) of those who completed questionnaires considered that the church's activities should not be exclusively in Latvian. Reasons given included the potential to be divisive:

> No – for many people, especially the younger generation and their friends/family the Latvian language is a barrier to them being able to fully participate in services/church life. (L21)

> No – we live in Australia. Many of our children are married to non-Latvians. Many of our grandchildren do not speak Latvian. (L28)

> No – it is important to keep the language alive (Latvian that is) but even more important to keep the community together and not drive away those whose command of the language is limited because they are made to feel inadequate. They will learn through encouragement not harassment. (L36)

> Restricts those who speak very little Latvian or none at all. Our doors should be open and cater to spiritual needs of non-Latvian speaking people too. (L9)

One participant felt that the provision of some activities in English, far from being divisive, enabled families with different language needs to worship together in the one church:

> *Ģimenes kas ir jauktas laulības var nākt uz abām. Bērni kuriem ir gruti sapras latviski var nākt uz angļu dievkalpojumiem un citreiz iet ar vecākiem kopā.* (Families who have mixed marriages can come to both. Children who have difficulty understanding Latvian can go to the English services and otherwise go together with their parents.) (L10)

Other reasons for not restricting activities to the Latvian language included the 'inevitability' of assimilation:

> No – Latvians are a diminishing race and often marry other cultures/ nationalities. To only conduct Latvian services is going to see a steady reduction in the size of the congregation of the coming years as the original Latvians pass away. (L37)

Some services should be inclusive of people of mixed background as the Latvian society becomes more assimilated. (L2)

No – the increasing incidence of mixed marriages where it is not expected of offspring to attend Latvian school or speak the Latvian language. These children are still christened Lutheran and may want to attend church but don't see the point if they can't understand services. (L38)

The pastor also referred to the diminishing Latvian community, claiming that ethnic and linguistic exclusivity would be detrimental for the future of the church:

The make-up of the congregation has changed over the years, becoming more assimilated, and to neglect this fact ['Latvian only'] will decrease our effectiveness and potential for any growth beyond the diminishing Latvian speaking population. (L20)

Among the participants who felt strongly that Latvian should be the only language used in the church came the view that the Latvian language linked the church to its past, and was also its hope for the future.

Ja šī ir latviešu celta latviešu baznīca, tad visām darbībām vajadzētu notikt latviešu valodā. (If this is a Latvian-founded Latvian church, then all activities should happen in the Latvian language). (L11)

This church was built by our Latvian people for preserving our culture and language. (L4)

While conceding that flexibility in language use in the church was a necessity, one participant emphasised that the languages must remain distinct and discrete:

Due to increasing numbers of mixed ethnic marriages, allowance needs to be made for this fact. However each service should be conducted in one or other language only – switching between languages in one services is distracting. (L16)

A discussion of participants' attitudes to code-switching may be found in Chapter 6.

Views on language in the church – the place of English

Do you feel that English has any place at all in the activities of this church?

Participants' responses:

Yes	No	No response
37 (80.4%)	6 (13%)	3 (6.5%)

The parallel question of whether English has any place in the activities of the church was also asked. In line with the previous question, the great majority of participants believed that English did have a role to play. Preventing the alienation of non-Latvian-speaking members was a key reason for including English:

> Yes – to reach out to the younger generation/non-Latvian family members and friends and ensure the church has a future after the first generation of Latvian migrants have passed away. (L21)

> *Angļu valodai ir jādod vieta baznīcas darībā un dievkaplojumos jo mūsu asimilizēšanas un jaukto lauliba to prasa lai visi varētu ņemt līdz dalību.* (English must have a place in the activities of the church and its services because our assimilation and mixed marriages require it if everyone wants to take part.) (L35)

> Although it is essentially a Latvian congregation and there is ample scope for English services outside this congregation, there is a segment of the congregation who would have a greater sense of 'belonging' if activities in English were incorporated. (L16)

> *Es domāju, ka angļu valodai ir vieta angļu valodas dievkalpojumos, kas domāti jaukto laulību dalībniekiem un viņu piederīgiem un draugiem.* (I think that the English language has a place in English language services, which are meant for partners of mixed marriages and their relatives and friends.) (L11)

Some participants acknowledged the need for some English activities but qualified how and when these might take place:

> Yes – on special occasions, e.g. weddings when one partner does not understand Latvian. (L43)

> *Jā – atsevišķi. Saprotu ka kaut kas ir vajadzīgs tām ģimenēm ar maisītiem(?) angļu un latviešu locekļiem.* (Yes – separately. I understand that something is necessary for those families with mixed English and Latvian members.) (L24)

Among those participants who felt that English had a role to play in the church came the following sobering responses:

> Yes – all the old Latvians' traditions will die with them unless they can be incorporated into Australian mainstream. (L31)

> Yes – we [the congregation] will die if we do not have English services or other activities in English.' (L28)

One participant felt that the use of Latvian in the church was hypocritical if Latvian was not also used in the home:

> There may be a handful of families in all of Melbourne who speak only Latvian at home. Most of the children at Latvian school speak English at recess, etc. So why not be comfortable at church without a façade? (L14)

Those participants who felt that English had no place in their church expressed the view that any claim to Latvian ethnicity should be partnered by Latvian language proficiency. Another participant pointed to the existence of other English-medium Lutheran churches as a justification for continuing a Latvian-only tradition:

> Nē – tādēļ, ka latvietim latviešu valoda labāk saprotam. (No – because Latvians understand Latvian better.) (L8)

> No – it seems that the majority of people, if not all, are Latvian and can speak and/or understand the language. (L33)

> No – I prefer a traditional Latvian Lutheran service in Latvian. If I wanted to hear a service in English then I could attend the Australian Lutheran church, of which there are two in my area. (L45)

Views on language in the church – the existence of language-related issues

> *Do you feel there are any language issues in particular which your church is struggling with?*

Participants' responses:

Yes	No	No response
23 (50%)	18 (39.1%)	5 (10.9%)

Half of the participants believed that the church was struggling with language-related problems. The root of these conflicts is summed up by the following comments:

> Yes – conflict between some first generation Latvians who want to maintain what has been and keep everything as Latvian as possible and the younger / more progressive generation for whom language is not the issue / purpose of being in church. (L21)

> Yes – some believe that in a Latvian church only Latvian should be used. This view is held by an ignorant minority. (L22)

> Yes – there are members in the congregation that do not approve of services in English and object to other nationalities joining the congregation. (L28)

> Use of the English language in any form is not accepted very easily. There seems to be a fear that the Latvian language will be lost or forgotten the more English is used. (L19)

The pastor's comments were in line with those of these participants, summing up the situation in the following way:

> Do we swing back to a more 'Latvian-only' congregation? Do we discriminate against non-Latvian speakers and origin people [*sic*.] as far as membership qualifications / requirements go (the latter is an actual proposal submitted for consideration to our council!). (L20)

Some participants considered the language of certain church members as problematic, singling out the pastor in particular for linguistic transgressions.

> [The absence of] correct grammar. (L17)

> The minister using English words and phrases in sermons which are presented in Latvian. (L15)

> Yes – the minister is of the younger generation and as a result does not have fluent knowledge of the language. (L34)

> Yes – the English and Latvian languages used in this church are of an elementary standard. I prefer the richness of an educated sermon. Traditional Lutheran pastors were highly educated articulate well-read men. I like a sermon which test my intellect and pleases my ear. (L45)

> *Ikkatram vajadzētu uzmanīgāk izteikties tīrā latviešu valodā. Pašlaik daudziem nejauši pasprūk par angļu vārdam vai izeticienam.* (Everyone should be careful to speak in pure Latvian. At the moment many people accidentally let English words and phrases slip out.) (L11)

This theme of linguistic purity was evident in the responses of many participants:

> Yes – there are many who wish to maintain 'pure' Latvian – not mixed with English. Many fear a type of 'pidgin' Latvian. (L29)

> Yes – mixing of languages is not tolerated in Latvian services. Sometimes a point is 'clarified' in English when most seem to be uneasy. English service attendees seem to be more tolerant. (L32)

One participant expressed the hope that a resolution might be reached eventually:

> *Draudzē ir nevienprātiba par angļu valodas lietošanu, bet es ļoti ceru ka tās problēmas ar laiku izkārtosies.* (The congregation disagree about the use of English, but I hope very much that in time the fighting will end.) (L35)

Views on language in the church – communicating the Gospel to youth

> *Do you feel that there is a problem communicating the Gospel to the younger generation of Latvians because the younger and older generations relate better to different languages?*

Participants' responses:

Yes	No	No response
30 (65.2%)	10 (21.7%)	6 (13%)

The majority of participants felt that there were language barriers in witnessing to Latvian youth. These barriers were often viewed as the result of English-medium education, which participants felt had strengthened the position of English in relation to Latvian for the younger generation. For one participant, the very weakness of young people's Latvian warranted the obligatory use of Latvian at church:

> *Nenoliedzmi, ka jaunā paaudze daudz labāk saprot angliski, jo viņa ir šeit skolujusies angļu valodā vairāk kā latviešu. Tādeļ vajadzētu klaustīties un vairāk vingrināties saprast dievkalpojumus latviski.* (It cannot be denied that the younger generation much more easily understand English because here they are educated in English more than Latvian. Therefore they should listen and practise more to understand Latvian services.) (L11)

Some participants referred to the need for proficiency in the Latvian religious register, which may be particularly poor amongst youth:

> The younger generation do not have the fluency or vocabulary to cope with sometimes complex emotive and philosophical issues. (L16)

> Yes – while many young Latvians speak Latvian fluently, the vocab used in a service is not everyday vocab and therefore requires concentration. Even then misunderstandings occur. (L37)

Some participants felt that any difficulties in attracting youth to the church were the result of the poorness of the message, rather than the medium:

> If there is a problem in communicating the Gospel to young people I think it's a problem of style of service and content of service [relevant issues] rather than language. (L19)

> It doesn't really matter which language is used, the younger generation seem to have lost faith in the church and what it stands for. Times have changed. (L6)

> Yes – the older generation (Latvian) have a greater emphasis on church tradition. The younger generation are looking for 'the meaning of life' which tradition does not answer. (L32)

> Yes – I think many members of the younger generation not only find it difficult to understand the sermon in Latvian, but also find it difficult to relate to the traditional style in which it is presented. (L21)

One participant laid the fault for the absence of youth in the church at the feet of their families, for creating an environment in which English is seen as 'second-best' to Latvian:

> I think the younger generation is not receptive to the Gospel because of lack of Christianity in the home; they would be 'chastised' for going to an English service rather than Latvian. (L14)

Views on language in the church – best language for communicating the Gospel to youth

> *What language do you feel is best to use in presenting the Gospel to the younger generation of Latvians?*

Participants' responses:

Latvian	English	Both/Depends	No response
12 (26.1%)	12 (26.1%)	20 (43.5%)	2 (4.3%)

Participants tended to suggest that some of the acknowledged difficulties in presenting the Gospel to young people could be counteracted by flexibility in the language(s) used with them:

> English with Latvian backup. Not many know unusual or technical words, etc, eg. blasphemy. For many, their Latvian is of a 'common' or 'garden' level and deeper discussion would have to be held in a type of children's language or the words would have to be defined every time they're used. I couldn't put up with that in English! (L29)

> Latvian for Latvian speaking members and English for English speaking members. Flexibility will allow you to still retain the Latvian culture but also keep up with the changing times. More mixed marriages (hence less Latvian spoken and more English) enabling God's Word to reach across language, nationality barriers. The true purpose of the church is God's Word not the language spoken and shutting out those who do not speak Latvian. (L38)

> In whatever language they are most conversant in. Our one and a half year old daughter currently understands Latvian better than English but I couldn't generalise that for all 'the younger generation of Latvians'. (L20 – the pastor)

> Latvian and English – I think there are some younger generation Latvians for whom Latvian is very important and who are working very hard to maintain it in their families, while there are others whose Latvian is poor and who have difficulty understanding a sermon preached in Latvian. (L21)

> Both! (However in the future, i.e. 50 years, English.) It is possible to structure a service that uses both languages 'seamlessly', i.e. singing could be in Latvian and service order could be in English. (L26)

English was seen by some participants as the best language to use with youth, either from the positive perspective of the great strength of their English or from the negative perspective of the great weakness of their Latvian skills:

English – because they are illiterate in Latvian (L45)

Domaju ka angļu valodā – tad viņi labāk sapratīs spredika saturu un lūgšanas jēgu. (I think English – because they understand the content of the sermon and the meaning of the prayers better.) (L35)

Several participants held strongly to the view that true Latvian identity is inseparable from the Latvian language and that it would be in the best interest of all Latvian youth if the church persevered with the task of evangelism via the medium of Latvian:

Latvian – the church is the only place where they hear the Gospel in Latvian. If and when they desire additional explanations or knowledge they can easily pick up a Bible in English. (L40)

Latvicšu katram latvicš jaunictim, ir jāmāk runāt, sava Tcva valoda. (Latvian – every Latvian youth must speak their native language.) (L13)

Latvian – interestingly, my own teenagers have reacted more negatively to introduction of English to sermons than expected. Much depends on how the material is presented. (L16)

Views on language in the church – a 'multicultural' church?

Do you want this congregation to be one which caters for Latvians only or for Christians of other backgrounds who might also want to attend?

Participants' responses:

Latvian-only church	Church for all, regardless of background	No response
11 (23.9%)	32 (69.6%)	3 (6.5%)

Participants were asked whether or not they wanted their church to have an 'open-door' policy as far as ethnicity is concerned. One of those who indicated that the church should be for Latvians only declined to give a reason but reasons given by participants in favour of inclusiveness included Biblical mandates:

'Therefore go and make disciples of all nations' (Matthew 28:19). Although this congregation should cater for anyone to come, its primary focus, in my opinion, should be towards persons of Latvian descent, their relatives, and to anyone interested in participating in services and fellowship with this group of persons. (L26)

God is not selective about who should enter His kingdom. It is open to all who seek it: our church should have the same attitude and preach the Good News to everyone. (L17)

Our Lord commanded us to 'go into the world' which I interpret as the whole world – not just the Latvian community. (L32)

We are all Christians – regardless of nationality and colour. God loves us all. We have no right to keep people out of church. (L28)

Because this would be God's will. (L9)

Some participants criticised the pre-eminence of Latvian culture in the church but still felt that membership of the church should be subject to meeting certain conditions:

The church is the House of God not the House of Latvia. However, being Lutheran should still be a criteria for attendance (regular) as all branches of Christianity are slightly different, e.g. Catholics, Orthodox. (L38)

There isn't (I'm sure!) a special place in Heaven for those who speak Latvian. I don't believe we can turn anyone who wants to worship away (as long as there is no basic difference in beliefs). (L29)

One participant expressed the view that meeting with other cultures in the context of the church could be a mutually rewarding experience:

I think all people should be welcomed – language should not be a barrier to being a part of the church. People from other backgrounds can teach us a lot about ourselves (being Latvian) and give us a new and healthy appreciation of our culture. It can only be unhealthy to be insular, as it is for individuals. (L19)

Other reasons for favouring an 'open door' policy focussed on being able to include friends and family:

A Latvian-only church does not cater for the next generation born in Australia or the mixed marriages. (L6)

We are all God's children so why close a door to a relative. (L14)

To maintain an ethnic identity does create a sense of isolation to those of different ethnic and language backgrounds. (L16)

Reasons for maintaining an ethno-specific church included the valid desire for services in the mother tongue:

Because the majority of the congregation still needs to receive all the services, etc., in Latvian. If we had to change completely to English language, then most people would select a congregation closer to their homes. (L15)

Tie latvieši, kas tagad apmeklē šo baznīcu drīz izmirs un tad baznīcā būs jālito cita valoda domājams – angļu valoda. (These Latvians who at the moment attend this church will soon die out and then the church will have to use another language, presumably English.) (L8)

One participant, while noting the need for mother-tongue services, pointed to the necessity of an English ministry for the sake of the church's future:

I think it is very important to cater for the first/second generation Latvians who have grown up and feel more comfortable in the Latvian church, but without catering for other backgrounds the congregation will die with the Latvians. (L21)

Other reasons for maintaining the Latvianness of the church were expressed more forcefully – as the hard-earned right of those who worked to build it:

This is a Latvian church and was built for Latvians. If other churches wish to use [it] they should be able as long as it isn't together. (L23)

I want to be among people of my own ethnic background and customs. (L42)

Tā ir latviešiem domāta un celta baznīca. (It is a church intended and built for Latvians.) (L46)

A person has a choice which church he/she wishes to attend. If he/she decides to attend the Latvian church, it is expected that it will cater for Latvian speaking people. You do not have English or Greek services conducted in Latvian. (L34)

One participant indicated that while they were in favour of a 'multicultural' church, they did not necessarily want a 'multilingual' one:

Church doors should be open to all, but services should be conducted [in] *either* Latvian *or* English – depending on language preference of those attending. (L39)

Finally, the pastor indicated that this is a burning issue for his church, writing:

I can't wait for the results of this one! The Gospel should be available to not only our Latvian-speaking members but also their friends and neighbours who may not speak Latvian. Our future growth and outreach depends on it.

Views on the future of the church

Where do you see this church in 50 years' time?

The answers provided by participants for this question proved quite interesting. While it was to be expected that those in favour of an English ministry would see the future as bleak without it, what came as a surprise was that those participants who wanted a Latvian-only church also held a grim view of the future:

If we do not let English-speaking people in – [the church will be] dead. (L28)

Most of the participants felt that the Latvianness of the church would not be as strong in the future:

Interdenominational church with services conducted in English. A very small group of English-speaking elderly people might have some special services to commemorate the church's Latvian beginning. Some Latvian church decorations may still survive. (L39)

Due to laziness of people, they will use the easy way out and gradually convert to English which will be a great pity. (L34)

Ne vairs latviešu. (No longer Latvian.) (L46)

One participant, who did not regularly attend any church, felt that the Christian Church, in general, was facing a gloomy future:

With the general trend being away from the church I believe that there will be no churches in 50 years – Lutheran, Catholic, Orthodox, etc. People have been steadily losing interest in the church due to a number of factors, e.g. allegations of child molestation, allowing homosexuals to practise ministry. Instead, small groups of people will meet regularly out or at home to discuss spiritual matters. (L38)

In contrast, other participants saw the future as promising:

(1) Services held in Latvian *and* in English (i.e. two separate services). (2) I see this congregation as one which *really* cares for people's needs – a warm and friendly place where both the first time visitors and long time members are made to feel welcome to come and participate in worshipping the Lord. (L26)

I see it as a vibrant, live, spirit-filled congregation active in missions and outreach, but that still acknowledges its Latvian heritage and beginnings, however Latvian will no longer be the primary reason for its existence. (L21)

Other comments from participants

Participants were given the opportunity at the end of the questionnaire to add other comments as they wished. Some participants used this opportunity to air specific grievances:

I think our pastor would prefer to preach in English and is pushing in that direction. However, there are still a lot of older Latvians whose English is very limited and they would have nowhere else to go. The English speakers have many churches to choose from. (L43)

Due to excessive use of English and missionary zeal of current pastor to bring in other ethnic groups to our church, Latvians are leaving the congregation. I see that the Latvian language and customs are not important to current pastor as he drives towards English services. It is the Latvian language that has kept us together to date. (L42)

Milder comments included the following:

By attending Latvian Church, I do not only receive spiritual teaching, but also participate in traditional activities, have an opportunity to speak Latvian, and receive and extend friendship unique to my ethnic group, the Latvians. (L40)

The rawness of the English *versus* Latvian debate came through clearly in such comments as the following ones:

Another element of the particular Latvian congregation I irregularly attend is the *politics* which evolves out the generation gap. Some of the older generation . . . do not differentiate nationality/ethnicity and belief in God. They are particularly 'un-Christian' in their viciousness towards the pastor. They are unable to put aside prejudice and acknowledge the changing nature of Latvian society in an Australian environment. (L2)

The language has certainly been a barrier to the friends we have brought to church and to us becoming more involved in the church. (L6)

You might find this quote by Tolstoy relevant: 'Loving your country and loving your family are good things; however they can be both a virtue and a vice when they become overwhelming and violate the love for your neighbour'. (L19)

It's sad to admit one's fellow countrymen are racist. (L14)

Closing Remarks

As can be seen from these data, there are many tensions within this church, tensions which are particularly related to perceptions of the role of the Latvian language in the church. These tensions exist at both the individual and collective level, being influenced by individual language skills and preferences, as well as by the long-preserved identity of the church as a 'Latvian' church, thereby implying that one must be a Latvian (however being Latvian is defined) to participate. The pastor's role as linguistic role model is also evident, resulting in harsh criticism where his language behaviour does not conform to notions of purity held by some of the congregation. The church's part in preserving its cultural heritage during the fight for a free Latvia resulted in the Latvian language taking on a sacred value in the religious domain. Theological arguments are also used on both sides of the language debate, questioning whether the 'Great Commission' of Matthew 28:19 validates the existence of a church which seeks to focus on the pastoral care of one particular ethnic group or, in fact whether it is an argument against ethno-centrism.

These questions will be further illuminated by an examination of the Indonesian congregation of the Uniting Church in the following chapter.

Note

1.   All English translations which follow Latvian statements are the author's own.

Chapter 5

Case Study 2: The Indonesian Church

Introduction

The results from the second of the two case studies – an Indonesian congregation of the Uniting Church – are presented and discussed in this chapter. Differing from the Latvian church in migration history, language and cultural background, it provides another perspective on the issues faced by ethnic churches.

The Indonesian Church in Social, Historical and Theological Perspective

Until 1988, this congregation was one of three Indonesian congregations in a parish of the Uniting Church in Australia which spanned three eastern/southeastern suburbs of Melbourne (Box Hill, Wheelers Hill, Mulgrave). Since 1998, when a separate facility was built, these three congregations have been worshipping together as one. As this portion of the research was conducted in 1997, the information presented here depicts the situation prior to the move to the new premises and thus focuses on one of these congregations, situated in Mulgrave, a southeastern suburb close to Monash University.

Each of the three constituent Indonesian congregations is attached to an English-medium church. Meetings for the Indonesian youth of these congregations are held on Saturday nights at the Box Hill church and despite the location, is known as 'MYF' or 'Mulgrave Youth Fellowship'. A 'Family Fellowship' also runs on a Saturday night, after MYF. The Mulgrave Indonesian congregation has been gathering together for worship since the mid 1980s, with the present minister having held his position since 1995.

The vast majority of those in this particular Indonesian congregation are of Indonesian background, with many Chinese Indonesians among them. Those who are not Indonesian themselves typically attend with their Indonesian spouse or because they are part of the growing number of those who, having learned Indonesian as a subject offered at school or university, are keen to practise their skills. Others who come might be those more generally interested in the Indonesian culture or those members of the English congregation interested in meeting the other members of their church and who are keen to see continued interaction.

The congregation includes a significant number of students who come to Australia for the university year and then return to Indonesia for holidays. This means that the size of the congregation is quite variable according to the time of the year, being largest (around 120) between March and November, following the Australian university year. Numbers drop to around 80 from November to March.

The weekly Indonesian service at the church is, for the most part, conducted in Indonesian. English is used in an intentional manner at certain points in the service for the benefit of visitors who are not Indonesian. Newcomers are asked to stand and introduce themselves and if the newcomers are not Indonesian, this request – and welcome – is given in English, the assumption being made that this is the language they understand best. Almost all parts of the service – prayers, welcome, notices, sermon – are simultaneously translated into English by a translator who sits in the foyer, which is separated from the church by a glass wall. The translation is heard through headphones which are offered to non-Indonesian visitors. Because the church owns only ten sets of headphones, when combined services with the English-language congregation of the church are conducted, the translator stands at the front of the church with the minister, translating out loud sentence-by-sentence.

English is also used for any interaction with children during the service: it is used when the minister gives the 'children's talk' – a brief period of teaching for children in the early part of the service before they go to their Sunday School class – and also if the children play any role in the service such as performing songs for the congregation that they have learned in their classes.

The minister also uses some English during his sermons. Sometimes this occurs when he is quoting from an English text but often this is spontaneous and unprepared. English words and phrases often appear in his Indonesian monologue, including English second-person pronouns.

Other activities of the congregation include council meetings and elders meetings (see later). Where these activities are held at the congregational level, Indonesian is used. If the meetings are combined gatherings with the other English and Indonesian congregations of the parish, they are conducted in English.

A good relationship exists between the English and Indonesian congregations in the parish – they regard themselves as equal members of the one parish. They intend to improve this relationship by increasing the dialogue between the congregations through more joint meetings and activities.

While many of the congregation possess skills in languages other than Indonesian or English – for example, regional languages such as Javanese or Sundanese or the Jakarta dialect which is popular among the younger generation – none of these other languages are used in services or other official activities of the church. The use of Indonesian in this setting is a mark of respect and reverence, and is, at the same time, a common language to all members. While the use of the highest speech level of a regional language such as Javanese would be considered more polite and reverent than the use of Indonesian, it is not as practical an option. Very few people possess adequate fluency and religious vocabulary to be able to communicate with God (or about or on behalf of God) in this speech level. The minister claims it would be impossible for him to preach in Javanese, although his brother, the minister of a Pentecostal church in an Indonesian village, preaches regularly in Javanese.

Prior to coming to Australia, members attended a range of different churches and denominations in Indonesia, such as Pentecostal/Charismatic, Reformed, Lutheran and Seventh Day Adventist. As a part of the Uniting Church in Australia, the congregation is given some freedom to develop its own liturgy appropriate to its needs: the congregation has been encouraged to incorporate the Indonesian culture as well as the language into worship. The liturgy that is used in the present congregation is similar to that found in the traditional mainstream Reformed churches in Indonesia. This similarity adds to the 'comforting familiarity' of the service. The liturgy is, however, unique to this congregation and is not used by any of the other 13 or so Indonesian congregations in Melbourne. The minister is continuing to adapt this liturgy to suit the changing needs of his congregation. In order to balance the preferences of those from Charismatic backgrounds with those from other traditions who are used to the structure which liturgy gives to a service, certain compromises are made in the running of the service. This largely results in the incorporation of modern songs and times of 'free' singing.

The Interview

The minister of the congregation is an Indonesian of Chinese descent with a background very strongly influenced by Javanese culture. While his Indonesian is fluent in all areas, his English receptive skills are much more strongly developed than his productive skills. He is also fluent in some levels of Javanese, which he calls his 'mother tongue', though he claims to have forgotten the Javanese script and cannot write it. At home he and his wife use Javanese, while Javanese is rarely used with his children in preference to Indonesian. His children also speak Indonesian amongst themselves at home. While he is pleased that his children possess such strong Indonesian skills, he encourages the use of English so that his own proficiency might benefit from theirs: 'I ask, let us speak English at home so we can practise and I can learn from you because you speak English all the time when you are at school – but they don't want to speak like that'.

The minister finds that the weakness of his English language skills results in some personal difficulty in communicating with younger members of the congregation. Those who have been educated in Australia for a number of years, and particularly those born in Australia, have strong English skills and, in some cases, very poor Indonesian. Though the minister sees it as important to communicate with them in English, he feels limited by his lack of proficiency:

> [Because] my English is not fluent as them, I don't have any, maybe, [the] capability to explain [the] deeper meaning of the Bible as I explain in Indonesia[n] and so maybe it is [a] barrier [when] I explain or com-municate with them, because if I explain in Indonesia[n] I can use everything . . . with many media [I can] talk to the children, but because [of] my barrier for them in language . . . I can't speak freely in many ways.

The minister sees language as being an important part of a person's Christian faith and the expression of that faith. He is in two minds about whether certain languages are more appropriate or proper than others for use in a church. On the one hand, he feels that language can create a sense of intimacy, a link between the heart, mind and spirit. On the other hand, he believes that some languages are better equipped for use in a religious context and other languages may benefit from borrowing suitable vocabu-lary from them.

The minister, however, does feel that it is necessary to use a style of language which shows appropriate respect for God. This means that the Biblical view of Jesus as a 'friend' and 'brother' still does not permit the use of familiar or intimate language. The relationship of an Indonesian Christian to God is always one of a servant to their King. A person's standing as a Christian in the community would be diminished if they were overheard using a language or style of language less than the most respect-ful one they have mastered.

The minister acknowledges that there are some who oppose the English translation ministry within the church and the use of English with the younger generation:

Every ethnic [group] and every people, I think they have some kind of racism, not just racism but ethnicism. Among the ethnic groups [in Indonesia] we are very strong, we don't have . . . good relations in [some ways] with the other ethnic [groups] sometimes. But [in] the church we should . . . practise what we believe, that all people are the same before God, and so we should try . . . to be one. And so this is part of the church education, . . . to go beyond their own thinking about the ethnicity and the racism, because every people have their own feeling sometime of racism, ethnicity.' [*Sic.*]

The minister sees the future of the congregation as promising but with two distinct groups. One, he envisages, would be made up of those who are content to integrate with the English-speaking church but who might add some Indonesian flavour to Australian spirituality. He also sees a need for a service for those who are part of the continual stream of short-term students and new migrants, to offer them a place to gather as a community and worship in a way to which they have been accustomed in Indonesia.

The Questionnaire

A total of 80 questionnaires were distributed to those attending the 11 am Indonesian-language service on a particular Sunday in October, 1997. Thirty-two of these 80 questionnaires (40%) were completed and returned. Possible reasons for the relatively low return rate may include timing – the approaching end-of-year examinations and subsequent return to Indonesia by many students within the congregation may have affected their ability to complete the questionnaire (however, as Figure 5.1 illustrates, the majority of actual participants were, nonetheless, under 24). It may be that an evaluation of language as a 'non-issue' by some potential participants within the Indonesian congregation (see later) resulted in a lack of interest in the research. The qualitative data obtained are valuable in shedding light on the linguistic situation within this congregation.

Nineteen participants (59.4%) completed the questionnaire using English only, five (15.6%) used Indonesian only and eight (25%) used different languages for different questions.

The participants

Of the 32 participants, 15 (46.9%) were male and 16 (50%) were female. One participant did not answer the question and unfortunately no clues were given elsewhere as to this participant's gender. The majority of participants were under the age of 24, with the next greatest number being in the 25–34 age group.

Because the congregation involved is made up of a large number of

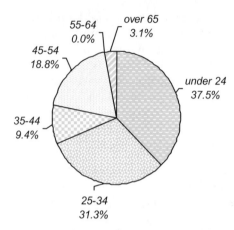

Figure 5.1 Age distribution of participants

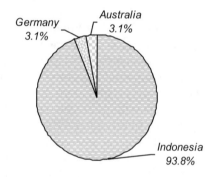

Figure 5.2 Distribution of participants by birthplace

students, citizenship and residential status was quite varied. Eleven participants (34.4%) were Australian citizens, ten (31.2%) were Indonesian
citizens. A further two (6.2%) claimed to be Indonesian citizens and
permanent Australian residents, while seven (21.9%) claimed simply to be
permanent residents in Australia and two (6.3%) were temporary residents.

Nearly all participants were born in Indonesia, with only one participant
each born in Australia and Germany. All of the participants' parents were
born in Indonesia.

Figure 5.3 presents the ethnic background of participants' parents, from

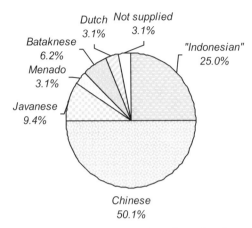

Figure 5.3 Distribution of participants by ethnic background of both parents

which participants' ethnicity may be determined. However, ethnic background is difficult to discern clearly for some participants. One-quarter of the participants gave the ethnic background of their mother as 'Indonesian' rather than providing more specific ethnic group membership such as 'Javanese'. Note also that one participant failed to provide information on the ethnic background of either parent, though it was indicated that they were born in Indonesia.

Of the 32 participants surveyed, 18 were married, with 17 of the 18 spouses born in Indonesia and one born in The Netherlands. While it is clear that all participants were, broadly speaking, 'Indonesian' (based on Figure 5.3) and all but one were married to 'Indonesians' (based on Figure 5.4), this does not, in fact, tell us much about the ethnicity of this group. Because of this more complex question of ethnicity it is difficult to classify a mixed marriage: if this definition is made on grounds of 'nationality' then the only mixed marriage amongst this group of participants is between an Indonesian woman and a Dutch man. Even were this definition made on grounds of (regional and/or national) ethnic grouping, there is still no other 'mixed marriage' in this group other than the aforementioned one.

Participants' language skills

Self-assessments of language skills were made for speaking/understanding/reading/writing on a scale which included the categories 'fluent', 'very well', 'moderately well', 'a bit' and 'not at all'.

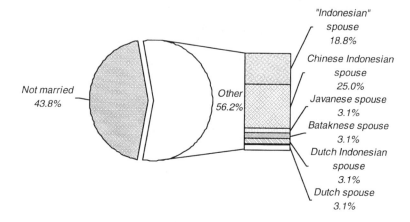

Figure 5.4 Distribution of participants by ethnic background of spouse

Adding together the percentages for the 'fluently' and 'very well' categories to form a single 'good' category, the distribution of responses becomes more reliably representative. A greater number of participants were proficient at Indonesian than English, with the percentage of participants with 'good' proficiency hovering around the nineties for Indonesian (speaking 90.7%, understanding and reading 93.8%, and writing 87.5%) but much lower for English (speaking 43.8%, understanding 53.1%, reading 65.7% and writing 50%). The considerable difference between English reading skills and other language skills is likely to be attributable to the high proportion of students in the group, each of whom would be required to read text books and other English-language materials during the course of their studies in Australia.

Participants were asked to indicate whether or not they were familiar with any other language or dialect other than English or Indonesian. As

Table 5.1 Participants' self-assessments of Indonesian language skills

	Fluently	*Very well*	*Moderately well*	*A bit*	*Not at all*	*Missing*
Speak	26 (81.3%)	3 (9.4%)	1 (3.1%)	2 (6.3%)	–	–
Understand	24 (75%)	6 (18.8%)	1 (3.1%)	1 (3.1%)	–	–
Read	27 (84.4%)	3 (9.4%)	1 (3.1%)	1 (3.1%)	–	–
Write	24 (75%)	4 (12.5%)	2 (6.3%)	1 (3.1%)	1 (3.1%)	–

Table 5.2 Participants' self-assessments of current English language skills

	Fluently	Very well	Moderately well	A bit	Not at all	Missing
Speak	7 (21.9%)	7 (21.9%)	15 (46.9%)	2 (6.3%)	–	1 (3.1%)
Understand	8 (25%)	9 (28.1%)	14 (43.8%)	1 (3.1%)	–	–
Read	9 (28.1%)	12 (37.5%)	9 (28.1%)	1 (3.1%)	–	1 (3.1%)
Write	7 (21.9%)	9 (28.1%)	13 (40.6%)	2 (6.3%)	–	1 (3.1%)

expected, the percentage of participants familiar with one or more additional languages was very high – 31 out of 32 participants (96.9%). Sixteen languages or varieties were mentioned in total, with many participants giving more than one language in their answer. Javanese was the most commonly known language, with half of all participants claiming to have some proficiency. Other regional languages of Indonesia included Sundanese and varieties of Batak; Chinese varieties such as Mandarin and Hakka were also known by some participants. One participant (I10) who had been born in Germany to Chinese Indonesian parents and educated in Brazil had fluent Portuguese language skills and weaker Indonesian than English skills.

Table 5.4 provides participants' self-assessments of their skills in these other known languages and indicated that comprehension skills are considered the strongest (65.7% having 'good' proficiency), while writing skills are the weakest (46.9% having 'good' proficiency). (Note that participants who indicated that they had skills in more than one language other

Table 5.3 Languages other than English or Indonesian known by participants

Language	No. of speakers	Language	No. of speakers
Javanese	16	East Javanese	1
Sundanese	4	Mandarin	1
Batak	3	Ambonese	1
Batak Karo	2	Madurese	1
Chinese, nfd	2	Portuguese	1
Hakka	2	Dutch	1
French	2	German	1
Jakarta dialect	1	Japanese	1

Table 5.4 Participants' self-assessments of skills in known language(s) other than English or Indonesian

	Fluently	*Very well*	*Moderately well*	*A bit*	*Not at all*	*Missing or n/a*
Speak	10 (31.3%)	8 (25%)	11 (34.4%)	6 (18.8%)	2 (6.3%)	4 (12.5%)
Understand	10 (31.3%)	11 (34.4%)	12 (37.5%)	5 (15.6%)	–	3 (9.4%)
Read	9 (28.1%)	9 (28.1%)	11 (34.4%)	5 (15.6%)	4 (12.5%)	3 (9.4%)
Write	7 (21.9%)	8 (25%)	10 (31.3%)	7 (21.9%)	6 (18.8%)	3 (9.4%)

than Indonesian or English did not differentiate between proficiency in those languages when answering this question.)

Interestingly, overall proficiency in these additional languages is higher than in English: a reflection of the migrational recency of the majority participants from an environment in which regional languages fulfil many of the functions of daily life. English is for many participants, a third – rather than second – language.

Many of these participants also indicated that they used their additional languages (Javanese, Batak, Sundanese, Ambonese) during church-related activities. In all of these cases, participants indicated that they would only use these languages with close friends.

Language use in the home

A 'home language' question was included on the questionnaire to gauge the linguistic environment in which most participants lived. None of the 32 participants lived alone and so the question was applicable to all. Indonesian figured prominently in home language use: 30 out of the 32 participants indicated that some Indonesian was used in the home environment. The higher rate of community language use in the home amongst Indonesian participants than Latvian participants would appear to confirm general trends for these communities as a whole in Australia (see section 1.2.2).

The greater variety of ages amongst the Indonesian participants when compared to the Latvian group has resulted in a wider range of home environment configurations.

Language used with spouse. Fifteen of the 32 participants (46.9%) indicated that they lived with a spouse, with equal language choices being made in both directions of the interaction. Indonesian or Indonesian with some English was clearly favoured by participants for communicating with

Table 5.5 Language use in the home (P = Participant)

	Spouse		Children		Mother		Father		Grand-parents		Siblings		Friends	
	To P	By P	To P	By P	To P	By P	To P	By P	To P	By P	To P	By P	To P	By P
Indonesian only	3	3	–	–	2	1	2	1	–	–	3	2	2	2
Indonesian with English words	5	5	4	4	3	3	1	2	–	–	5	6	1	1
English only	1	1	1	1	–	–	1	1	–	–	1	1	2	2
English with Indonesian words	–	–	3	2	–	1	–	–	1	–	–	–	–	–
Other language(s)	6	6	2	3	3	2	–	–	1	–	2	1	1	1

spouses. Only two participants mentioned using a regional language with their spouses. Of these 'other language' combinations, one used Dutch, German, Indonesian and English; another used Javanese, Indonesian and English; another three used Dutch, Indonesian and English; and one used Indonesian with some English words as well as Batak Karo (the Batak language spoken in central/northern Sumatra, west/north-west of Lake Toba).

Language used with children. Ten participants (31.3%) lived with their children. English was used more in child/parent interactions than in other situations, with four of the ten using Indonesian along with some English words and one using English only. Three participants indicated that their children used English with some Indonesian words to them, while only two used the same combination to their children. The third participant here used Javanese to their children. Two other participants indicated that they used other languages or combinations of languages in interaction with their children: one used Dutch only, while another participant claimed to use both Indonesian and English equally with her child who she said was 'still learning to speak'.

Language used with mother/father (or mother/father-in-law). Eight participants (25%) indicated that they lived with their mother/mother-in-law. Some participants made use of regional languages, with Javanese and Sundanese featuring. However, Indonesian was the preferred language of communication, with slightly more being used by the parent to the participant than the reverse. Four participants (12.5%) indicated that they lived with their father/father-in-law. The same pattern was evident with participants' fathers as for their mothers: Indonesian was claimed to be used slightly more by the parent to the participant than the reverse.

Language used with grandparents. Two participants (6.3%) indicated that they lived with a grandparent (or grandparents), but both of these provided information only as to the language(s) spoken by that grandparent to them and not *vice versa*. One participant was spoken to in English with some Indonesian words, while the other participant was spoken to in Javanese and Chinese.

Language used with siblings. Eleven participants (34.4%) indicated that they lived with siblings, although one participant failed to indicate which language they used with that sibling. Javanese and 'Chinese dialect' were mentioned by some participants. Indonesian was the language predominantly used in both directions of interaction, though most also used some English.

Language used with friends. Because the congregation is made up of many students who come from Indonesia without their families to study at university, a number of participants (six: 18.8%) indicated that they lived with friends. No information was supplied as to whether these friends were of Indonesian ancestry but the frequency of Indonesian language use implies that this was typically the case. Language choice patterns were shown to be equal in both directions of interaction.

Language use in church-related activities

Other language use questions were also asked. The first of these related to the language(s) used in church-related activities.

Table 5.6 Language use in church-related activities

	Elders' meetings	Council meetings	Sunday School	Bible study	Ladies Group	Music rehearsals	Youth activities	Other
Indonesian only	2	2	–	2	1	3	1	2
Indonesian with English words	2	1	1	5	–	6	9	6
English only	–	2	1	–	–	–	–	1
English with Indonesian words	–	–	3	–	–	–	–	–
Other language(s)	–	–	–	–	–	–	–	–
Depends on circumstances	2	–	–	1	–	1	–	1
No response/not applicable	26	27	27	24	31	22	22	22

Language used during elders' meetings and church council meetings. Six participants (18.8%) indicated that they were involved in elders' meetings. While Indonesian or Indonesian with some English words was used by four of these participants, two participants suggested that the language used depended on the circumstances. These latter two participants explained that they used Indonesian only or Indonesian with some English words in 'Indonesian' elders' meetings but English only in combined council/elders meetings or in meetings with English-speaking people.

Five participants (15.6%) indicated that they were involved in church council meetings, with two indicating that they spoke Indonesian only, two indicating that they spoke English only and one speaking Indonesian with some English words. One of the participants who indicated that they used English only explained that this was for combined council or parish meetings (i.e. those held with the English-language congregation of the church).

Language used during Sunday School classes. Five participants (15.6%) indicated that they were involved in teaching Indonesian Sunday School classes. There is some ambiguity in calling the Sunday School class which runs during the Indonesian service an 'Indonesian Sunday School', as those involved indicated that it is run largely in English. One participant indicated that they used Indonesian with some English words, while three indicated that they used English with some Indonesian words and another participant claimed to use English only. No participants indicated that they taught the 'English' Sunday School class, i.e. the class held during the English services.

Language used during small group/Bible study meetings. Eight participants (25%) indicated that they were involved in a 'small group' or Bible study. All but one claimed to use Indonesian only or Indonesian with some English words. The remaining participant suggested that the language used depended on circumstances, as 'the book may be in English or Indonesian'. This may refer to the Bible or to other texts and materials used during the meeting such as Bible study guides.

Language used during 'ladies group' meetings. One participant (3.1%) indicated that she was involved in a Ladies Group, claiming to use Indonesian only during meetings. However, no such group officially exists.

Language used during choir/church band rehearsals. Ten participants (31.3%) indicated that they were involved in music rehearsals. All used Indonesian only or incorporated in some English words. One participant commented that they used Indonesian exclusively but would use English on those occasions where an English-speaking band member was present.

Language used during youth group meetings. Ten participants (31.3%) indicated that they were involved in a youth group, with nine participants using Indonesian with some English words and one participant using Indonesian only. This language-use pattern was confirmed by the minister who indicated in the interview that Indonesian was used during these meetings, although English is used with children of Sunday School age. It is also not certain whether those who answered this question were referring to youth group meetings other than the 'Mulgrave Youth Fellowship' meetings which are held regularly. While the minister did not mention other kinds of youth activities, some participants seem to have distinguished between the 'Mulgrave Youth Fellowship' (MYF) and other 'youth group meetings' in their questionnaire responses (see the following question).

Language used during other church-related activities
    Ten participants (31.3%) indicated that they were involved in another activity, four of these referring to some type of activity for youth. One participant referred to a 'youth meeting', where they used Indonesian with some English words, while another two referred to MYF, one using Indonesian only, and the other using Indonesian with some English words. Another participant referred to a 'camp/youth fellowship', where English only was used.
    Two participants indicated that they helped to serve morning tea in the kitchen and to clean up after the service and used Indonesian with some English words. One participant was involved in a prayer fellowship and used Indonesian only. The remaining three participants failed to identify the activity in which they were involved but two of them used Indonesian with English words and the remaining participant claimed to use Indonesian only or English only, depending on the situation.
    Questions were also asked of participants' language use habits in other religion-related activities.

Language used when talking after the service. Participants' responses to this question indicated a tendency to converse in Indonesian after attending an Indonesian service, although very many also acknowledged that they would incorporate English into their speech.

Language used when discussing religion away from the church. Similar results were also found when participants were asked to recall the language

Table 5.7 Language use in other aspects of the religious domain

	Talking after service	Discussing religion away from church	Informal private prayers	Formal private prayers	Lord's Prayer in questionnaire	Bible for personal use	Bible used in Bible study	Meeting Indonesians in the workplace
Indonesian only	7	10	19	24	18	19	16	6
Indonesian with English words	16	12	9	3	–	–	–	8
English only	1	1	2	1	2	5	2	2
English with Indonesian words	2	3	1	1	–	–	–	3
Other language(s)	1	–	–	–	–	1	–	2
Depends on circumstances	4	4	1	1	–	7	2	–
No response / not applicable	1	2	–	2	12	–	12	11

they would use when discussing religious matters away from the church setting: most reported that they would use Indonesian or Indonesian with some English. Two participants claimed that they did not discuss religious matters outside of the church environment.

Language used for informal private prayers (said away from the church).
Indonesian was the favoured language for personal prayers, though many claimed to use some English words in their otherwise Indonesian prayers. Perhaps not surprisingly (given the earlier discussion of speech levels and religious discourse), no participants indicated that they would use a regional language, such as Javanese, when praying.

Language used for formal private prayers (said away from the church). As Table 5.7 illustrates, participants also showed a preference for the Indonesian language when reciting formal prayers. Two participants claimed that they did not recite any formal prayers such as the Lord's Prayer outside of the church context.

Language of Bible for personal use and in Bible study meetings. A strong preference for using Indonesian Bibles can be seen from Table 5.7, whether for personal use or in the small group context.

Table 5.8 Versions of Bibles for personal use

Language	*Version*	*No. of participants*
English	New International Version	11
	Good News Bible	3
	King James Version	3
	New Revised Standard Version	2
	New King James Version	1
Indonesian	'Terjemahan Baru' ('New Translation', Indonesian Bible Society 1974)	7
	Indonesian, not further defined	6
	'Terjemahan Lama' ('Old Translation' – terminology may have been used by the participant to contrast what is officially called 'New Translation' above, or may indicate some confusion between 'testament' and 'translation')	1
No response/do not read the Bible		5

Versions of Bible for personal use. Participants were asked to indicate the version of the Bible they used most for personal study/reading. The most commonly used versions are given in Table 5.8 (note that some participants named two different versions in their answers):

Indonesian Bibles are not available in as great an array of versions as English language Bibles and some participants pointed out that there is only one Indonesian Bible. The minister of this congregation suggests that there are three versions of the Indonesian Bible. The first is a translation into Indonesian from Dutch, which he claims is very unsatisfactory as it is effectively a second-hand translation. The second is a translation into formal Indonesian from the Hebrew and Greek completed in the 1960s: this is the version used in the church. The third version is a popular modern translation, closely related to the style of the English Good News Bible.

Other aspects of language use

Language use in the workplace. Language use in the place of work/study was also investigated. Participants' occupations varied, though predictably there was a large percentage of students (56.3%) among this group.

A total of 19 of the 32 participants (59.4%) indicated that they came into contact with other Indonesians in their place of work/study and most of

Table 5.9 Participants' occupations

Occupation	No. of participants
Student	18 (56.3%)
Bus/tram driver/mail officer/process worker	5 (15.6%)
Engineer/Information Technology	3 (9.4%)
Unemployed	3 (9.4%)
Retired/pensioner	2 (6.3%)
Self-employed	1 (3.1%)

these preferred Indonesian or Indonesian with some English for communicating with them.

Code-switching. In order to gauge attitudes on a general level to notions of language purity, participants were asked about their code-switching behaviour.

> *Do you ever find you begin a sentence in one language and finish it in another? For example, do you begin a sentence in Indonesian (or another language which you are able to speak) and finish it in English? Can you think of an example when this happened? Why do you think this happened?*

Participants' responses:

Does code-switch (Yes)	Does not code-switch (No)	No response
22 (68.8%)	5 (15.6%)	5 (15.6%)

While some participants responded to this question with a firm 'never' (or other negative response), others indicated that code-switching was a frequent part of their conversational style. Some reasoned that they did this because they lacked the appropriate vocabulary for the topic at hand:

> Yes – I usually do this when I cannot remember the words either in English/Indonesian. (I3)

> Sometimes it is very hard to complete the conversation fully in Indonesian and it is hard to speak fully in English especially meeting with Indonesian people so I [often] speak both languages, sometimes in broken English or incomplete Indonesian. (I8)

Yes – when I speak with my Indonesian friends. I just use some terms that I usually use in English. (I31)

Yes – when I want to express myself and find it difficult to choose the right word in my mother's tongue. (I4)

Terkadang tidak semua bahasa punya kekayaan kata dan dengan mudah diterjemahkan kedalam bahasa lain. Ada kata dalam bahasa Jawa yang artinya akan lain kalau diterjemahkan Inggris – Indonesia. (Sometimes, not all languages have the richness of vocabulary and can be easily translated into other languages. There are words in Javanese which have a different meaning if translated into English or Indonesian.) (I26)

Sometimes you would like to explain something in English but in the middle of the sentence you couldn't think of the appropriate phrase in English, or, sometimes when you speak in one language you'd find it more comfortable/ better explained in another. (I19)

Yes – sometimes it's easier to express something in certain languages. (I1)

For some participants, the need to convey a message clearly was also accompanied by a desire to help their listener understand the message:

Yes, if I think that will make the message easier to be understood. (I15)

Yes, it . . . happened during the first approx. five years living in this country. Because my vocabulary of English language was so poor [I code-switched] in order to explain something to other people clearly. (I16)

I sometimes speak Indonesian and end it in Javanese. My friend is from Jakarta and [when I spoke to her] I finished in Javanese. She couldn't understand it. (I12)

In addition to lexical and stylistic reasons, another participant referred to the presence or entry into the conversation of a non-Indonesian (or non-English) speaker as a reason for switching during their own turn:

Usually [I] begin [in] Indonesian, finish [in] English – when it gets too technical and there [are] no Indonesian words for it; when a non-Indonesian speaker comes and joins; when there is a phrase/expression that fits better than the Indonesian equivalent. (I23)

Some participants indicated who their usual interlocutors were in a typical code-switching situation, as well as who they would not code-switch in the presence of:

Yes – it usually happens when I speak to my brothers and / or friends all of whom are bilingual. However, I never do this when I speak to my servants back home as they are monolinguists. I believe this phenomenon is caused by my bilinguality. (I5)

Kadang-kadang – ini terjadi waktu saya berbicara dengan teman Jawa saya/ pacar saya. (Sometimes – this happens when I speak with my Javanese friends / my boyfriend.) (I9)

Yes, when I spoke with another Indonesian student. I don't know, I think [it's] reflex. (I21)

Kalau berbicara dengan orang tua saya dan family *saya.* (If I'm talking with my parents and family.) (I17)

Another participant felt that they could code-switch more easily with someone they shared a closer relationship with:

Dalam segala pembicaraan. Mungkin merasa lebih dekat, dan mesra, dan lebih penuh arti. (In all discussions. Maybe I feel closer [to this person], and intimate, and it has more meaning.) (I6)

Some participants were able to be more specific about the instances when they code-switched, recognising the mood of the conversation as a trigger for a switch:

Pernah bahkan seringkali, terjadi pada saat kita berbicara diawali dengan pembicaraan kurang serius (misal, bercanda) tetapi pada akhirnya menjadi pembicaraan serius, atau sebaliknya. Hal ini dapat terjadi jika berbicara dalam keluarga atau dengan teman akrab. (Sometimes, it happens when we are talking, preceded by a less serious discussion (for example, joking around) but eventually the discussion becomes serious, or the other way around. This happens when talking with family or with close friends.) (I30)

Another participant referred to grammatical difficulties – more particularly, differences in word order – as a reason for switching:

Yes, it happens when I try to explain something in English to other Indonesians and I can't seem to find words to explain it. This might [happen] because sometimes for a non-English speaker it's hard to find and arrange words into [a] sentence. (I13)

One participant indicated that he was proud of his code-switching abilities:

> Yes – in my place, [at] school and with friends, [it] naturally happens and I like it. (I24)

Many participants indicated that they code-switched between turns:

> *If an Indonesian speaker says something to you in Indonesian do you ever find you respond in English? Can you think of an example when this happened? Why do you think this happened?*

Participants' responses:

Does code-switch (Yes)	Does not code-switch (No)	No response
17 (53.1%)	9 (28.1%)	6 (18.8%)

Ease of expression was given as a primary reason:

> Yes – when I want to make myself understood better by the listener. English can express [the] situation more aptly in certain cases. When speaking with the youth, especially, I use English because they seem to understand my point better. (I4)

> Again, this usually [happens] when speaking to other Indonesians who are bilingual. Sometimes I find it easier to express myself in English. (I5)

> Yes, this is quite often [happens]. The reason is I sometimes [can] not find a proper answer in Indonesian language so I use English to finish it off. (I8)

> At times it is only a matter of which language you're comfortable with. (I19)

One participant also indicated that she switched languages if she wanted to refer to something someone else had said:

> Yes – sometimes when it's more appropriate to say it in English or if we quote other people's [words]. (I2)

Participants also indicated the importance of which interlocutors are present and involved in the conversation as a determining factor in whether or not they felt code-switching was appropriate:

> Yes, when I talk to my brother, sister and my girlfriend. (I24)

If someone speaks to me in Indonesian and among us are some English speaking people, I prefer to answer/respond . . . in English (polite reason). (I16)

Sometimes when I speak to people who are [close] to me, and usually we use both languages too. (I3)

Some participants recalled more specific instances in which they were aware of their code-switching habits:

Pernah, pada saat pertama kali (bulan pertama saya berada di Melbourne) karena saya harus melatih anak bungsu saya yang baru saja keluar dari sekolah berbahas indonesia memasuki sekolah dengang bahasa Inggris. Hal ini terjadi dengan maksud agar anak ini lebih cepat ber-adaptasi dengan lingungan sekolah yang baru. (Once, the first time [the first month I was in Melbourne] was because I had to train my youngest child who had just left an Indonesian-speaking school to enter an English-speaking school. This happened intentionally so that this child could adapt more quickly to the new school environment.) (I30)

Kadang-kadang, waktu ada discussion *mengenai* subject *di sekolah.* (Sometimes, if there's a discussion about a school subject.) (I9)

Yes, it happens when I feel like speaking English all day long and my brain is set to think in English and say things in English. This might happened because sometime you just feel like talking in English and probably you want to improve your English even with your Indonesian friends. (I13)

Some participants firmly indicated that they did not consider switching languages between turns as being polite or showing appropriate respect:

Tidak, karena saya menghormati bahasa Indonesia. (No, because I respect the Indonesian language.) (I11)

Tidak, karena kita akan dikira sombong oleh orang yang mengajak bicara. Tapi kalau orang itu bisa bahasa Indonesia dengan bicara Inggris dengan saya, saya bisa jawab Indonesia. (No, because we are considered arrogant by the person who initiated the conversation. But if the person can speak Indonesian, but speaks English to me, then I can answer in Indonesian.) (I26)

Kalau orang yang berbahasa Indonesia berbicara dengan saya dalam bahasa Indonesia, saya tentu mejawabanya dalam bahasa Indonesia juga. (If a person who can speak Indonesian speaks to me in Indonesian, of course I also answer them in Indonesian.) (I32)

As with the Latvian case study, two additional questions were asked in order to gauge participants' attitudes towards code-switching in the church (concerning their feelings during code-switching events in a church service, and their attitudes towards the person who was carrying out the code-switch). Similar difficulties were encountered by the Indonesian participants as with the Latvians: the results of these two questions are thus considered too inconclusive to warrant analysis.

Summary

Participants involved in this part of the research were members of an Indonesian congregation of the Uniting Church. Using parents' ethnicity as a guide, over half of the participants were Chinese Indonesians, one-quarter were 'Indonesian' (not further defined) and the remaining quarter were of Javanese, Bataknese, Menado and Dutch ancestry. The complexity of the concept of group membership is apparent here: while all participants could claim Indonesian group membership, some, for example, also claim Chinese group membership, which is then further broken down into Hakka subgroup membership, etc.

Due to the proximity of the church to Monash University, the congregation attracts many Indonesian students and, thus, the majority of the participants in this research were under the age of 24. Over half of the participants were students; other occupations were more varied.

Participants were overwhelmingly proficient in Indonesian, with self-assessments of English skills indicating a more moderate proficiency. The high level of Indonesian proficiency amongst participants – including youth – is due to the large number of Indonesian-born students who travel frequently between Indonesian and Australia. It might be expected that English proficiency would exceed proficiency in Indonesian amongst youth born and educated in Australia. In fact, this was shown to be the case for the one Australian-born student participant in this study.

A large range of Indonesian regional languages, Chinese varieties and former-colonising languages (Dutch, Portuguese) were also claimed to be known, again with typically moderate levels of proficiency.

It is somewhat surprising then that regional languages and Chinese varieties did not feature greatly in home language use. Indonesian was the language most used between participants and spouses. English featured more in the interaction between participants and their children, with more English being used by the children than the participants. Surprisingly, Indonesian was used more by participants and their siblings than

English, though English words and phrases were claimed to be readily incorporated.

Participants were involved in a range of church-related activities and in nearly all of these Indonesian featured heavily. The only activities in which English was the main language used were those which were specifically designed for those with poor or no Indonesian language skills – the Sunday School and its related activities, such as performances by the Sunday School children. English is also used during the service in simultaneously translating the proceedings with the use of headphones. Indonesian appears to be linked to most activities of the religious domain, in particular to prayers and to the Bible, although the most commonly used Bible is the English *New International Version*. Informal private prayers, post-service conversations and discussions about religious matters outside of the church context tended to be accompanied by the use of some English along with Indonesian.

Given the Indonesian cultural understanding of showing respect and honour through the way language is used, it is not surprising that language choices in the religious domain did not vary widely from Indonesian (which acts as a *lingua franca* for this ethnically diverse group) or English (which caries a great deal of prestige). While certain regional languages such as Javanese and Sundanese have particular speech levels which carry more prestige than either Indonesian or English, fluency is difficult to achieve and is rarely claimed.

The need to convey – through language choice – appropriate respect for one's interlocutor clearly governs code-switching behaviour, although when compared to the Latvians, a much larger percentage of Indonesian participants claimed to code-switch.

Questionnaire findings

In this section, the responses of participants to the remainder of the open-ended questions included in the questionnaire are presented and discussed. Note that any square brackets included in responses indicate additional information not given by participants. Where rounded brackets are found, these form part of the participant's own response. Italics are used for Indonesian text; if unbracketed regular type English text is found in an otherwise Indonesian text, this represents an instance of code-switching by the participant. All English translations are the author's own.

Reasons for church attendance

Twenty-nine (90.6%) of those who completed questionnaires claimed to regularly attend the church, with participants having been at the church for an average of six years. Reasons given for attending the church regularly

included the need to maintain Indonesian identity through worshipping in
the Indonesian language and in the company of other Indonesians:

> Because I'm Indonesian people. [*Sic.*] (I29)

> *Sebab berkhotbah dalam bahasa Indonesia.* (Because it has sermons in Indonesian.) (I7)

> To worship and to praise the Lord with the Indonesian congregation. (I20)

Being a part of an Indonesian congregation in Australia also reflected an
Indonesian–Australian identity for some:

> this church is the first church I attended in 1986 and I have attended it
> since then, therefore I feel that the church is part of my life here in
> Australia. (I3)

Feelings of familiarity and comfort were important for many participants –
feelings which were aided not only by the use of Indonesian in the church
and by the presence of other Indonesians but also by the use of a style of
worship accustomed to in Indonesia:

> By attending this church we are sure that all doctrines taught by the
> priest are exactly the same [as] those we had in Indonesia. (I25)

> We are comfortable with the service (similar with those in Indonesia).
> We like the people. (I4)

> *Merasa cocok dengan semuanya (tata cara ibadah / cara berbakti).* (I feel
> satisfied with everything (customs and manner of worship, the way
> services are run.) (I26)

Other reasons given by the participants for attending the church included
its proximity to home, the desire to serve in a role in the church (such as
through teaching Sunday School), and – for some young people – because it
was the decision of the participant's parents. One participant indicated that
he felt he had been divinely directed to the church:

> *Karena Tuhan telah menempatkan saya di gereja ini (Dia menjawab doa saya).*
> (Because God put me here (He answered my prayers.) (I9)

Only five participants (15.6%) indicated that they attended the church
alone, the vast majority attending with a family member also of Indonesian
ancestry. Eleven of the participants (34.4%) surveyed had children, with six
of these 11 indicating that their children attended the Indonesian services of

the church and one indicating that their children attended the English services of the church. Five of the 11 indicated that their children attended the Indonesian Sunday School – which is run largely in English – while one indicated that their children had attended when they were of the appropriate age. Two indicated that their children attended the English Sunday School, though it is hard to be certain whether this actually referred to the Sunday School held during the English service or whether this was a reflection of the fact that the Sunday School held during the Indonesian service is run in English.

A total of six participants (18.8%) claimed to attend another church regularly, with denominations mentioned being 'Baptist', 'Assemblies of God/Pentecostal/charismatic', 'Presbyterian' and 'Catholic'. One participant also claimed to attend an English-speaking Baptist church service, 'because it provides me an opportunity for growth, fellowship and services, and it's easier for me to invite friends over' (I10). Another participant claimed to occasionally visit Presbyterian, Baptist and Assembly of God church services held in English: 'I do not attend the service regularly, only held every Tuesday (part of my study)' (I8). This participant gave her occupation as student but provided no information as to her field of study. Only one participant who attended other churches indicated that these other churches were Indonesian.

Table 5.10 Services regularly attended by participants

Indonesian services only	Indonesian services and occasional English service	English services only	English services and occasional Indonesian service	Both Indonesian and English regularly	No response – do not attend church regularly
29 (90.6%)	3 (9.4%)	–	–	–	–

The majority of the participants claimed to attend only Indonesian services at the church. However, just over half of the participants claimed to have attended an English service at least once, whether the weekly 9.30 am English service or the monthly 'combined' service.

Have you ever attended the English services of this church?

Participants' responses:

No, never	No but planning to	Yes, once	Yes, a few times	Yes, regularly	No response
11 (34.4%)	2 (6.3%)	9 (28.1%)	8 (25%)	–	2 (6.3%)

Participants were asked to indicate why they had a preference for attending the Indonesian and/or English services of the church. On the whole, participants answered this question in relation to the Indonesian services, providing similar reasons for attending as given in the previous question. The language of the service was the most frequently given reason for attending – largely due to the comfort provided by worshipping in Indonesian or the ease with which this could be done by participants, when compared with using English for the same purpose:

> Because I found that it is easier for me to digest and understand the sermon in Indonesian. (I3)

> *Karena lebih baik menerima firman dengan bahasa Indonesia.* (Because it's better to receive God's word in Indonesian.) (I11)

> *Saya memilih kebaktian berbahasa Indonesia agar saya dapat lebih mendalami/memahami arti atau penjelasan atas Firman Tuhan.* Because Indonesian language is language of my 'mother tongue'. [*Sic*] (I choose the Indonesian services so that I can deepen my understanding of the meaning or explanation of God's word. Because Indonesian language is language of my 'mother tongue'.) (I30)

> Because it is quite difficult to understand services in English. (I31)

> *Saya mengikuti kebaktian Indonesia sebab saya rasa dengan berbahasa Indonesia saya benar-benar mengerti makna dari penyampaian Firman tapi kadang-kadang saya pun mengikut kebaktian di* Campus (chapel) in English. (I attend Indonesian services because I feel that with Indonesian I can truly understand the meaning of God's word, but sometimes I even attend services on campus (chapel) in English.) (I8)

The comfort and familiarity which the Indonesian language was reported to provide meant that for some participants, the use of Indonesian was strongly associated with activities in the religious domain – to the point that the use of any other language would feel unnatural:

> Because this church use Indonesian language; also I feel uncomfortable attending the service if they use English language. (I14)

> I have always attended Indonesian services (in both Singapore and Australia). Thus I found it odd to attend services in other languages. Moreover, Indonesian is the language I use when communicating with God in my personal prayers. (I5)

Fellowship with other Indonesians was also an important reason for attending Indonesian services rather than English services:

> I only attend the Indonesian service because I want my children to grow in this environment. [The] Indonesian cultural background – to a certain extent – creates a more friendly atmosphere for spiritual growth. Another reason is [that] we are more comfortable [expressing] our spiritual life in our mother tongue. (I4)

> I feel more comfortable when attending the service in Indonesian as it is my mother tongue and also I may meet my fellow countrymen during the service. (I20)

> Most of the Indonesians attend the Indonesian service so we [would] not be able to see them if we [attended] the English service. Besides, my wife and I are not comfortable with the English service (of the Uniting Church). (I23)

Familiarity with the style of the service was also considered an important reason for some participants:

> Because I feel at home. (I22)

Knowledge about and interest in the activities of the English-speaking congregation, as well as 'combined' activities of the two congregations, seemed to vary between participants. While one participant indicated that they had not inquired about any other services held in the church, another participant wrote:

> *Karena gereja kami telah bersatu dengan gereja yang berbahasa Inggris* (integrate) *jadi kadang-kadang kami mempunyai kebaktian gabungan.* (Because our church has become one with the English speaking church (integrate), we sometimes have combined services.) (I6)

Views on language in the church – the 'appropriateness' of language

> *Do you feel that certain languages are more appropriate/proper than others for use in the church?*

Participants' responses:

Yes	No	No response
12 (37.5%)	19 (59.4%)	1 (3.1%)

Interestingly, reasons given for answering 'yes' and 'no' to this question were similar. Responses mainly centred around the argument that languages are more appropriate if they are more easily understood by the congregation. In other words, if a language cannot be understood properly, it is *inappropriate* for use:

> *Ya – sebab kita harus menyesuaikan dengan jemaat yang ada di gereja tersebut, kalau jemaatnya mayoritas orang Indonesia sebaiknya memakai bahasa Indonesia.* (Yes – because we must adapt to the congregation which exists in the church; if the majority of the congregation is Indonesian it's best if Indonesian is used.) (I28)

> Yes – because with the first language, i.e. Indonesian, I can understand more and absorb the meaning of the sermon. (I2)

> Yes – some Indonesians do not understand English well, so it is better for ethnic church such as this one to use Indonesian language. (I23)

Some participants who considered no language to be more appropriate than another for church use, also gave ease of understanding as a reason. These participants implied that any language could be considered appropriate, as long as the congregation was able to understand the language used. Language is thus considered a tool, a means of communicating a message:

> No – because any language which makes it easier for people to communicate and understand better the Bible and God is appropriate. (I10)

> No – I believe every group has [the] right to worship in [the] language most suitable for everybody. (I14)

> No – because language is just one way of getting the message through and no language is more appropriate than others. [When you] listen to [a] sermon with your first language you really understand it better, so that you can get the right message. (I13)

> No – language is just a matter of choice, whichever you're comfortable with. The words of God are the same in all different languages. (I19)

> *Tidak – Di mana para jemaatnya yang fasih dalam suatu bahasa tertentu merupakan mayoritas, bahasa itulah yang harus dipergunakan di gereja itu.* (No – where the members of the congregation who are fluent in one

particular language form the majority, it is that language which must be used in the church.) (I32)

Another reason commonly given for thinking that no language is more appropriate than any other for use in the church focussed on the notion that just as all people are equal and are equally loved by God, so are all languages:

all languages are appropriate for use in the church since God speaks all languages. I think it is personal preference. (I3)

I believe that God understand all languages and He does not discriminate. (I5)

Tidak – Bahasa-bahasa apapun juga yang dipergunakan di gereja sama tepat / pantas sebab semua bahasa merupakan anugerah Tuhan. (No – whichever language is used in the church is equally suitable / proper because all languages are a gift from God.) (I30)

Views on language in the church – Indonesian language only?

Should all activities of the church, including the services, be conducted in Indonesian only?

Participants' responses:

Yes	No	No response
3 (9.4%)	27 (84.4%)	2 (6.3%)

The great majority of participants considered that Indonesian should not be used exclusively in their congregational activities. Many of these participants referred to the younger generation of Indonesians, particularly those born in Australia, as well as non-Indonesians, whose Indonesian may not be as strong or may be non-existent:

Tidak – sebab anak-anak remaja dan Sunday School *mereka adalah generasi kedua yang kurang mengerti bahasa Indonesianya.* (No – because teenagers and Sunday School children, they are the second generation who don't understand Indonesian as well.) (I7)

Tidak selalu – harus ada translator *yang menterjemahkan bagi orang asing yang mau mendengarkan kotbah di kebaktian berbahasa Indonesia.* (Not always – there must be a translator who translates for foreigners who wish to hear the sermon in an Indonesian service.) (I9)

No – it would be very selfish [of] me because not everyone understands Indonesian. (I5)

Tidak – karena di Melbourne yang tinggal bukan orang Indonesia saja. (No – because Indonesians aren't the only ones living in Melbourne.) (I28)

No – because a church needs to cater its service according to its audience needs. (I31)

Some participants went further with this concept of the need to accommodate those with poorer Indonesian skills, suggesting that the language used should be altered for the benefit of those who may be from other ethnic backgrounds. This was also considered by some to be a means of evangelism and of extending Christian fellowship beyond the Indonesian community:

We have to blend the two languages because I notice that some of the comers are non-Indonesian speakers. (I2)

No – because by mixing two languages we can attract more people to come to church, but not only Indonesians, so that we can really have a multicultural surroundings. (I13)

No – I feel that we need to communicate with different ethnic groups so we [can] make more friends. (I12)

The use of English was also considered by some as a necessary and unavoidable part of life in Australia, which if allowed to flow into religious activities would provide the congregation with the benefit of improved English language skills:

No – I think that every now and then there should be a service in English to familiarize everyone with the 'English' jargon used for church talk. (I10)

No ... English/any other language can also be used for variation, and this will make students/listeners practise English more. (I25)

No – [the longer we live] in Australia, [the more] we realise that we have to live like Australians – integration to a certain extent has to be initiated, therefore English should also be applied in some activities especially when English speaking [members of the] congregation are present. (I4)

One of the participants who felt that Indonesian only should be used for activities of the church indicated that this is what most would expect of an 'Indonesian' church:

> Yes – as much as possible. People [who] come to the Indonesian service expect [that the] Indonesian language will be used. For some people it's OK if [a language] other than [the] Indonesian language is used. But for the others, because they didn't expect [English], they might not understand or understand fully, or just understand but [find it] difficult to absorb ([it's] easier to absorb if 'mother language' is used). (I15)

Views on language in the church – the place of English

Do you feel that English has any place at all in the activities of this church?

Participants' responses:

Yes	No	No response
27 (84.4%)	2 (6.3%)	2 (6.3%)

The parallel question of whether English has any place in the activities of the church was also asked, with reasons for believing that English does have a role to play centring on the need to include those whose Indonesian is poor or non-existent:

> Yes – because we also have to [be concerned] for those who can't speak Indonesian. Praise and worship can be conducted in both languages. (I2)

> Yes – because we have also non-Indonesian background families such as husbands or wives or visitors who don't speak Indonesian, so of course there is always [the] possibility to have English activities in this church. (I8)

> Yes – we have a translator every week to translate the language used during the service to those with non-Indonesian speaking background. We communicate to them also using English. (I19)

> Yes – because we live in [an] English speaking country and it is unavoidable for the children who were born here that they speak only

English or maybe [a] little Indonesian. Therefore the church has to have some activities that can embrace these children. (I3)

Yes – for Sunday School children, English is their mother language. For them, English should be used as much as possible. (I15)

Ya – penting juga terutama buat orang-orang muda (youth). (Yes – it's important especially for the youth.) (I6)

Others felt that English should be used only on special occasions such as Christmas, while one person, a newcomer to the church, claimed to have seen no evidence of English being used in the five weeks he had attended. Observation undertaken in the present research proved otherwise – not only are the services simultaneously translated into English via headphones but English words and phrases are frequently used during the sermon, as well as in any interaction with Sunday School children (such as performances by them during the service).

Views on language in the church – the existence of language-related issues

Do you feel there are any language issues in particular which your church is struggling with?

Participants' responses:

Yes	No	No response
6 (18.8%)	25 (78.1%)	1 (3.1%)

Interestingly, the vast majority of participants (78.1%) did not feel that the church was struggling with any language-related issues. Among the few participants who did feel there were issues, some mentioned the task of effectively relating to the youth:

Yes – to bridge the gap between the Indonesian-speaking generation with the English speaking (children). (I4)

Yes – the Sunday School and teenagers in our church are taught in English. (I2)

Other issues included the perceived 'alienation' of those who cannot speak Indonesian:

Yes – by using [the] Indonesian language in the service, we discourage non-Indonesian speaking people from coming. (I23)

Yes – not everyone feels comfortable speaking English, so many of the English-speaking people are a bit left out. (L1)

Views on language in the church – communicating the Gospel to youth

Do you feel that there is a problem communicating the Gospel to the younger generation of Indonesians because the younger and older generations relate better to different languages?

Participants' responses:

Yes	No	No response
16 (50%)	11 (34.4%)	5 (15.6%)

Reasons given by participants for thinking language problems exist in trying to communicate the Gospel to Indonesian youth included the following:

Yes – the different language acquisition between generations is accompanied by a cultural problem. Besides that, children who grow up in Australia start to have a different perspective compared to their parents. Sometimes they question values that their parents believe. (I4)

Yes – I am not totally certain – but I feel that the younger generation is having a bit of trouble relating to the service. Most of them understand Indonesian but tend to speak in English. Yet communicating the Gospel in Indonesian is of great benefit to Indonesian students who come here temporarily. (I10)

Ya – karena kebanyakan anak-anak Indonesia tidak pasih bahasa Indonesia. (Yes – because the majority of Indonesian children are not fluent in Indonesian.) (I11)

One participant indicated that this generational difference in language abilities had the potential to result in misunderstandings about the Gospel, with the message being miscommunicated. Many other participants referred not just to the communication problems faced between the younger and older generations but more specifically to those problems experienced by those of the younger generation who are born and educated in Australia, and whose English is considerably better than their Indonesian:

Yes . . . because younger generations [are used to speaking] in English, especially those who were born outside Indonesia (Australia). Therefore, there is a little problem communicating the Gospel to them in the Indonesian language. (I8)

Yes – it is a problem because of the language barrier, but I do not think it is a big problem. I think it is better if children are taught by someone who is fluent in English, preferably an Indonesian who grew up here. (I23)

Other participants did not think there were any language problems which hindered communication of the Gospel to the youth, some saying that young Indonesians could still understand Indonesian well enough:

No – we all learn and understand our language (Indonesian) fluently. Your question will not happen unless the young generations live in an English-speaking country since their childhood. [*Sic.*] (I25)

No – because Indonesian is still our first language. [One] problem that might arise is probably [the] different point of view [between the] young generation and old generation. (I13)

Other participants felt that any language problems could be overcome by creative means:

No – because we can communicate the Gospel through 'doing' instead of 'speaking/telling'. As long as they know the words through the Sunday School, and the older generation can reinforce them by example. (I3)

No – there is always someone in the middle to translate. (I1)

Views on language in the church – best language for communicating the Gospel to youth

What language do you feel is best to use in presenting the Gospel to the younger generation of Indonesians?

Participants' responses:

Indonesian	English	Both/Depends	No response
6 (18.7%)	12 (37.5%)	11 (34.4%)	3 (9.4%)

Responses to this question were quite divided, with a large number of people saying that both languages should be used, either in combination or with different individuals depending on their language skills and preferences:

> For international students (Indonesians) Indonesian is more adequate. For local people English is. Because that's the language they're more at ease with. (I10)

> Both (English and Indonesian) *supaya* [in order to] meet the needs. [*Sic.*] (I9)

> Indonesian/English – those who come from Indonesia understand Indonesian better, however those who are born in Australia or grew up here since [they were] babies/small kids understand English better. (I1)

> English for Sunday School children, Indonesian (and English translation) for the youth. Every year, a lot of new coming students from Indonesia attend the Youth Fellowship. They need Indonesian language to understand and absorb the message. (I15)

Some felt that both should be used because fluency in both languages is both desirable and necessary:

> Both – because we are now living in Australia therefore we ought to speak/at least use both languages (we have to consider that [the] majority [of] people here . . . speak English. (I8)

> Both languages – so that they will understand, but [so] at the same time they do not lose the ability to master Indonesian as their second language. (I4)

> Indonesian, but combined with English, because students in Australia should learn more English than Indonesian. Still use mostly Indonesian so that way we can probably understand better. (I13)

> *Tergantung situasi dan kondisi – Untuk generasi muda Indonesia yang berada di Australia (di mana mereka sudah tidak fasih dengan bahasa Indonesia) maka sebaiknya diberikan dalam bahasa Inggris (sebagai bahasa yang mereka pahami dengan baik.* (It depends on the situation and conditions – for the young generation of Indonesians who are in Australia (where they are already fluent in Indonesian), then it's best if it's given in English (as a language they understand well.) (I30)

Other participants referred to the need to understand one's identity as an Indonesian:

> English and a bit more Indonesian – to tell them that they are Indonesian. (I24)

> English for those who were born here. More appropriate for them but on the other hand we have to remind them about our language because it will be useful for them. (I2)

Participants who thought that English was the best language to use in communicating the Gospel to younger Indonesians largely referred to the English proficiency of the young, and to the usefulness of English in an English-speaking country:

> English – as English is their everyday language and they are more comfortable using English rather than Indonesian. (I20)

> *Bahasa Inggris – karena mereka bisa berintergrasi dengan jemaat bahasa Inggris.* (English – because they can integrate with the English congregation.) (I11)

> English – because most of them could not speak Indonesia any longer. (I31)

> English – because they understand English better than Indonesian. (I3)

Interestingly, some participants thought the converse was true:

> *Indonesia – karena lebih dimengerti bahasa Indonesianya.* (Indonesian – because they understand Indonesian better.) (I17)

> Indonesian language – to avoid misunderstanding, because even though English language is very important in Indonesia, [only] a few people speak English fluently. (I25)

> *Indonesia – karena mereka tetap lebih nyaman mengunakan bahasa mereka sendiri.* (Indonesian – because they are still more comfortable using their own language.) (I26)

Views on language in the church – a 'multicultural' church?

> *Do you want this congregation to be one which caters for Indonesians only or for Christians of other backgrounds who might also want to attend?*

Participants' responses:

Indonesian-only church	Church for all, regardless of background	No response
–	31 (96.9%)	1 (3.1%)

In recent times, some denominations (notably the Uniting Church) have moved towards the concept of a 'multicultural church' as the ideal. In the light of this, participants were asked whether or not they wanted their church to have an 'open-door' policy as far as ethnicity is concerned. The percentage of those wanting a 'multicultural' congregation was extremely high. This finding was confirmed by the author's own experience attending the church, in which the minister greeted her personally after the service with the words, 'You are very welcome, we want this to be a multicultural church'.

Reasons for thinking that the congregation should be open to non-Indonesians as well include the belief that everyone is equal in the eyes of God and it would, therefore, be wrong to discriminate:

Karena Tuhan tidak memandang suku bangsa. (Because God takes no notice of ethnic background.) (I29)

Because we are all the same [before] Jesus Christ. (I25)

Karena gereja adalah untuk semua orang dan kita hanya memuja Tuhan yang satu yaitu Allah! (Because the church is for all people and we only worship one God, our Lord!) (I6)

Karena kita harus adil dan Tuhan pun tidak pernah membeda-bedakan kita. Oleh karena itu jangan membeda-bedakan. (Because we must be fair and God has never treated us unequally. [For that reason], neither can we discriminate.) (I9)

Di gereja kami tidak terbatas pada orang-orang tertentu. Siapapun mereka / golongan maupun memiliki bahasa selain Indonesia & English also welcome – in God we all one. (Our church is not restricted to particular people. Whoever they are, whether they have a different background or language besides Indonesian and English [they are] also welcome – in God we [are] all one.) (I8)

Other participants felt that the notion of the unity of the 'Body of Christ' (the Church) was an important reason for not restricting those who attended their congregation to Indonesians only:

We want to be united with other believers from different backgrounds. (I1)

Unity – *lebih merasakan pengalaman berbagi suka dan duka dalam Kristus dan suku bangsa lain.* (Unity – [we can] can better experience and share the ups and downs in Christ and [with] other ethnic groups.) (I26)

Unity within the congregation itself was also seen as important, but not if it excluded those of other ethnic backgrounds:

Since we have a translator, this facility should be used. Moreover, some members of our congregation are intermarried and their spouses might be coming as well. (I5)

Because I think the reason we have a congregation [is] for Indonesians just to unite together, but basically all Christians are brothers and sisters in God. (I13

Hard to say because actually I have two arguments. First I would like this congregation to cater only for Indonesians who live in Melbourne and [want to] grow together in Christ. But on the other hand we will be too selfish if we only cater for particular ethnic [group]. (I2)

Opening the church to those of other backgrounds was also seen by some as being important for the spiritual and physical growth of the congregation:

It will be good for the growth of the congregation – so that the congregation will learn how to be Christ's body. (I4)

We need to expand our relationship to other ethnic groups. (I16)

Other participants saw the 'Great Commission', the words of Jesus as given in Matthew 28:19 ('Therefore, go and make disciples of all nations'), as being an undisputable reason for not limiting the membership of their congregation to Indonesians only:

Karena misi gereja ini adalah membawa injil kepada semua manusia. (Because the Church's mission is to take the Gospel to all mankind.) (I7)

Because of Matthew 28, it says to preach to all nations. There is a place for ethnic churches, but there should be an opening for people of other nations. (I10)

Karena 'injil' harus diberitakan pada semua bangsa dan jika ada jemaat lain yang mau bergabung maka sudah selayaknya kita menerima dengan senang hati. (Because the Gospel must be told to all nations and when there are other congregations who want to gather, then it's only right that we receive them with warm hearts.) (I30)

Evangelisation. (I27)

Some participants saw the welcoming of non-Indonesians into the congregation as a means of integrating into Australian society:

Karena orang-orang Indonesia yang tinggal di Australia harus berintegrasi di mana mungkin. (Because Indonesians who live in Australia must integrate in whatever way possible.) (I32)

Although this is an Indonesian service, we are a part of the Australian community, which means that we would have to accept [people of] other ethnic backgrounds who are also members of the Australian community. (I19)

One participant wanted the congregation to be open to those of any background 'so people will like our service' (I12). Another participant also saw a church made up of those from many different ethnic backgrounds as being unproblematic, saying:

we, Christians, should speak only the 'language of love'. (I3)

Views on the future of the church

Where do you see this church in 50 years' time?

Many participants responded to this question with a view that the church would grow numerically and spiritually over time:

Seharusnya berkembang baik Quantity *maupun* Quality. (It should grow in both quantity and quality.) (I9)

I hope that more people will only put their faith in Jesus and the quality of the faith will increase and deepen. (I25)

Pasti bertumbuh kalau kita tetap setia dan penuh dengan pelayanan ke padanya. (It will certainly grow if we stay faithful and serve Him fully.) (I6)

I don't know. I hope and pray that it grows much more and still serves all the people in need, not only Indonesians. (I15)

Tidak tahu sebab 50 tahun adalah waktu yang terlalu jauh ke depan dan saya percaya jika gereja ini tetap berjalan dalam 'terang Kristus' maka gereja ini akan bertahan bahkan berbuah dalam Kristus. (I don't know because 50 years is too far into the future and I believe if this church still walks in the light of Christ, then this church will survive, even bear fruit in Christ.) (I30)

Other participants described how they imagined the activities of the congregation would be structured, including which roles certain languages would play:

Having an Indonesian service in the morning and Australian [*sic*] service in the afternoon. (I4)

Tetap ada kebaktian dalam bahasa Indonesia sebab terus akan ada pengunjungi dan pendatang dari Indonesia, tetapi akan ada kebaktian dalam bahasa Inggris juga. (There will still be services in Indonesian because there will still be visitors and newcomers from Indonesia, but there will also be services in English.) (I7)

It may change in its services and approach to the congregation but the fundamental and basic teaching I think will remain the same. (I20)

It will be still [an] Indonesian congregation, the language we'll use will be still mostly Indonesian. We'll have translator to translate all the words during the service. (I13)

Some participants felt that the future of the Indonesian congregation was not certain because of the possibility of complete assimilation into Australian society:

I think that in fifty years' time the Indonesian ethnic group will disappear and dissolve into [the] English ethnic group. (I16)

Pendapat saya ialah bahwa pada 50 tahun mendatang gereja ini sudah akan menjadi gereja yang berbahasa Inggris karena anak-anak kami, orang-orang Indonesia, tentunya sudah tidak berbahasa Indonesia lagi. (My opinion is that in 50 years time this church will have become an English-speaking church because our children, Indonesians, no longer speak Indonesian.) (I32)

Difficult to see so far ahead. I think if things as they are now (no change in church policy), then the church cannot grow much. The attendants would be the old generations (such as us), new migrants and students. Our children would likely attend other churches because they do not understand Indonesian. (I23)

Other participants referred again to the desire to fulfil the 'Great Commission' by spreading the message of the Gospel beyond their own ethnic group.

> I really hope that this church will still serve all [the] people's needs, religiously or/and socially. They can be Indonesian, Australian or [from another] race. (I3)

> I think if we hold on together with the same vision and mission and value our togetherness, I believe this church will be used amazingly by God to reach not only Indonesians but also non-Indonesians. (I2)

Other comments from participants

Additional comments provided by two participants provide a good summary of the general attitude of this congregation towards the place of language in relation to faith and worship:

> *Kalau orang Indonesia lebih tahu bahasa Inggris dengan Indonesianya, lebih baik kalau berdoa pakai bahasa Inggris, dan sebaliknya?!!* (If an Indonesian knows English better than Indonesian, then [it's] best if they pray using English and *vice versa*.) (I17)

> *The suitability or choice of language depends on the objective/mission of the church. Whatever its mission, it has to keep an open mind and be attentive to the changes taking place. This includes learning to adapt to cater for the second or third generation of Indonesians' children growing up here. And also to maintain contact with other ethnic groups. (I10)*

Closing Remarks

The situation faced by the Indonesian congregation differs markedly from that of the Latvian church. The 'Indonesianness' of the congregation benefits from the presence of longer-term migrants as well as the constant yearly flow of university students from Indonesia. While the number of Australian-born-and-educated Indonesians in the church is growing, the influence of English is not seen as problematic in the way that it has been by many members of the Latvian church. Indonesian clearly plays a different role in the Indonesian church than does Latvian in the Latvian church. Among the Indonesian community there is a preparedness to accommodate non-Indonesian speakers through the provision of simultaneous translation during the services and an English-medium Sunday School. English ministry is seen as a necessary part of the pastoral care of the wider Indonesian community: it is not considered a betrayal of Indonesian ethnicity. There are many possible reasons for this positive evaluation of English in the church when compared to the Latvian church: the prestige which English carries in Indonesia, the cultural and linguistic diversity of the Indonesian community which requires the use of a *lingua franca* (a role which English could also play), the general acceptance of multiculturalism in Australian society over the last 20 years when many Indonesians have come to Australia and the Uniting Church's active promotion of multicultural ministry. It is also significant that Indonesia is predominantly an Islamic country, while almost all Latvians are nominally Lutheran. The strong nationalism of Latvians is reinforced by the traditional use of Latvian in church, whereas the Indonesian language has not been traditionally associated with any particular religion – amongst Christian churches in Indonesia (particularly rural ones) regional languages, rather than Indonesian, are often used.

In the following chapter, these themes will be discussed in greater detail as the issues faced by all 16 congregations are compared and evaluated.

Chapter 6

Some General Trends

Introduction

In this chapter, findings from this research which contribute to the wider understanding of language in the religious context are summarised.[1] (The reader is also referred to the Appendix for detailed presentation of results.)

Findings Concerning Language in the Religious Domain

In all but one of the congregations involved in this research (English-medium Reformed), *community languages* were predominantly used for services. The community language may be chosen as the main language of the church for many reasons. First, it is often claimed to be the language most easily and comfortably used by parishioners. The use of the community language also provides a sense of familiarity for church members. This is particularly true for congregations whose members may have only recently arrived in Australia, such as the Oromo Uniting (Oromo refugees), Indonesian Uniting (overseas students) and Chinese Anglican (East Timorese refugees). Second, for some communities (and individuals) the use of a particular language may be so strongly associated with religious activities, that it is seen as the only 'appropriate' language (see later). Third, it is clear that the church is often seen as a vehicle for religious *and* cultural maintenance – therefore it is also seen as having a responsibility for language maintenance. This is particularly the case for communities that see the church as an integral part of their cultural heritage. In this sense, the language used is part of the tradition of religious expression for a community.

English is used in ethnic churches to facilitate communication with particular groups of church members. Typically, English is used in varying degrees and via a diverse range of methods (see later) for the benefit of the youth of the church, whose community language skills may be inadequate for the religious domain. Similarly, exogamous marriages may also be targeted. In some cases, English may be used in ethnic churches for its perceived prestige value. This is usually only found when English has strong prestige in the home country and is often realised through code-switching during sermons or notices. Finally, English may be used in the church because of a deliberate decision to assimilate to the wider (English-speaking) society. Under such conditions, English may eventually become the language best understood by the community: as a result of this kind of language shift English may be used almost exclusively.

Bilingual or *multilingual* services or activities are typically chosen by ethnic churches over the exclusive use of just one language in order to maximise the size of the community gathering together for worship: bilingual activities are seen as a way to include those on the 'periphery' of ethnic community life – youth, and those in 'mixed' marriages. There is often a strong resistance to the change which accompanies the move to bilingual activities. Such resistance tends to come from the older members of the community and is especially felt by those who see the church as having a responsibility for passing on the community language. Some services, such as the Orthodox, are already bilingual by virtue of using the community language for sermons and the ecclesiastical variety for the liturgy. In this case, the opposition is not to bilingualism but to trilingualism, referring to the often controversial addition of English in the service. Bilingual activities may also be held where eventual 'assimilation' into the wider 'Australian' Church is the long-term goal. Language shift may be the eventual result.

Language and liturgy

Where a liturgy is used in a church, the tendency is to have this liturgy in the community language where possible. Liturgies tended to be similar to or influenced by those used in the home countries. For example, the liturgy of the Indonesian congregation of the Uniting Church has been developed with reference to liturgies used in Protestant churches in Indonesia. The liturgies used may be 'official' translations *or* 'homemade' translations into the community languages.

While most churches choose the language used for liturgy on the basis of that which is most easily understood by the congregation (to facilitate communication), for other churches it is considered more important to use the language which upholds the continuity of church tradition, whether or not this language is understood by the congregation. The classic example of this is the use of Latin in the Catholic Church, but even today some people go to church to worship in a language they do not understand. Within the Orthodox Church, Old Church Slavonic and particularly Ecclesiastical Greek provide an important element of continuity – and, therefore, authenticity. An incomprehensible language may also seem 'beautiful' and 'refined' in the church environment, compared to the perceived crudeness of everyday language. Particularly important to the continued use of such a language is the sense of mystery which is evoked by the sound of incomprehensible words – it makes the act of worship seem more sacred. Such churches tend to be strongly opposed to language change – particularly where this would be simply for purposes of better communication.

Language and music

The hymns and songs used by the congregations in this research were often brought over from the home countries. The Persian congregation also used popular Persian love songs, changing the lyrics to reflect Christian themes. Modern songs (choruses, for example) are often sung in the preferred language of the congregation, while hymns are often in the standard variety of the community language. Sung responses within the liturgy may be in the most formal style of the community language. Like prayer, songs provide an opportunity for congregational participation and, thus individual language production and variation. Within some congregations, songs and hymns have been translated so that they may be sung in more than one language simultaneously.

Language and prayer

The language of prayer in church services is largely influenced by the language of liturgy: even the recitation of formal prayers away from the church setting is usually done in the liturgical language. Informal spontaneous prayers are usually said in whichever language the person praying is most proficient. However, even in these situations (as discussed in Chapter 1), the language used for prayer may be influenced by perceptions of what is considered appropriate when addressing God directly. In languages which have speech levels, such as Javanese, the highest level must be used in prayer and, indeed, in any reference to God. Even the New Testament view of Jesus as 'friend' does not permit a more intimate level of speech by Christians in cultures with strict language rules.

Times of prayer during a church service are often opportunities for congregational participation (such as the recitation of the Lord's Prayer). Churches which seek to include some bilingual elements may see these as opportunities for variation in language use; for example, the members of the congregation may be invited to say the Lord's Prayer in whichever language they prefer. Intercessory and extemporary prayers provide the greatest opportunity for language variation.

Language and the Bible

Most of the congregations in this research have access to a complete translation of the Bible in their community language; however, not all translations are in a modern, readable variety of the language. For example, only the New Testament is currently available in the modern Oromo script and the Arabic Bible is only available in a very 'high' form of Arabic. Church tradition and / or political influences may also result in many ethnic congregations relying on Bibles published in the official language of their home country (which may not be their preferred language).

Language and other resources

Common to many of the congregations involved is the difficulty experienced in acquiring suitable resources in the community language. The Tamil Uniting minister, for example, related how he had been forced to leave behind his personal library of theological literature when fleeing war-torn Sri Lanka. The Persian Anglican minister reported that there was a lack of theological literature available even in Iran, as many of the church leaders and religious writers were killed during the Revolution. While some ministers reported a new ease in locating resources, thanks to the Internet, most referred to the great cost of importing resources from the home countries. A significant issue for ethnic churches is finding resources which are appropriate to the Australian context. Sunday School resources which provided some cultural input, whilst not requiring community language proficiency, were mentioned as being particularly difficult to find.

Language and sermons

While the relative importance ascribed to sermons may differ between ethnic congregations (and especially between denominations), all of the congregations in this research made some effort to facilitate understanding for their members during this part of the service. Concessions made particularly included oral or written translation (in part or whole) into English or another community language. For example, in the Greek Orthodox Church, while Ecclesiastical Greek is used for the liturgy, the brief sermon is given in Modern Greek and then repeated in English. Code-switching is also often found during sermons, as an attempt to reach younger members of the congregation, among other reasons (see next section).

Language and worship style

Patterns of language use in ethnic congregations appear to be associated in part with the style of worship and level of formality found in the congregations. Congregations which allow bilingual activities often adhere less rigidly to formal liturgy. Those with no liturgy or with charismatic tendencies (and therefore greater congregational participation) tend to be those who use (combinations of) languages most freely and, in particular, who may move to a predominant use of English. For example, the Latvian Lutheran church has two regular services: one is traditional liturgical and Latvian-medium, the other is modern liturgical and English-medium. It may be that where one kind of change (the use of English) is embraced, another (a charismatic style) is also welcomed.

Code-switching

While code-switching is reported to occur amongst parishioners in informal settings (such as after a service), not all of the clergy interviewed claimed that code-switching formed part of their multilingual speech behaviour, clearly seeing themselves (and being seen by their parishioners) as role models for 'correct' language behaviour. Clergy tended to indicate disapproval of any 'mixing' of languages in a formal setting, such as during a sermon, except where a brief switch to English would facilitate understanding.

Code-switching occurs for a number of reasons in the religious domain. As mentioned earlier, code-switching between the community language and English often occurs in ethnic churches which see English as having 'prestige'. The type of code-switching behaviour found in this situation is typically carried over from the language-use patterns of the home country (for example, where the use of certain English pronouns is seen as prestigious). Code-switching often occurs where the appropriate words are not found in one of the languages. The need to express certain concepts particular to the English-speaking religious domain may also trigger code-switching. Code-switching, however, can cause conflict within churches and congregations which have strong beliefs in upholding language 'purity'. Switching languages may be perceived as evidence of laziness, a lack of intelligence, self-discipline or loyalty to the culture. These reactions may be especially destructive when they are directed by the congregation at the clergy.

Various types of code-switching behaviour exist in each of the ethnic congregations in this research. In the congregations which make the most use of formal liturgy, code-switching is less likely to occur within the services. When it does, it may occur in sermons or notices (for example, when the author attended the Russian Orthodox church, the priest switched to English to reprimand the children for talking during the notices which were otherwise given in Russian) or it may occur in other activities such as youth groups. Churches which are strongly liturgical and formal tend to use the community language more rigidly. The degree of passivity of the congregation also influences this: if there is little opportunity for the congregation to participate in the service, language choice is determined by the service leader. In contrast, in churches which make little or no use of a written liturgy, congregational participation may be more frequent and code-switching may occur more freely and regularly.

Strategies for communication

The congregations in this research employed a range of innovative strategies to facilitate communication with parishioners whose community language and / or English skills may be inadequate. Among these strategies were the following:

- use of simultaneous translation by interpreter via headphones (Indonesian Uniting, Slovak Lutheran);
- use of simultaneous translation by interpreter (up front or person-to-person) (Arabic Baptist, Chinese Anglican, Chinese Reformed);
- oral translation of sermon (in whole or part) by clergy (Persian Anglican);
- written translation of sermon (in whole or part) in the form of a handout or overhead (German Lutheran);
- written translation of liturgy (in whole or part) in the form of a handout, overhead, or printed booklet (e.g. prayer book) (Greek Orthodox); and
- code-switching by clergy, e.g. during a sermon (Chinese Anglican, Persian Anglican, Croatian Catholic, Italian Catholic, Latvian Lutheran, Slovak Lutheran, Russian Orthodox, Chinese Reformed, Indonesian Uniting, Tamil Uniting).

Each of these strategies has both advantages and disadvantages. The use of headphones, for example, is an expensive option and somewhat distances the listener from direct involvement in the service, as well as being dependent on the skills and availability of an interpreter. Oral translations (sentence-by-sentence) make a service rather lengthy and some parishioners find it distracting to hear the continuous switching of languages. Written translations, such as those found in a prayer book, may require a high level of literacy, and – particularly in Orthodox churches – can detract from the multi-sensory worship experience. As a strategy for communication, code-switching can be controversial. It seems clear that no single strategy would work equally well for every congregation.

Language and clergy

Several of the ministers interviewed came from backgrounds other than those of the majority of their congregation. For example, the minister of the Slovak Lutheran congregation was born in Slovakia, while most of his congregation were born in the former Yugoslavia. In the Spanish Baptist congregation, the pastor is the only person to have been born in Spain – all others were born in Latin America or Australia. In the English-speaking Reformed congregation, the minister was a Sri Lankan Burgher, although an estimated 70% of his congregation were of Dutch heritage. The Greek Orthodox priest was the only Australian-born church leader involved in this research.

Interestingly, the minister's role as a bridge linking the community of speakers is often emphasised by this cultural disparity and, in some cases, results in a high value placed on language and cultural maintenance. For example, language maintenance is viewed very highly in the Slovak Lutheran and the Spanish Baptist congregations, with each congregation seeing itself as playing an important role in achieving language maintenance goals. All the clergy interviewed were proficient in the relevant community language, with the exception of the previously mentioned Sri Lankan-born minister of the Dutch-heritage Reformed congregation. English-language proficiency of the clergy was more variable and depended largely upon their place of birth, their migrational recency and their exposure to English during education.

The theological training of the clergy involved in these churches was generally undertaken overseas (though not always in the home country), with only the Chinese Reformed and Chinese Anglican ministers having studied in Australia (although the Persian Anglican minister completed some additional studies in Australia; no information was available for the Russian Orthodox priest). Insufficient information was obtained to be able to determine the impact of the type of training – and the circumstances in which it was undertaken – on the language use and language attitudes of the clergy; however, it seems clear that this would contribute to some degree to the linguistic environment of the congregations in which they serve.

The variety of language used by the clergy in ethnic churches can be a potential point of controversy. This is particularly the experience of churches using a pluricentric language, such as Spanish, in their activities. The variety used by the church leader often influences his 'standing' before the congregation: the use of a variety considered 'more pure' may result in an enhanced view of the priest as community role model. In contrast, a priest's use of a variety not considered 'proper' may result in perceptions of him as 'uneducated' (see Chapter 4 for a discussion of how the linguistic behaviour of the Latvian pastor affected his parishioners' attitudes).

The clergy in ethnic churches bear great burdens as linguistic (and spiritual) role models, as targets of linguistic criticism and as the mediators in language-related conflict. They do indeed each walk their own 'cultural tightrope' (Overberg, 1981: 27).

Church links

Links to other churches of the same ethnic background within Australia are stronger for some groups than others, with some clergy being 'shared' between congregations in different states. Ecumenical involvement is generally high among the Protestant churches.

Of the congregations involved in this research, the ones with the strongest links to a church body overseas are the Orthodox and Catholic Churches. The Greek Orthodox Church is under the jurisdiction of the Patriarchate of Constantinople; the Russian Orthodox Church (non-canonical) is part of the Russian Orthodox Church Abroad, which has its headquarters in New York; and the Catholic Church is under the Pope. Other churches such as the various Lutheran ethnic churches (whether or not they are associated with the Lutheran Churches of Australia), previously had much stronger links to their counterparts in the home country; with the passing of years, some of these links are less prominent and thought to be less necessary.

Links with the Church beyond Australian shores are also enhanced where clergy are provided by the home country, as in the case of the Croatian Catholic priest. The provision of clergy, funding or resources from the home country has the potential to influence the way in which a church functions, including its political stance: some churches have, therefore, sought to sever or weaken their ties.

Language and the congregation

Community-language proficiency was reported to be generally high amongst members of the congregations involved in this research, with proficiency generally increasing with age and with recency of migration. Community-language proficiency was reported to be weakest amongst school-age children of the second or third generation, for whom English has become the preferred language, and amongst spouses not of the same ethnic background. English language skills also tended to be high, with school-age members of the congregations being the most proficient group overall. English language skills amongst the older members of the congregations appear to depend largely on their exposure to English in their home country, their migrational recency and their exposure to English in their work environment.

The congregation play a great role in determining the linguistic climate of an ethnic church, particularly through their reaction to the leadership of the clergy in the area of language use. The older members of a congregation (regardless of migration vintage) tend to cling most tenaciously to the 'old' way of doing things – whether this means the use of a special liturgical language or the use of the community language. If the clergy wish to change any aspect of language use in the church, it is the older members who tend to be the most distressed and dislocated by it, often seeing faith and language as being more intimately connected than younger members of the church. The youth of ethnic churches have their own set of language-related problems. These increasingly disparate language needs can cause great fissures in previously close-knit communities of Christians.

Language and youth

A special area of concern in ethnic churches is effectively ministering to the youth of the community. The majority of the clergy interviewed felt that language-related problems existed in communicating the Gospel message to younger members of their churches. Many clergy reported differences in the language preferences of youth depending particularly on their place of birth, their country of education and their age upon arrival in Australia. Haugen's (1953) distinction between what he calls generation 1a (equating to those who came to Australia as adolescents or adults), generation 1b (those who came to Australia before reaching the age of 12) and the second generation (those who were born in Australia) highlights how the youth of an ethnic community may be far from being an homogenous group. For some young people within the community, English-language skills may be stronger than community-language skills, and are often better than the English-language skills of their parents. Issues such as these were particularly apparent in the Indonesian and Chinese churches, which have many recently arrived younger members in their congregations (such as overseas students), as well as young people who were born and raised in Australia. Amongst some clergy there appeared to be a reluctance to deal with the cross-generational language differences. One of the clergy – the Croatian Catholic priest – suggested that youth who were not proficient in the community language could be catered for by an English-speaking church elsewhere (and therefore he did not perceive the existence of language-related issues for the youth in his church), while another – the Russian Orthodox priest – suggested that the passing of time would ultimately resolve the issues.

English was perceived by most clergy as the best language to use with the youth of their churches: the additional use of the community language was suggested in order to facilitate communication. The only member of the clergy who felt that the community language should be solely used with youth was the Oromo minister, who perceived it to be their preferred language. As the smallest and most recently migrated group – and one having come from a tense political and linguistic background – it is not altogether surprising that support for language maintenance is strong, even among the youth.

The Australian Church as a whole is aging: many churches have a non-existent or visibly declining youth presence. From this research – and particularly the results of the Latvian church study – there appears to be a link between churches which prioritise language maintenance *over* effective communication and those which have a low youth membership/involvement. Clearly, the reason for disinterest in church activities amongst ethnic youth is not solely due to inappropriate language use – a perceived lack of relevance ascribed to the Christian faith was also suggested by some participants – however, it is certain that a church which pays little attention to the most elementary level of communication (speaking a language they understand) will soon lose its appeal to the youth of ethnic communities.

Language-related conflict

Not all clergy perceived the existence of language issues in their church. Amongst those who did, the lack of community-language proficiency amongst youth was both directly and indirectly mentioned as a language issue with which the church was struggling. Information gathered from responses to subsequent questions revealed the existence of other tensions related to language.

Attitudes to language in ethnic churches

Views concerning the 'appropriateness' of language can cause conflict in ethnic churches. The question of whether any language is more appropriate/proper than another for use in the church was asked of participants in order to determine whether the congregations involved viewed specific languages as inseparably linked to religious practice. Clear answers to this question were not obtained from six of the 16 clergy interviewed: in part this is the result of the lack of clarity in the phrasing of the question (from responses of case-study participants, it is clear that there were many interpretations). However, the majority of clergy (eight out of ten) who did respond did not consider any language to be more appropriate than another for use in a church. This is true also of the majority of the members of the Latvian (60.9%) and Indonesian (59.4%) churches, whose views were sought via questionnaires. However, it is true that for at least some Latvian members (particularly those who oppose an English ministry), the Latvian language is strongly linked to their expression of religious faith. In the Indonesian church, notions of the appropriateness of language in the religious domain are evident in the culturally conditioned use of languages or varieties of language which carry prestige or convey respect and honour to God. This attitude was reflected in the response of the Indonesian minister, one of the two clergy to suggest the existence of appropriate languages for church. The other was the Greek Orthodox priest, who maintained that Ecclesiastical Greek was most appropriate. These two responses indicate the presence of different interpretations of the question: for the Indonesian minister, an appropriate language for use in the church need not be a specific named language but rather one which fulfils a specific communicative function, whereas a named language – Ecclesiastical Greek – was considered to be solely appropriate in the Greek context.

Should all activities of the church, including the services, be conducted in the community language only?

To further examine the link between language and religion, case-study participants were asked whether all activities and services of the church should be conducted in the community language only. It is interesting that while similar percentages of Indonesian and Latvian participants considered no language more appropriate than another for use in a church, a greater difference in percentages was found in response to this question dealing with specific languages. In response, 17.4% of Latvian participants felt that Latvian only should be used, compared to 9.4% of Indonesian participants in relation to the Indonesian language. This is indicative of a difference in attitude towards language in the church: in the Latvian church it is the Latvian language which is linked to religion, regardless of whether it is understood by all parishioners, while for the Indonesian congregation, it is the language which conveys appropriate respect which is linked to religion, however this language must be one which is understood by the people.

Do you feel that English has any place in the activities of this church?

This question was again asked only of case-study participants. In response, 13% of Latvian respondents felt that English had no place in their church, compared to 6.3% of Indonesian respondents. Again, these figures represent the relative flexibility of the Indonesian congregation in regard to language use and the perception amongst many in the Latvian church of an English ministry as posing a threat to the maintenance of their ethno-religious identity.

Goals of the church

Many of the clergy interviewed perceived their primary goal as spreading the Gospel message but also often cited it as being to minister to a particular ethnic group. A few of the clergy indicated that a multicultural ministry was part of the church's goal. (Interestingly, for the Chinese (Hakka) congregation of the Anglican Church, language-related problems have occurred as a result of functioning as a bilingual congregation: the minister and congregation feel that those more comfortable with English than Hakka (and *vice versa*) would be better catered for in a separate service.) Only the Latvian church, in its constitution (see Chapter 4), expressed precisely what part language was to play in achieving the goals of the church.

Ethno-specific or multicultural churches?

Ethnic churches differ in their evaluation of the concept of 'ethno-specific' and 'multicultural' churches. Most of the clergy felt that it was 'unbiblical' to reject membership of the church on the basis of ethnicity but claimed that they felt they were called to minister to one ethnic group in particular. Some churches faced internal division over the issue: the Latvian church was divided in its responses between those were in favour of an 'open door' church (the pastor and some of the congregation) and those who wanted it to stay closed to 'outsiders' (the majority of the congregation).

The degree of openness to Christians of other cultures seems to be related to theological viewpoints of the clergy or denomination, as well as those of members of the congregation. The Uniting Church, for example, has strongly supported multicultural ministries and has officially declared itself a 'multicultural Church'. Each of the Uniting Church congregations which participated in this research expressed their endorsement of this attitude (for example, the Tamil minister serves in a parish which has adopted the motto of 'parish of all nations'). The 'Great Commission' of Jesus recorded in Matthew 28:19, 'Therefore go and make disciples of all nations' was referred to by participants from many different churches: it is interesting to note that it was seen by some participants as a mandate for seeking and welcoming a mix of ethnicities and by others as a justification for the existence of churches catering for the needs of only one particular ethnic group.

The future of ethnic churches

Many of the clergy saw the future of their churches depending largely on continued migration. Those, such as the Spanish Baptist and Indonesian Uniting, who saw multicultural ministries as a goal, were positive about their future. Conversely, those who saw their future as relying on 'ethnic continuity' were less positive: many members of the Latvian Lutheran church felt that their church would no longer exist in 50 years' time. Aside from issues of continuing migration, perceptions of the future appear strongly linked to language-use patterns. Churches which are innovative in their approach to language (using communication strategies such as simultaneous translation) and who see language as a means for communicating the faith (as opposed to mere cultural transmission) also tend to view their future as bright. Where the role of the church is seen as reaching only to members of one ethnic group, the future is seen as less certain and even grim for the older community groups. It is interesting to note that these churches also see their decline and eventual extinction as inevitable. The survival of the church is not, in some cases, sufficient motivation to change traditional patterns or beliefs about language use.

The role of ethnic churches in language maintenance

Ethnic churches appear to play a vital role in language maintenance but not for all sections of an ethnic community. The use of community languages in ethnic churches is of most benefit to those who already have some community-language skills: such people tend to be the first genera-tion, for whom church attendance is culturally embedded and who have forged strong social networks in which the community-language is again reinforced. Ethnic churches do not seem to be as successful in raising the level of community-language skills of the younger generation. The general experience of the congregations involved in this study is that the younger members of the church are more familiar with, skilled in and comfortable using English rather than their community language. As a result many ethnic church leaders feel that English is the best language to use with youth in order to communicate the Gospel message most effectively.

In churches in which language maintenance is regarded as a goal, the community language is seen as the best language to use with youth. These language choices may or may not be at odds with the preferences and skills of the youth of the church. The role of ethnic churches in language mainte-nance may be enhanced where the church is linked to other community activities and organisations, such as through the provision of funding, teachers or a venue for a Saturday School in the community language.

Closing Remarks

In ethnic churches language is both a means by which the community is united and a cause of fragmentation. For some communities, language, culture and religion are so strongly intertwined that language change is perceived as a threat to community life. Some church members would rather leave the church than have to use and respond to a new language, even if they could not understand the 'old' one (Boyd, 1985: 163). The language has effectively taken on a sacred value and it is difficult for some to see another language as fulfilling the same role. The use of English may be considered a threat to both community cohesion and the 'true' expres-sion of ethnic and religious identity. Fishman (1996: 18–19) puts it this way:

Wherever fidelity is well-defined, there apostasy is likely to be well defined as well. Where language maintenance is viewed as moral rectitude, there language shift is likely to be viewed as tantamount to moral transgression ... In this view, maintaining the beloved language is a supreme commandment, one that is even more important than keeping the faith itself. The language which is a companion, key and expression of the faith may, indeed, become not only an article of faith but a faith in its own right.

It is clear that inflexible language maintenance goals can cause conflict in ethnic churches, particularly over the question of whether serving cultural interests can become a form of idolatry. Theses issues will be summarised in the concluding chapter.

Note
1. It needs to be noted that not all questions were adequately answered by clergy during the course of interviews conducted with them – for this reason it is difficult to quantify results exactly, other than for members of case-study churches whose questionnaire answers could be more precisely analysed.

Chapter 7

Towards a New Framework

Discussion and Application of Findings: Some Introductory Remarks

What has become quite clear from the research described here is that the each of the churches and congregations involved has its own story to tell: each is unique in its historical, political, social and theological background; and each has reacted differently to the dynamics of Australian society. They can be grouped together under the term 'ethnic churches' because each is associated with the use or one of more languages other than English. However, those who attend may represent the first *or* subsequent generations of the particular ethnic community in Australia, may be of mixed ethnic descent, may have married into the community or may simply choose to worship within that community despite the absence of any family ties. Nonetheless, it is important to examine the ways in which these churches are the same and those in which they differ. In the following section, a number of ethnic church models are presented and discussed and, based on these, the congregations involved in this study have been categorised according to the attitudes they hold towards their own and other cultures and languages.

Models of ethnic churches

A number of models, and groups of models, have been developed which categorise the structures and attitudes of ethnic churches. For instance, Clyne (1991: 132) outlines four alternative models which relate to the use of community languages in the religious domain in Australia. These are:

(i) *Rapid assimilation*: There are no community language parishes. Periodic services in community languages for the benefit of recent migrants are phased out as soon as possible so that the newcomers are integrated into monolingual English-speaking parishes.

(ii) *Transitional assimilation*: No link is perceived between religion and the community language. Ethnic parishes or community language services and activities are seen only as a transition to either a complete integration into an English-medium denomination or to the 'de-ethnicization' of an originally ethnic one.

(iii) *Structural bi- or multilingualism*: This model provides for self-contained ethnic congregations conducting different community language or bilingual services within a wider, English-dominated denomination. The bilingualism is intended to cater for both the older and younger generations and to provide a link between the ethnic congregation and the wider church.

(iv) *Pluralism*: This model maintains a close relationship between language and religion. Religious groups adhering to model (iv) vary in the concessions they make to the younger generation (for example, occasional English or bilingual services and/or youth groups) to prevent dropout. Basically, the community language remains the language of the congregation.

Clyne's *rapid assimilation* and *transitional assimilation* refer to similar structural organisations for the congregation/church/parish/denomination but describe different goals of the host denomination concerning the extent to which the community language may be used in the religious domain. Essentially this difference lies in perceptions of the time which is required or allowed for the ethnic group to assimilate. Similarly, the primary difference between *structural bi- or multi-lingualism* and *pluralism* is attitudinal: both describe situations in which ethnic congregations or churches function somewhat autonomously; however, in the latter, the community language is seen as an irremovable part of the religious experience.

A second group of models for the 'incorporation of ethnic Christians within the church', has been posited by Charles Wilcox (1994: 30–1)). His framework is as follows:

(1) *Assimilationist*: This expects people to adopt the language, culture, and religious form of the host or dominant culture. 'Become like us.'

(2) *Integrationist, multiethnic or multiracial*: People from a variety of ethnic backgrounds meeting as one congregation, but with separate language/culture Bible studies, group fellowships etc. as needed with, ideally, a multicultural pastoral team.

(3) *Multicultural and multicongregational*: One church, yet meets as separate congregations, but linked in common fellowship, regular services of celebration, communion, and in social activities through joint organisation. These are now referred to as 'cluster' or

'satellite' churches. A multicultural pastoral team is an essential feature.

(4) *Mono-ethnic*: Separate churches of separate language/culture groups. Complete autonomy.

In Wilcox's framework, Clyne's *rapid* and *transitional assimilation* categories are collapsed into the one *assimilationist* category. At the other end of his framework, Wilcox posits a category called simply *monoethnic*, which approximates Clyne's *pluralism* category. In between the two extremes, Wilcox suggests two other types of ethnic church set-ups. The first of these, which he calls *integrationist, multiethnic or multiracial* describes a congregation made up of different ethnicities, with language-specific activities. The second type is a *multicultural or multicongregational* church, in which many language-specific congregations co-exist. Neither of these two categories exactly corresponds to Clyne's *structural bi- or multi-lingualism* category.

The frameworks of Clyne (1991) and Wilcox (1994) examine the same picture from different perspectives. Clearly, each has something to offer the other but both could go further in expounding the link between language and religion. A more complete description of language–religion relationships and language practices is, therefore, presented in a revised framework in the following section.

A revised model for language attitudes and practices in ethnic churches

What is clear from the results of this research is that ethnic churches differ widely in the extent to which the community language is used and in the value ascribed to maintaining the use of that language in the life of the church, as well as in the wider community. The following framework incorporates the language–religious ideology (LRI) continuum introduced in Chapter 2, providing a means for describing the *attitudes and practices of an ethnic congregation* in relation to languages. This framework adds an additional and vital dimension to the Clyne (1991) and Wilcox (1994) models.

This two-dimensional framework highlights the dynamic nature of language practices and attitudes. The horizontal continuum represents the strength of the relationship between language and religion (its language–religious ideology), while the vertical continuum represents the practices of a congregation in relation to the language(s) used, with English at one end of the continuum, and the community language at the other end (of course, these could be replaced by combinations of languages relevant in other environments). The midpoint of the vertical continuum, thus, represents mixed use of English and the community language: different

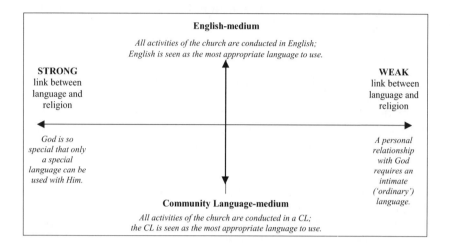

Figure 7.1 Language attitudes and practices in ethnic churches

languages may be thought appropriate for different activities of the church (as opposed to exclusive language use represented by either end of the vertical continuum). Points between the two extremes represent the use of combinations of languages with various weightings. Thus, the 16 congregations involved in this research may be described according to how they fit into this framework.

Application of the framework of language attitudes and practices in ethnic churches

Each church or congregation involved in this research has been placed within the framework introduced in Figure 7.1 (revised as Figure 7.2), according to the results as reported in Chapters 3–6.

For purposes of comparison, the LRI continuum (introduced in Chapter 2) on which the denominations involved in this research have been placed according to the strength of the relationship which they exhibit between language and religion, is reprinted as Figure 7.3.

A comparison of Figures 7.2 and 7.3 shows the extent to which the ethnic congregations in this research reflect the LRIs of the denominations of which they are a part.

Exclusive English-medium
One of the 16 ethnic congregations in this research uses only English in

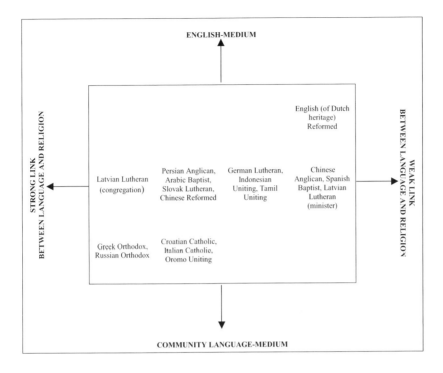

Figure 7.2 Language attitudes and practices of ethnic churches involved in this research

its services and activities. While it might seem at odds with the definition of 'ethnic church' as being related to the use of languages *other than* English, this is an example of an ethnic church which has shifted over time from the use of a community language to the use of English only (or predominantly). Some ethnic churches (and indeed some denominations) see the eventual shift to English as being ultimately desirable and as evidence of being truly 'Australianised'. This is true of the early attitude of the Christian Reformed Churches of Australia (CRCA), which began essentially as an ethnic church of Dutch migrants and then went through a period of de-ethnicisation. Historically, the Christian Reformed Churches of Australia have fitted into both of Clyne's (1991: 32) two *assimilation* models, having deliberately sought a shift to exclusive use of English. As discussed in Chapter 3, the LRI of the Reformed Church since the late 1960s has been one in which the Dutch language has not been strongly linked to religion and may be characterised by an openness to the influence and use of English. Language is seen

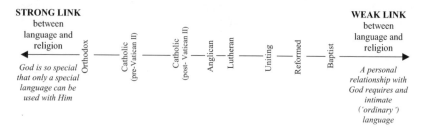

Figure 7.3 Application of the LRI continuum

as a tool of evangelisation. This LRI has been the inheritance of the Reformed English-medium congregation involved in the present research. The Sri-Lankan-born pastor of this church is responsible for the main congregation, whose members are predominantly of Dutch background. However, Dutch-language services were phased out over 20 years ago and the only regular Dutch-language event which continues to this day is a Christmas service. From the pastor's perspective, it is best to continue to move away from the 'European' model of a church to a more 'Australianised' church – with English as the unifying language. This congregation, therefore, exhibits a very weak link between language and religion, due to the well-documented high rate of language shift amongst the Dutch community, the non-Dutch ethnicity of the minister and many of the congregation, and the lack of emphasis on the Dutch language within the LRI of the Reformed Church.

From the indications of the present research, English-medium ethnic churches may well become more numerous over the next decade, particularly where migration ceases and the culture does not view language and religion as inseparable.

Mixed community language/English-medium

It is interesting that another member of the Christian Reformed Churches of Australia which, in fact, uses the facilities of the previously mentioned church – has a different approach to the use of English and their community language in church life. When this particular Chinese congregation was first established, Cantonese was chosen as the language of services; however, this was then replaced by Mandarin in order to facilitate better communication between the members who variously originate from Taiwan, China, Hong Kong, Singapore and Malaysia. English is used during the services and in activities where children are present and is considered the best language to use with youth. However, the pastor feels that a bilingual 'open-door' congregation is the best model to follow. This congregation fits into the *third* of Clyne's four alternative models, which he terms *structural bi- or multilingualism*. In the revised framework of Figure 7.2, this congregation may be described as exhibiting a *moderate* link between language and religion. The greater emphasis on language in this congregation as opposed to the English-medium Reformed congregation described earlier is most likely due to the much lower rate of language shift in the Chinese community, together with the evaluation of Chinese as a core value. However, as a Chinese community (whose linguistically diverse character requires the use of a *lingua franca*) within the CRCA (whose LRI does not strongly link language and religion), the Chinese Reformed congregation may well shift to exclusive English use with the passing of the first generation.

Both of the Anglican congregations involved in this research – Persian and Hakka – appear towards the *moderate–weak* end of the LRI continuum. These two churches are structurally different. In the first, the Iranian minister is responsible for an English-language congregation (generally not of Persian-background), who worship together weekly, in addition to a Persian-language congregation which is only able to meet once a month. In the second Anglican congregation, the Malaysian-born minister is responsible for a large bilingual congregation which has worshipped together weekly until recently, but which has since decided to split into two separate language-specific congregations – one for those who prefer Hakka (principally those from East Timor and Southern China) and another for those who prefer English (those from Malaysia, Singapore and Hong Kong). However, the ministers from both of these churches ascribe great value to language maintenance and to the role that language can play in getting across the message of the Gospel: both have been active in translating Anglican and other church resources such as songs and prayers into their community languages, but the desire to 'get the message across' means that both feel that English is the best language to use with youth. It is interesting, however, that facilitating communication within the Chinese (Hakka) congregation means that a *bilingual* congregation has decided to split into *two monolingual* congregations to ensure that their needs are adequately met. The pastor of this church has a vision not for a *multicultural* church but rather for a *multicongregational* church, with new language-based congregations being established within it as the need arises. It is also significant that the Chinese congregation uses a charismatic style of worship. Both these congregations (Hakka and Persian) exist within the Anglican LRI in which language is seen as quite important in the religious context, particularly its written forms (liturgy, hymns, Scripture). However, the Hakka congregation (with illiteracy an issue for a proportion of the congregation) demonstrates a weaker commitment to this same type of LRI, showing greater flexibility towards the language–religion relationship than is traditionally Anglican (and, in the context of this research, than the Persian congregation).

Two out of three of the Uniting Church congregations – the Tamil and the Indonesian – use both their community language and English in the church context. The Tamil-speaking minister is in a similar situation to the Persian Anglican minister in that he is responsible for an English-speaking (largely non-Tamil background) congregation as well as a congregation where his community language is used.[1] One of the bi-monthly services for the Tamil community is run by the youth, with youth as the target audience, and predominantly uses English. The other Tamil service predominantly uses the Tamil language. The second of the Uniting Church congregations uses both English and Indonesian in each of the weekly services by means of simultaneous English translation heard through headphones. Again, youth activities are conducted in English, and the minister has a strong 'multicultural church' ethos, warmly welcoming non-Indonesian visitors to the church. Both the Tamil and Indonesian congregations reflect the Uniting Church's LRI, which is marked by flexibility towards language use and tolerance for pluralism of worship styles. However, both the Tamil and Indonesian congregations perceive some sort of a link between language and religion. While the prestige which English has gained in Indonesian society has resulted in a great openness to the use of English in the religious domain, the Indonesian congregation has culturally embedded views about the appropriateness of language in the religious domain (and the need to convey honour and respect). As mentioned in Chapter 1, research by Smolicz *et al.* (1990) has suggested that Tamil Hindus, but notably not Tamil Christians, consider language a core value. The findings of this research suggest that the Tamil language is considered important in the religious context to this group of Christians, perhaps due to Uniting Church support for a language-specific ministry.

An openness to English but an emphasis on community language use is characteristic of two of the three Lutheran congregations involved in this research. The Slovak congregation uses a similar communication strategy to the Indonesian Uniting congregation, providing headphones for simultaneous translation during services. The pastor of this congregation is very active in the wider (non-Slovak) community, having helped to establish a Christian bookshop and school, running regular outreach services and touring with the church's youth band. At the same time, the pastor considers himself a role model for 'proper' Slovak, having come from Slovakia, unlike most of his parishioners who come from the former Yugoslavia and so are said to speak are mixture of Slovak and other languages such as Serbian. While clearly being open to the use of English, the historically developed cultural tenacity of the Slovak people has resulted in great importance being attached to the maintenance of the language in the religious domain.

The German Lutheran church runs English services twice a month and German services two to three times a month but verbal or written summaries in English of the sermon are always provided. Youth activities are also generally in English, except for a German-language play group in which the emphasis is on the German-language acquisition of pre-schoolers. It is interesting to note that although a German-language Sunday School was established in response to demand from parents, it was forced to close due to low and irregular attendance. A previously well-attended Saturday School was also run by the parish. This church reflects the experience of many German churches in the Lutheran Churches of Australia and the accompanying low-level link between language and religion.

Devotion to language in the religious context, paired with strong nationalistic feeling, pervades the third of the Lutheran churches involved in this research – the Latvian church. As a case study, both the views of the pastor and the congregation were sought and, in some cases, they differed considerably. Broadly speaking, the minister places high priority on maintaining the Latvian language through its use in a church in which Latvians may go to hear the Gospel preached in their language. However, in response to the increasing number of mixed marriages and youth who have little or no Latvian language skills, he considers the use of English in appropriate situations vital to the communication of the Gospel message. In a Latvian service, this may mean providing an English translation of a phrase or the use of an English word where the Latvian does not convey the desired meaning. Officially, (exclusive) Latvian-language services are held weekly and (exclusive) English-medium services bi-monthly but while the minister sees the combined use of English and Latvian as being the best arrangement, the majority of the congregation and church council are strongly nationalistic and wish to use Latvian exclusively in all activities of the church. In the face of such great opposition to the use of English, the minister's stance may be seen as even more *open* to the influence of English than it might have been otherwise and, in this sense, it is more open than that of the German and Slovak ministers. The minister's interest in charismatic worship also influences the link he perceives between language and religion. The Latvian church is thus divided and sits at either end of the continuum, displaying two types of LRI. Likewise, the church is simultaneously following two of Clyne's models, that of *structural bilingualism* and *pluralism*.

Like the pastor of the Slovak Lutheran congregation, the Spanish Baptist pastor is one of a small number in his congregation who speak the variety of the community language that is spoken in the country of its origin: the Spanish pastor is from Spain, while most of his congregation have migrated from Latin American countries. The Spanish congregation also uses simultaneous translation in its weekly services. While Spanish is considered the most appropriate language for the congregation overall, the pastor's goal is for a church in which a number of communities make their home, existing on an equal level with the English-speaking community. Services would be held in large numbers of languages other than English each week. Thus while the pastor's focus is currently on the Spanish community, he is open to other communities and sees a 'multicultural' church in this literal sense as being ideal. This view ties in with the discussion of the Baptist LRI in Chapter 2, which suggested that the characteristic emphasis on an individual relationship with God and the lack of emphasis on structures have meant that Baptist theology is easily integrated within a new culture and language without becoming the exclusive property of that same culture and language.

Both Arabic and Spanish, as pluricentric languages, work as unifying factors in ethnically diverse congregations; however, the Spanish congregation appears to perceive a weaker link between language and religion than the Arabic Baptist congregation. Although the Arabic pastor warmly welcomes those of other ethnic backgrounds to the church, he claims to have a special love for the Arabic language, linking it strongly to his expression of religious faith. The strength of the relationship between language and religion in the Arabic church is likely to be due in part to the very high level of language maintenance evident in the Arabic community. It may also be that the sacredness of Arabic for Moslems (as the language of the Koran) has been 'de-Islamicised' in the Christian context – Arabic is still seen to convey a sacred character but one which is instead distinctly Christian.

Exclusive community-language-medium

Few congregations involved in this research use a community language exclusively. The Oromo fellowship, which is affiliated with the Uniting Church, is a very small, recently migrated group. Its members are united by their language and, like the Latvians, are proud of having maintained it in the face of political oppression. The fellowship is made up of Oromo Christians from a number of denominational backgrounds but has a general charismatic leaning. Their more fundamentalist theology distances them somewhat from Uniting Church tradition. The leader of this group sees himself as having the dual role of reaching the Oromo people, and teaching the Oromo language through its use in services. Language maintenance is perceived as being very important, as the leader feels that their mother tongue is the best for understanding spiritual matters. However, the leader welcomes those who are not of Oromo background to attend the services. While a preference for charismatic worship tends to be accompanied by greater flexibility in attitudes towards language, the cultural tenacity of the Oromo people has resulted in a strong link between language and religion (and therefore only partial openness to English).

A greater link between language and religion exists in the Catholic tradition and was evident in the present research. The priest of the Croatian parish of the Catholic Church sees the best model for his church as being an exclusively Croatian one. The church's position as part of a Croatian community centre where the boundaries between religious activities and other community activities are, to some extent, blurred results in an increased emphasis on the maintenance of Croatian. However, loyalty to the Catholic Church is paramount and the priest emphasises that his church differs from any other Catholic church around the world only in that it uses the Croatian language. This is also used as a justification for advising those whose Croatian skills are poor to attend one of the English-language Catholic churches – instead of providing English-language services, activities or resources within the Croatian Church.

In discussing the situation of Italian Catholics, it needs to be remembered that the Italian priest interviewed for this research was not attached to any one parish and, thus, provided general observations concerning his chaplaincy. While he indicated a commitment to Italian ministry as long as it was required within the community and feels that the church plays an important role in language maintenance for the community, this priest believes that language maintenance should always be subordinate to worship. In this sense, the Italian Catholic tradition exhibits slightly less emphasis on language in the religious context than the Croatian Catholic tradition. This is likely to be influenced by the differing roles of the Catholic Church in Italy when compared to Croatia, where the Church has taken on a political and strongly nationalistic role. Clyne (1991) points out that the Catholic Church in Australia has at times fitted the description of each of the four alternative models he posits, having initially been very *assimilationist* in its attitudes towards ethnic groups within its care. Since the Vatican II ruling on the use of the vernacular, the ethnic parishes of the Catholic Church have tended to follow Clyne's *pluralism* model, using the community language almost exclusively.

The Orthodox Churches are perhaps the best example of ones in which language and religion are immutably linked. Both the Russian (despite its non-canonical status) and Greek Orthodox churches in this research have a strong attachment to the community language. In the Greek church, modern and Ecclesiastical Greek are used at different times (and English translations of the sermon, creed and Lord's Prayer may also be given); however, the priest rejects the idea of English-language liturgies – like the Croatian Catholic priest he feels that there are enough English-language churches already within the denomination to meet those needs. The Russian Orthodox church uses Old Church Slavonic and modern Russian, and may use some English for youth activities and Bible studies. The Russian priest does not reject English liturgies outright but admits he has never asked the younger generation whether they would prefer English in the service. While in both the Greek and Russian situations, Christians from another Orthodox jurisdiction are welcome and may share in communion, these two Orthodox churches are reluctant to allow language shift away from the liturgical languages which are valued for their distinctiveness from 'everyday' languages. The Greek and Russian churches may, thus, be characterised as exhibiting strong links between language and religion according to the present framework.

Implications of This Research

This chapter has so far drawn together the results of the present research concerning 16 ethnic congregations in Melbourne. From these results some general trends were outlined and a number of frameworks for categorising ethnic church models discussed. A revised framework, in which an individual church could be placed according to its language practices and the attitudes it holds towards its own and other languages, was then presented. Using this framework it became clear how great a role the LRI of a denomination plays in determining the relationship between language and religion for particular churches. The potential of religious subcultures, such as the charismatic movement, to influence the strength of the relationship also became clear. Trends in language maintenance and shift, as well as the evaluation of language as a 'core value' also play a part in the extent to which a church exhibits the general LRI of its 'parent' denomination. Let us now consider the implications of this research.

Implications for ethnic churches

The title of this book incorporates the deceptively simple question *Medium or Message?* Indeed, it is clear that this is anything but a simple issue for the clergy of ethnic churches and their parishioners. Clearly, many tensions arise in efforts to balance the transmission of faith (the 'message') with the transmission of a community language (the 'medium') and its associated culture, and it requires not insignificant creativity and wisdom to work this balance out.

With the acknowledgement that this research is conducted within the field of linguistics and not of theology, some implications for ethnic churches have become apparent and are listed here:

- Ethnic churches are not necessarily linguistically homogenous: levels of proficiency will vary, particularly between generations. Dialogue between leaders of ethnic churches and youth (in particular) is recommended in order to explore any language-related issues: important also is a willingness to make changes in response to the concerns expressed by youth.

- The specific language used is unlikely to be the sole reason for poor youth attendance or general disinterest: language issues may, in fact, obscure other issues. Shifting from the community language to English in church activities may not be of any help where the problem is not being unable to understand the language but rather being unable to understand the relevance of faith.

- The use of a liturgical language or a register which requires familiarity with complex or archaic religious terminology may render a service inaccessible to those with struggling community-language skills. While the 'mystery' of God is particularly important in some denominations, it needs to be questioned whether the mystery of God is, in fact, the same as obscurity of language.[2]

- Creative use of language is recommended: different communication strategies may work better than others and no single strategy works for all ethnic churches and all individuals within them.

- Ethnic churches may be able to increase their contribution to community-language maintenance where additional resources such as Bibles, Sunday School materials, prayers, songs and sermons as well as age-appropriate teaching materials and Christian literature, are made available in an accessible form of the community language or in bilingual format. Even English-language materials may be of benefit to cultural maintenance where they are given an ethno-specific context.

- Language-related goals must be defined and prioritised alongside other goals. While faith needs to be conveyed in a specific cultural context, the Gospel message is not bound to one culture and one language: it is not the exclusive domain of Ecclesiastical Greek or Latvian or Latin or English. The description of Pentecost given in Acts 2 affirms the serving role of language in conveying the message of the Gospel: when the Jews 'from every nation under heaven' who were staying in Jerusalem for the feast of Pentecost heard the believers speaking in their own languages, they were amazed. But the miracle of that Pentecost was not simply that many different languages were spoken but that because the 'heart languages' of many different peoples were spoken, the message of the Gospel was proclaimed *and understood*: 'Are not all these men who are speaking Galileans? Then how is it that each of us hears them in his own native language? . . . We hear them declaring the wonders of God in our own tongues!' (Acts 2: 7–8,10). It is the medium which *serves* the message. If the message can best be understood in one language rather than another, then the use of that language in the religious context needs to be encouraged and supported.

- Ethnic churches need to make their needs known to the denominations of which they are a part.

Implications for denominations

The following implications are offered at the denominational level:

- First and foremost, denominations need to be convinced of the vital contribution of multicultural ministries to the 'Body of Christ'[3] – the Church – and be prepared to live out this belief through the giving of time and resources.

- Denominations need to be aware of the great importance of the community language to Christians of non-English-speaking backgrounds in the context of worship. It is the 'heart language' of a group of people needing to express their deepest sentiments in the language most intimately known and it carries with it a sense of shared heritage which provides comfort in what may often seem to be 'foreign' surroundings.

- Denominations need to be aware of the 'core values' of the ethnic groups which worship within them and the reasons for the centrality of these values; for example, previous experience with minority language status or linguistic persecution may result in strong commitment to the preservation of that language in any environment. Language maintenance within the religious domain may be seen as particularly important to the maintenance of that community's identity.

- Denominations need to be aware of ethnic churches (or parishes/ chaplaincies) which are struggling with cross-generational issues of language, culture and faith and must seek to work sensitively with ethnic churches to make progress in reconciling language-related conflict.

- Denominations need to work with ethnic churches (or parishes/chaplaincies) in designing, funding and implementing suitable strategies to communicate the Gospel message appropriately to youth within the ethnic community context.
- Denominations need to examine their own LRIs. These have implications beyond the ethnic church context, determining how language in a general sense is used in a ministry: for example, whether a church embraces language reform and whether it alienates some members because its services require a high degree of literacy.

Implications for the wider Church

The wider Church must understand the importance of the relationship between language and religion. Understanding why a denomination places high value on using a particular language or a particular style of language in a church may enhance ecumenical relationships. Shared appreciation of this relationship will go some way towards breaking down some of the barriers existing between branches of Christendom.

Concluding Remarks

This research has undertaken to examine the ways in which language, culture and the Christian faith intersect in the specific instance of ethnic churches. This issue can, of course, be investigated from many perspectives (anthropological, sociological, historical, theological, to name but a few) and while endeavouring to give due attention to these, the focus has necessarily been on ethnic churches as a linguistic phenomenon.

The central objective guiding this research has been to move towards a thoroughly documented response to the question: *What is the role of language in ethnic churches?* In this investigation of 16 ethnic congregations in Melbourne – Protestant, Catholic and Orthodox – this question has received its fullest treatment to date: research which looks at Christians within a large number of ethnic communities as well as spanning different denominational affiliations has been conspicuously absent.

In the course of this research, two significant developments were made towards future research. First, a discussion of the ways in which community languages are more generally incorporated into particular religious traditions lead to the introduction of the notion of *a language–religion ideology*, a term which describes the linguistic climate of a religious body such as a denomination. Second, a new framework was developed in which the churches involved in this study were placed according to the attitudes held towards their own and other languages in the religious context. Such a framework goes some way towards expounding the complex relationship between language and religion.

What specific conclusions may be drawn from this research?

This research has demonstrated clearly that language has different roles in different ethnic churches. These roles are determined by two sources of influence – the ethnic community and the church community (i.e. the denomination). This interchange of perspectives may be summarised as follows:

(1) *how the ethnic culture places language and religion within its context* (which can be determined in part by reference to rates of language maintenance and shift, as well as by deterring whether language and religion are 'core values' of the culture, to use Smolicz's terminology); and

(2) *how the religion places language (and other cultures) within its context* (which refers to the concept of LRI introduced by this research).

The mutual interaction and influence of these factors is significant in shaping the environment in which an ethnic church functions.

It has become clear that in ethnic churches, language is both a means by which the community is united and a cause of fragmentation. At one level, the reasons for this dual ability of language in the ethnic church context are the cross-generational differences in language abilities, needs and preferences. The older generation, who are typically proficient in the community language and are part of established church-related social networks in which the community language is also used, benefit most from community-language use in the church. However, the younger generation (particularly those born in Australia), whose education and social networks are dominated by English use and who may have only minimal community-language skills, may find the community language used in the church of no benefit to increasing proficiency. This is particularly the case where the church uses a special register of the community language and specialised religious vocabulary or where the language most used in the church is an older variety of the community language which has been preserved for liturgical use. Ethnic churches have, therefore, been found to provide a valuable source of community-language input but with differing consequences.

At a deeper level, however, the reason for language either unifying or dividing a church is the theological emphasis placed on language and particular languages in the various religious traditions. In other words, language-related problems can occur when the social changes in an ethnic church (such as the younger generation's proficiency in English rather than the community language) interact with the LRI of a denomination. The language used in a church has the potential to unite by its ability to express the spiritual and the cultural simultaneously. Language has the potential to cause fragmentation by virtue of the sacred value it takes on as a result of being used in a religious context. Depending on the strength of the link between language and religion, any change to this language may be perceived as a threat to the 'true' expression of ethno-religious identity.

This research has shown that inflexible commitment to the medium of communication can obscure the message and alienate the listener. Ethnic churches which are looking forward to the brightest futures are those which perceive the need for some flexibility in language use in order to cater for the younger generation and those in mixed marriages. Such churches are willing to loosen the link between a particular language and religious faith enough to make the message of more importance than the medium.

It is hoped that this research will inspire offshoots into some of the areas which have been touched upon.

This research introduced the term 'language–religion ideology' to describe the place of language and particular languages in denominations. Further research could extend this concept to examine the LRI of different theological orientations (such as charismatic) which overlap traditional denominational boundaries – an area which was only briefly touched upon in the present research. Similarly, another interesting question raised by this research warrants further attention: Can 'national' churches (such as the Orthodox) be 'de-nationalised' and what would the implications of this process be for language? Do the LRIs of 'national' churches allow denationalisation?

The issue of young people within an ethnic community and their place in ethnic churches is one which begs further focused attention. There exists a sense of alienation amongst many of the younger generation who have grown up and been educated in Australia and whose first or preferred language is different to that of the older members of their families – even to that of their older brothers and sisters. Churches which hope to exist in the future, apart from relying on further migration from the home country, need to address the issue of how to keep their youth in the church family and, more importantly, how to pass on to them an active faith. Closely related to this is the issue of how the linguistic and spiritual needs of spouses from other ethnic backgrounds may be met, particularly given the high rate of exogamy in some communities.

A more in-depth exploration of code-switching in the ethnic church context would also be valuable. Such research would doubtlessly yield some exciting data, both in churches which are strongly oral and non-liturgical as well as in those which follow strict liturgical formulas and may see themselves as custodians of language purity.

At the outset of this research, it was determined that indigenous churches would not form part of the study: this is yet another opportunity for future exploration. With around 50 Aboriginal languages in use in Australia, the role of Aboriginal churches in language maintenance is a complex question which deserves separate and informed attention.

Finally, this research has reflected the issue of ethnic churches in the *Australian* context, with the range of ethnic communities involved representing some of those who make up the particularly Australian 'multicultural mosaic'. It would be valuable to examine these issues within an international framework, perhaps tracing the religious settlement (to use Bouma's terminology) of Christians from one particular ethnic background in different places around the world, thereby focusing on the impact of different language contact situations on language maintenance in the religious setting.

The present research has taken a detailed look at community languages in the religious domain. It is hoped that this, as a major comparative work, will contribute to the study of community-language maintenance in Australia, to the wider Christian Church and its body of ethnic church resources, and to the individual congregations who have participated as a means of clarifying their present and future directions.

Notes

1.   This might be indicative of an emerging type of ethnic church – another alternative model to add to frameworks such as that of Clyne (1991).

2.   Statement 6 (item 8) of the Lutheran Church of Australia's Commission on Worship makes this point well. It states that

> The language of hymns is also the language of worship. It needs to be clear and readily understood, since God uses words to communicate to his people in worship. It needs to also be rich, beautiful, and dignified, since in worship we glorify the Triune God and celebrate the mystery of his gracious presence. *But the mystery of God is not the same as obscurity of language.* (italics mine)

3.   'Now the body is not made up of one part but of many ... If the whole body were an eye, where would the sense of hearing be? ... The eye cannot say to the hand, 'I don't need you!' And the head cannot say to the feet, 'I don't need you!' On the contrary, those parts of the body that seem to be weaker are indispensable ...' (1 Corinthians 12:14, 17, 21–2).

Appendix: Summary Tables of Data Gathered from Interviews with Ministers

Reference	Denomination	Location	Ethnic background of minister/priest	Ethnic background of congregation	Language(s) officially/mainly used during church services/activities
Anglican Chinese (Hakka)	Anglican	Abbotsford	Chinese (Malaysia)	Chinese (southern China, Hong Kong, Singapore, Malaysia (migrants); East Timor (refugees))	Chinese (Hakka)
Anglican Persian	Anglican	Alphington	Persian (Iran)	Persian	Persian
Baptist Arabic	Baptist	Brunswick	Arabic (Egypt)	Egyptian, Lebanese, Iraqi, Syrian, Somali, Sudanese	Arabic
Baptist Spanish	Baptist	Dandenong	Spanish (Spain)	Latin American	Spanish
Catholic Croatian	Catholic	Clifton Hill	Croatian (Croatia)	Croatian	Croatian
Catholic Italian	Catholic	North Fitzroy (office)	Italian (Italy)	Italian	Italian
Lutheran German	Lutheran – affiliated with LCA only, not a member	Springvale	German (South African-born)	German, Swiss, Austrian	German
Lutheran Latvian	Lutheran (LCA)	Surrey Hills	Latvian (American-born)	Latvian	Latvian
Lutheran Slovak	Lutheran (LCA)	Laverton	Slovak (Slovak Republic)	Slovak (former Yugoslavia)	Slovak

Reference	Denomination	Location	Ethnic background of minister/priest	Ethnic background of congregation	Language(s) officially/mainly used during church services/activities
Orthodox Greek	Orthodox (canonical) Ecumenical Patriarchate	South Melbourne	Greek (Australian-born)	Greek	Ecclesiastical Greek
Orthodox Russian	Orthodox (non-canonical) Russian Orthodox Church Abroad	Dandenong	Russian (Serbian-born)	Russian (Manchuria, China)	Old Church Slavonic
Reformed Chinese (Mandarin)	Reformed (RCA)	Dandenong	Chinese (Taiwan)	Chinese (China, Hong Kong, Singapore, Malaysia)	Chinese (Mandarin)
Reformed English (Dutch heritage)	Reformed (RCA)	Dandenong	Burgher (Sri Lanka)	Dutch (70%), Sri Lankan (20%)	English
Uniting Indonesian	Uniting (UCA)	Mulgrave	Chinese/Javanese (Indonesia)	Indonesian (Chinese descent)	Indonesian
Uniting Oromo	Uniting (UCA) – affiliated only, not a member	Huntingdale	Oromo (Ethiopia)	Oromo (refugees)	Oromo
Uniting Tamil	Uniting (UCA)	Oakleigh	Tamil (Sri Lanka)	Tamil (refugees)	Tamil

Reference	Use of community language	Use of English
Anglican Chinese (Hakka)	Hakka is used as the main language for all activities, but is always accompanied by a translation into English or other Chinese variety.	An (oral) English translation of every service is provided; youth activities (Sunday school, youth fellowship) are conducted in English.
Anglican Persian	Persian is used for all church activities and business, other than youth activities.	An English summary of the sermon may be given if required; youth activities are conducted in English.
Baptist Arabic	Arabic is used for all church activities, other than youth activities and when youth are present.	English is used for prayers, songs, notices, readings when youth are present. Once a month a guest speaker may preach in English. English is used for youth activities, such as the Sunday School and youth group.
Baptist Spanish	Spanish is used during the main service and selected activities.	Simultaneous translation into English is provided through headphones during the main service; some Sunday School classes and Bible studies are conducted in English.
Catholic Croatian	Croatian is used during all services and official activities.	English is only used for special services by request, such as during marriage services.
Catholic Italian	Italian is used during mass, except (on occasion) during sermons/homilies.	English is used for special services by request but is most commonly used in Baptism services and with youth; English may also be used by priests during the homily, depending on their facility and confidence with Italian.
Lutheran German	German is used during services officially in German (three times each month), as well as during the playgroup established for language maintenance purposes.	English is officially used during the bi-monthly English services; during the German services, written English translations of the sermon are distributed and oral English summaries may also be provided; some hymns are sung in English; youth activities such as Sunday School are conducted in English.

Reference	Use of community language	Use of English
Lutheran Latvian	Latvian is used during all official activities.	English is officially permitted to be used during the fortnightly English-medium contemporary service and at certain Bible study groups.
Lutheran Slovak	Slovak is used during the main service and selected activities.	Simultaneous translation into English is provided through headphones during the main Slovak service; a contemporary English service is held on Sunday evening, and all youth activities are in English.
Orthodox Greek	Ecclesiastical Greek is used for the liturgy and Scripture readings; modern Greek is only used during the sermon, and for the recitation of the creed and the Lord's Prayer.	English is used for Sunday School; for Scripture readings (after they have been read in Ecclesiastical Greek); for an English rendition of the sermon (after it has been given in modern Greek); and for the recitation of the Creed and the Lord's Prayer (after they have been recited in modern Greek).
Orthodox Russian	Old Church Slavonic is used for most of the liturgy; modern Russian is only used during the sermon and notices.	English is used for some Scripture readings (parallel to Old Church Slavonic) and for some parts of the liturgy (*Kyrie Eleison* [Lord have mercy]) whenever the English-speaking non-Russian priest assists.
Reformed Chinese (Mandarin)	Mandarin is used for all church services / activities other than youth activities (Cantonese was originally used; the change was made to facilitate better communication).	English is used for youth activities such as the Sunday School and when children are present during services; the sermon may also be provided in English by a member of the congregation who stands near the minister and translates 'line by line'.
Reformed English (Dutch heritage)	Dutch services have long since ceased; Dutch is used only in an annual Christmas service (a Dutch-only service).	English is used for all church activities and business (except for the annual Christmas service).

Reference	Use of community language	Use of English
Uniting Indonesian	Indonesian is used for church services/activities, other than youth activities, or when youth are involved in services.	Simultaneous translation into English is provided through headphones during the entirety of the service for non-Indonesian-speaking visitors and spouses; it is also used by the minister for the children's talk, as well as for all youth activities such as the Sunday School.
Uniting Oromo	Oromo is used during all services and activities.	*Information not available*
Uniting Tamil	Tamil only is used during the second of two services held each month.	English is used during the first of two services held each month, which is a youth service; all other youth activities, including the Sunday School, are also conducted in English.

Reference	Service frequency	Congregational age breakdown	Occurrence of bi-/multi-lingual services/activities
Anglican Chinese (Hakka)	1 Chinese service weekly; held in the morning.	The majority are young professionals.	Multilingual services are the norm; Hakka is used together with English in sentence-by-sentence translation; informal translations into other Chinese varieties may occur during the service amongst groups within the congregation.
Anglican Persian	1 Persian service monthly; held in the morning.	*Information not available*	English/Persian bilingual services are held on special occasions, with hymns sung simultaneously in both languages; translation of the sermon into English is done by the minister from the pulpit.
Baptist Arabic	1 Arabic service weekly; held in the morning.	The congregation's ages vary, with a large number of young first generation migrants.	Each service is bilingual in that some English components will be incorporated (songs, etc.). Monthly guest speaker will preach in English, to be translated sentence-by-sentence into Arabic by a church member.

Reference	Service frequency	Congregational age breakdown	Occurrence of bi-/multi-lingual services/activities
Baptist Spanish	3 Spanish services weekly; held in the morning, afternoon and evening.	*Information not available*	Simultaneous translation from Spanish into English (via headphones) is a regular part of Sunday afternoon services; Spanish and English may both be used during youth activities.
Catholic Croatian	1 Croatian service weekly; held in the morning (number of services may vary according to church calendar).	*Information not available*	Bilingual components are typically only included during special services such as weddings.
Catholic Italian	(Around 40 Italian masses are celebrated each Sunday)	The majority are first-generation migrants.	Bilingual components are typically included during special services such as weddings; English and Italian may also be used by at different times during a mass depending on the priest's proficiency and confidence in Italian.
Lutheran German	3 German services and 2 English services monthly; held in the morning and evening.	The majority are over the age of 60.	*Information not available*
Lutheran Latvian	1 Latvian service weekly; 2 English services monthly; held in the morning.	The majority are over the age of 65.	No bilingual activities or services are conducted; as a result of conflict in the church, the pastor feels it is best to keep the languages as separate as possible.
Lutheran Slovak	1 Slovak service weekly, held in the morning; 1 English service weekly, held in the evening.	*Information not available*	Simultaneous translation from Slovak into English (via headphones) is a regular part of the main Sunday services; Slovak and English may both be used during youth activities.

Reference	Service frequency	Congregational age breakdown	Occurrence of bi-/multi-lingual services/activities
Orthodox Greek	1 Greek service weekly; held in the morning (number of services may vary according to church calendar).	The majority are first-generation migrants.	Bilingual components are typically included during special services such as weddings; the priest is known as one who does not object to using English on such occasions. In a sense all services are multilingual, using Ecclesiastical Greek, modern Greek and English at various times.
Orthodox Russian	1 Russian service weekly; held in the morning (number of services may vary according to church calendar).	The majority are first-generation migrants but with a good representation of second generation.	Bilingual components are typically included during special services such as weddings. In a sense all services are multilingual, using Old Church Slavonic, modern Russian, Greek and English at various times.
Reformed Chinese (Mandarin)	2 Chinese services weekly; held in the morning and evening.	The majority are over the age of 45.	Bilingual components are typically included during special services such as Baptisms; Chinese and English may both be used during youth activities; and combined services held together with the English congregation of the church (see below) are bilingual.
Reformed English (Dutch heritage)	2 English services weekly; held in the morning.	The congregation's ages vary; the services are transmitted on closed-circuit television for frail church members living in an adjacent hostel.	Combined services held together with the Chinese congregation of the church (see above) are bilingual.
Uniting Indonesian	1 Indonesian service weekly, held in the morning; 1 English service weekly, held in the evening.	The majority are students and young families.	Simultaneous translation from Indonesian into English (via headphones) is a regular part of the main Sunday services; children's involvement during services or other youth activities may be bilingual.

Reference	Service frequency	Congregational age breakdown	Occurrence of bi-/multi-lingual services/activities
Uniting Oromo	1 Oromo service weekly; held on Saturday afternoons.	The majority are between the ages of 20–30.	*Information not available*
Uniting Tamil	2 Tamil services monthly; held in the evening.	The majority are between the ages of 30–60 but there is a large Sunday School.	Combined services with other congregations in the Parish (English, Tamil, Cook Islander, Oromo) are bilingual; Tamil youth services, which are otherwise conducted in English, may include songs sung in Tamil.

Reference	Church administration structure	Attendance	Year established	Congregation's community language (CL) proficiency
Anglican Chinese (Hakka)	The congregation are the sole occupants of the church.	80 people.	1986	*Information not available*
Anglican Persian	The congregation are sharing the church with an English congregation of the same denomination; the Persian minister oversees both.	20–25 people.	*Information not available*	The congregation's CL proficiency is reported to increase with age.
Baptist Arabic	The congregation are renting the church facilities from a church of a different denomination.	60 people approx.	1977	The congregation's CL proficiency is reported to increase with age; children educated in Australia tend to have poor CL proficiency.
Baptist Spanish	The congregation are renting the church facilities from a church of a different denomination.	200 people.	1990	High CL proficiency exists across most age groups because migration is ongoing.

Reference	Church administration structure	Attendance	Year established	Congregation's community language (CL) proficiency
Catholic Croatian	The congregation are the sole occupants of the church.	800 people.	1962	The congregation's CL proficiency is reported to increase with age.
Catholic Italian	n/a	n/a	n/a	General speaking, CL proficiency in Italian congregations is reported to increase with age.
Lutheran German	The congregation are the sole occupants of the church.	60–80 people.	1960	The congregation's CL proficiency is reported to increase with age.
Lutheran Latvian	The congregation are the sole occupants of the church.	100 people (Latvian service), 10 people (English service); total membership of 1000.	1950	The congregation's CL proficiency is reported to increase with age; fluency is poor among non-Latvian spouses.
Lutheran Slovak	The congregation are the sole occupants of the church.	120 people.	1979	The congregation's CL proficiency is reported to increase with age; however many children have very good CL skills.
Orthodox Greek	The congregation are the sole occupants of the church.	200–300 people.	1965	The congregation's CL proficiency is reported to increase with age; however many children have very good CL skills.
Orthodox Russian	The congregation are the sole occupants of the church.	100 people approx.	1979–1981	The congregation's CL proficiency is reported to increase with age; however many children have very good CL skills.

Reference	Church administration structure	Attendance	Year established	Congregation's community language (CL) proficiency
Reformed Chinese (Mandarin)	The congregation are renting the church facilities from a church of the same denomination (see below).	60 people.	1993	The congregation's CL proficiency is reported to increase with age.
Reformed English (Dutch heritage)	This congregation is the main congregation of a church which also rents its facilities to another congregation of same denomination (see above).	350 people; total membership of 500.	1953	Only the elderly members of the congregation are proficient in Dutch; English might realistically be considered the 'CL' for this congregation.
Uniting Indonesian	The congregation are sharing the church with an English congregation of the same denomination; a different minister oversees each.	Fluctuates according to Australian university year.	1986	The congregation's CL proficiency is reported to increase with age.
Uniting Oromo	The congregation are renting the church facilities from a church of the same denomination.	40–45 people.	1990s	High CL proficiency exists across most age groups because migration is recent and ongoing.
Uniting Tamil	The congregation are sharing the church facilities with another congregation of the same denomination; ministers are shared throughout the parish.	100 people; total membership of 131 families.	The congregation began as an Anglican one in the early 1980s.	The congregation's CL proficiency is reported to increase with age and is dependent on an individual's migration vintage; however, many children have very good CL skills.

Reference	Congregation's English language (EL) proficiency	Minister's CL proficiency	Minister's EL proficiency	Minister's home language use
Anglican Chinese (Hakka)	The congregation's EL proficiency is reported to decrease with age but is dependent on migration vintage and level of English-medium education; youth, young professionals and those from SE Asia tend to be fluent.	Fluent oral/aural skills in Hakka and Mandarin; fluent Malay	Fluent	Malay, Mandarin, Hakka and English
Anglican Persian	The congregation's EL proficiency is reported to decrease with age but is dependent on migration vintage and level of English-medium education; youth and young professionals are fluent.	Fluent	Fluent	English and some Persian
Baptist Arabic	The congregation's EL proficiency is high amongst most age groups but is dependent on country of origin; youth tend to be fluent, and those from countries in which English is used in education.	Fluent	Very good	Arabic and English
Baptist Spanish	The congregation's EL proficiency is reported to decrease with age, but is dependent on migration vintage and level of English-medium education; youth and young professionals are fluent.	Fluent	Fluent (Spanish Spanish)	Spanish and English
Catholic Croatian	The congregation's EL language proficiency is very high across most age groups, although it is reported to be less so amongst the oldest members; youth are fluent.	Fluent	Good	Usually lives alone
Catholic Italian	The congregation's EL language proficiency is very high across all age groups, although it is reported to be less so amongst the oldest members.	Fluent	Fluent	Italian, Venetian

Reference	Congregation's English language (EL) proficiency	Minister's CL proficiency	Minister's EL proficiency	Minister's home language use
Lutheran German	The congregation's EL language proficiency is very high across all age groups, although it is reported to be less so amongst the oldest members.	Fluent	Fluent	German and English
Lutheran Latvian	The congregation's EL language proficiency is very high across all age groups, although it reported to be less so amongst the oldest members.	Fluent	Fluent (US English)	Latvian and some English
Lutheran Slovak	The congregation's EL language proficiency is very high across most age groups, although it reported to be less so amongst the oldest members.	Fluent	Fluent	Slovak and English
Orthodox Greek	The congregation's EL proficiency is dependent on migration vintage and level of English-medium education/employment; youth and young professionals are fluent, elderly may have limited proficiency.	Fluent	Fluent	Lives alone, except for 'bilingual' dog
Orthodox Russian	The congregation's EL proficiency is dependent on migration vintage and level of English-medium education/employment; youth are fluent, elderly may have limited proficiency.	Fluent	Fluent	Russian and English
Reformed Chinese (Mandarin)	The congregation's EL proficiency is dependent on migration vintage and level of English-medium education; youth and young professionals are fluent, elderly may have limited proficiency.	Fluent Mandarin and Hakka	Very good comprehension and reading skills; moderate speaking and writing skills	Mandarin, Hakka and English

Reference	*Congregation's English language (EL) proficiency*	*Minister's CL proficiency*	*Minister's EL proficiency*	*Minister's home language use*
Reformed English (Dutch heritage)	All age groups within the congregation have very high English proficiency.	Minimal	Fluent	English
Uniting Indonesian	The congregation's EL proficiency is dependent on migration vintage and level of English-medium education; youth and young professionals are fluent, elderly may have limited proficiency.	Fluent	Very good	*Information not available*
Uniting Oromo	*Information not available*	Fluent	Good to very good speaking and comprehension skills	Oromo, Swahili and English
Uniting Tamil	The congregation's EL proficiency is high amongst most age groups.	Fluent	Fluent	Tamil and some English

Reference	Code-switching in church-related activities	Links to denomination in Australia	Links to church overseas
Anglican Chinese (Hakka)	The minister claims he will sometimes code-switch in a sermon, for example, to clarify a concept.	*Information not available*	*Information not available*
Anglican Persian	The minister claims he often code-switches in a sermon, for example, to clarify a concept.	The congregation's links to the Anglican Church are strong; the minister also preaches to a Persian congregation in Sydney.	The congregation's links to the Anglican Church in Iran are strong; the congregation is also a member of Iranian Christian International, which links Persian congregations world wide.
Baptist Arabic	*Information not available*	The congregation is part of the Baptist Union (New Settlers Baptist Association).	*Information not available*
Baptist Spanish	*Information not available*	The congregation is part of the Baptist Union (New Settlers Baptist Association).	*Information not available*
Catholic Croatian	The minister claims he sometimes code-switches during church activities (not during services), for example, to clarify a concept, but claims to try to keep his language 'pure'.	The congregation's links to the Catholic Church are very strong.	The congregation's links to the Catholic Church worldwide are very strong, as is their relationship to the Catholic Church in Croatia; all of the Croatian Catholic priests have come from Croatia.
Catholic Italian	The minister claims he often code-switches during church activities (not during services), for example, to clarify a concept.	The priest is assigned by the Scalabrinian Fathers, but works within the Catholic Archdiocese of Melbourne.	The priest has strong links with his order – the Scalabrinian Fathers, which originated overseas, as well as with the Catholic Church overseas.

Reference	Code-switching in church-related activities	Links to denomination in Australia	Links to church overseas
Lutheran German	*Information not available*	The congregation are only in 'altar and pulpit fellowship' with the LCA (not full members), but in practice their links with the LCA are stronger than with the church in Germany from whom they receive some financial support.	The congregation's links to the Lutheran Church in Germany are of a financial and personal nature only.
Lutheran Latvian	The minister claims he will sometimes code-switch in a sermon, for example, to clarify a concept.	The congregation is now a member of the LCA.	The congregation was formerly part of the Latvian Church in Exile, now called the Latvian Church Abroad.
Lutheran Slovak	The minister claims he will sometimes code-switch when speaking to the youth of the church but claims that he is able to control his switches; code-switching amongst parishioners is said to be very common (typically using English, Slovak and Serbian).	*Information not available*	The congregation has strong links with the Lutheran Church in the former Yugoslavia because of the origin of the majority of the congregation.
Orthodox Greek	The minister claims he does not code-switch; he claims to try to keep his language 'pure'.	The congregation are within the Archdiocese of Australia; their links to Orthodox Christians of other ethnic backgrounds are also very strong.	The Archdiocese of Australia must submit to the Patriarchate of Constantinople, which is in communion with other Patriarchates; churches in Australia are thereby linked to Orthodoxy worldwide, regardless of the jurisdiction.

Reference	Code-switching in church-related activities	Links to denomination in Australia	Links to church overseas
Orthodox Russian	The minister claims he may intentionally code-switch in a sermon, in order to clarify a concept for the youth of the congregation but he claims to warn the older members first.	The congregation are within the Australian Diocese of the Russian Orthodox Church Abroad.	The congregation is under the jurisdiction of the Russian Orthodox Church Abroad, to which most Russians in Australia belong; it is a non-canonical Orthodox church.
Reformed Chinese (Mandarin)	The minister claims he will sometimes code-switch in a sermon, for example, to clarify a concept.	*Information not available*	The congregation has links to the Reformed Church in Taiwan, which originated in Korea, more than to the Reformed churches in the Netherlands
Reformed English (Dutch heritage)	The minister claims that code-switching frequently occurs amongst parishioners, and Dutch-speaking parishioners may code-switch in their conversations with him (although his Dutch is minimal).	The congregation is a member of the RCA.	The congregation has loose ties, based on theological similarity, with the Reformed churches in The Netherlands; they have a 'sister church' relationship only.
Uniting Indonesian	The minister claims he often code-switches in a sermon, for example, to clarify a concept. (Note: researcher's observation shows most code-switches occur with pronouns and phrases.)	The congregation is a member of the UCA and the minister feels that their relationship to the UCA is a strong one.	The congregation has loose links with many denominations in Indonesia, due to the varied Christian backgrounds of the congregation.
Uniting Oromo	*Information not available*	*Information not available*	*Information not available*

Reference	Code-switching in church-related activities	Links to denomination in Australia	Links to church overseas
Uniting Tamil	The minister claims he often code-switches in a sermon, for example, to clarify a concept.	The congregation is a member of the UCA, and the minister feels that their relationship to the UCA is a strong one; he considers the UCA to be very supportive of ethnic congregations.	The congregation has a strong relationship with the Church of South India.

Reference	Links to other Australian churches of same ethnic background	Liturgy used	Bible used
Anglican Chinese (Hakka)	The congregation have informal links with a group which unites all Chinese congregations in Melbourne, however they are not yet a member of this group.	The congregation have been involved in translating some services of the Anglican Church; however liturgy is not regularly used, as the congregation have a preference for charismatic worship which does not emphasise the use of formal liturgy, in addition to there being a high rate of illiteracy among the members of the congregation who came as refugees.	The congregation use a Mandarin Bible.
Anglican Persian	The minister also regularly leads Persian (Anglican) services in Sydney.	The minister is currently translating an abbreviated form of An Australian Prayer Book into Persian; previously they had used a version provided by the Anglican Church in Iran.	The congregation will soon be using a new Persian paraphrase Bible which has recently been published.

Reference	Links to other Australian churches of same ethnic background	Liturgy used	Bible used
Baptist Arabic	The congregation has no involvement with other Arabic congregations of other denominations (such as Melkite, Maronite), except on a personal level between individuals.	No liturgy is used.	The congregation use an Arabic Bible which is similar to the English New King James Version. Minister reports that no other version has been published.
Baptist Spanish	*Information not available*	No liturgy is used.	*Information not available*
Catholic Croatian	*Information not available*	The congregation use the Croatian liturgy provided by the Catholic Church.	The congregation use a Croatian Bible printed in 1974.
Catholic Italian	The congregation has no involvement with Croatian congregations of other denominations.	The congregation use the Italian liturgy provided by the Catholic Church.	*Information not available*
Lutheran German	The congregation has a good relationship with German congregations of other denominations.	While the congregation do use a liturgy, the minister claims that it is 'not specifically Lutheran'.	The congregation use a revised German Bible printed in 1984.
Lutheran Latvian	The congregation has occasional involvement with other Latvian Lutheran and Catholic congregations.	The congregation use the liturgy provided by the Latvian Church Abroad.	*Information not available*

Reference	*Links to other Australian churches of same ethnic background*	*Liturgy used*	*Bible used*
Lutheran Slovak	As the only Slovak Lutheran minister in Australia, the minister often leads services in other suburbs and interstate.	*Information not available*	The congregation use a Bible printed in1979; it is the 'official Slovak evangelical Bible'.
Orthodox Greek	*Information not available*	The congregation use the liturgy of St John Chrysostom provided by the Greek Orthodox Church.	The congregation use several Bibles, for example, one in which New Testament Greek appears in parallel with modern Greek.
Orthodox Russian	The church's links to the Canonical Russian Orthodox Church is 'cordial'.	The congregation use the liturgy of St John Chrysostom (325AD) in Old Church Slavonic (translated in the 10th century) , as well as the liturgy of St Basil.	The congregation use a Russian Bible (called the Synod Publication) which was produced before the Revolution.
Reformed Chinese (Mandarin)	*Information not available*	The congregation have access to a liturgy provided by the Reformed Church in Korea, but do not regularly use a liturgy.	*Information not available*
Reformed English (Dutch heritage)	*Information not available*	*Information not available*	*Information not available*
Uniting Indonesian	*Information not available*	The congregation have developed their own liturgy, based on that of the UCA as well as the liturgical preferences of members of the congregation.	The congregation use a modern Indonesian Good News Bible.

Reference	Links to other Australian churches of same ethnic background	Liturgy used	Bible used
Uniting Oromo	*Information not available*	The congregation, which prefer charismatic worship, do not use a liturgy.	The congregation use an Oromo New Testament which has been printed using the new Oromo script, but the Old Testament still only exists in the old Oromo script.
Uniting Tamil	The congregation has strong links with other Tamil congregations, particularly where the other congregation also has links to the Church of South India; the minister also leads services at independent churches in Sydney.	The congregation have developed their own liturgy, based on that of the Church of South India and the UCA.	The congregation use two different Tamil Bibles (one modern, one older), of which the minister reports there to be no English equivalent.

Reference	Other resources	Problems with resources	Reasons for use of particular languages
Anglican Chinese (Hakka)	*Information not available*	While the minister claims the congregation like liturgy and ceremony, there is a need for more resources suited to those with limited literacy; the Bible is written in a very educated Mandarin which is not easy to understand.	The congregation's / minister's choice of language is based on the desire for effective communication.
Anglican Persian	A number of hymns have been translated by members of the church.	There is a need for more books; many church leaders were killed during the Revolution, resulting in a shortage of theological literature.	The congregation's / minister's choice of language is based on the desire for effective communication.

Reference	Other resources	Problems with resources	Reasons for use of particular languages
Baptist Arabic	The congregation use a comprehensive English-language Sunday School program, chosen on the basis of its content, not the language used.	There is a need for more commentaries, Bibles and other religious books but they are expensive to have sent over. When Christian Arabic migrants arrive in Australia they seldom have an Arabic Bible with them because they are so heavy; the church gives away many Arabic Bibles.	The congregation's/minister's choice of language is based on the desire for effective expression of deep feelings. Arabic is also the language which allows the greatest freedom of expression and requires the least effort to use.
Baptist Spanish	*Information not available*	No shortage of resources is perceived, due to the strong evangelical tradition in South America which is continuing to produce church resources.	*Information not available*
Catholic Croatian	*Information not available*	No problem with resources is perceived.	*Information not available*
Catholic Italian	Many resources may be found at the Catholic Italian Resource Centre; the priest is also involved in translating the Diocese's publications.	While there are many Italian theological resources available, there is a need for inexpensive, unsophisticated, large-print religious books appropriate for the aging community.	The priest's choice of language is based on the desire for effective communication; he considers Italian to be the best instrument to communicate with other Italians.
Lutheran German	*Information not available*	There is a need for more resources such as hymns, songs and stories; the congregation feels isolated from the church in the homeland.	*Information not available*
Lutheran Latvian	*Information not available*	*Information not available*	*Information not available*

Reference	Other resources	Problems with resources	Reasons for use of particular languages
Lutheran Slovak	A new Slovak hymnal, printed in 1994, has now replaced the old Czech hymnal.	The Czech hymnal, which was used until 1994, contained racist lyrics such as 'O Lord save us from the Turks'.	*Information not available*
Orthodox Greek	Members of the congregation may use a small service book printed in modern Greek and / or English; in general, most of the congregation's resources come from Greece.	No problem with resources is perceived.	The priest's choice of language is generally based on the desire for effective communication; however a 'sense of mystery' is considered important in the Orthodox Church, which the use of an 'ancient' liturgical language provides.
Orthodox Russian	*Information not available*	No problems perceived – though geographical distance may be great, the Internet makes resources more accessible.	The priest believes that Old Church Slavonic is used because it is what people want to hear, both because of tradition and for its aesthetic value.
Reformed Chinese (Mandarin)	*Information not available*	There is a need for more Chinese resources, particularly those appropriate for Sunday School.	The congregation's / minister's choice of language is based on the desire for effective communication; this prompted the shift from Cantonese to Mandarin as the language of the congregation when it was first established.
Reformed English (Dutch heritage)	*Information not available*	*Information not available*	The congregation's / minister's choice of language is based on the desire for effective communication; English is the language in which the congregation are most proficient.

Reference	Other resources	Problems with resources	Reasons for use of particular languages
Uniting Indonesian	The congregation imports many hymns and songs from Indonesia.	*Information not available*	The congregation's/minister's choice of language is based on the desire for effective communication; using Indonesian provides a sense of familiarity for recently migrated members of the congregation; language choice is also based on cultural assumptions of what is appropriate for the religious domain.
Uniting Oromo	The minister has collected many songs from Kenya; other resources get sent from the USA.	There is a great need for Oromo resources; there are many more resources available in Amharic, and those resources which exist in Oromo are often not be printed in the new (more readable) script.	The congregation's/minister's choice of language is based on the desire for effective communication.
Uniting Tamil	*Information not available*	There is a need for Tamil resources which are relevant in the Australian, rather than the Sri Lankan, context. The minister has also suggested that resources in English, rather than Tamil, may be more appropriate as language maintenance in the younger generation is low.	*Information not available*

Reference	Appropriateness of particular languages for church use	Existence of language issues in the church
Anglican Chinese (Hakka)	The minister does not perceive any one language as being more appropriate than another for use in the religious domain.	The minister does perceive the existence of language issues; the congregation will split (in 1997) from a single multilingual congregation into separate congregations according to specific language needs; English is the preferred language of the youth and young professionals from South East Asia, while Chinese is the preferred language of those from southern China and of the refugees from East Timor. Members of the congregation feel their needs are not being met by the switching of languages in the current multilingual services.
Anglican Persian	The minister does not perceive any one language as being more appropriate than another for use in the religious domain.	The minister does not perceive the existence of language issues.
Baptist Arabic	The minister does not perceive any one language as being ore appropriate than another for use in the religious domain; however, English is more appropriate to use with those born in Australia.	*Information not available*
Baptist Spanish	*Information not available*	The minister does not perceive the existence of language issues, but feels issues may arise with the next generation.
Catholic Croatian	The priest does not perceive any one language as being more appropriate than another for use in the religious domain.	*Information not available*

Reference	Appropriateness of particular languages for church use	Existence of language issues in the church
Catholic Italian	The priest does not generally perceive any one language as being more appropriate than another for use in the religious domain; however, the use of dialects is considered to be inappropriate.	The priest does perceive the existence of language issues; providing appropriate care for the elderly Italians who are increasingly reverting to Italian is perceived as a task of the Catholic Church.
Lutheran German	*Information not available*	*Information not available*
Lutheran Latvian	*Information not available*	The minister does perceive the existence of language issues; there is strong opposition from some members of the congregation to the existence of an English ministry within the church and to the use of English in Latvian services.
Lutheran Slovak	*Information not available*	The minister does perceive the existence of language issues; there is strong opposition from some members of the congregation to the existence of an English ministry within the church and to the use of English in Slovak services.
Orthodox Greek	The priest does perceive certain languages as being more appropriate than others for use in the religious domain; Ecclesiastical Greek – the traditional language of the Church – is considered most appropriate.	*Information not available*
Orthodox Russian	*Information not available*	The priest feels that there are generational differences in language preferences but that there is no easy solution; time will solve any language-related problems.

Reference	*Appropriateness of particular languages for church use*	*Existence of language issues in the church*
Reformed Chinese (Mandarin)	*Information not available*	*Information not available*
Reformed English (Dutch heritage)	The minister does not perceive any one language as being more appropriate than another for use in the religious domain; however the use of different languages is considered to have different effects.	The minister does not perceive the existence of current language issues; however the cessation of Dutch services approximately 20 years ago was traumatic for some members of the congregation.
Uniting Indonesian	The minister does perceive certain languages as being more appropriate than others for use in the religious domain; within the Indonesian culture it is considered important to show appropriate respect for God through the use of the most prestigious language or speech level.	*Information not available*
Uniting Oromo	The minister does not perceive any one language as being more appropriate than another for use in the religious domain; however some are considered as being 'better equipped' (with resources, for example) than others.	*Information not available*
Uniting Tamil	*Information not available*	The minister does perceive the existence of language issues; the lack of Tamil proficiency among the youth of the church is considered problematic.

Reference	Existence of language-related problems for youth	Opinion of best language to use for youth evangelism
Anglican Chinese (Hakka)	Language-related problems are encountered by youth; Chinese Australian youth are perceived as struggling with cultural identity issues, and language is considered to be a marker of identity.	English in a 'simplified' form
Anglican Persian	Language-related problems are encountered by youth; there is a need for age-appropriate resources; the minister also wants to ensure that Persian youth feel a freedom to attend any church and do not feel bound to the Persian church.	*Information not available*
Baptist Arabic	Language-related problems are encountered by youth; however, much effort is made to accommodate the linguistic needs of young people by using English wherever required.	English
Baptist Spanish	*Information not available*	*Information not available*
Catholic Croatian	Language-related problems are not perceived as being encountered by youth; the priest encourages Croatian youth who are not sufficiently proficient in Croatian, to go to an English-speaking Catholic church instead.	English and Croatian (the priest feels that Croatian is necessary to supplement his less-than-proficient English)
Catholic Italian	Some language-related problems are encountered by youth; a lack of Italian proficiency amongst youth is an issue; however a greater problem is the lack of relevance that youth, regardless of ethnic background, perceive Christianity to have in their lives.	English (the priest feels that this is the best language choice because youth may speak an Italian dialect at home, not Standard Italian, and therefore their Italian proficiency may be poor)
Lutheran German	Some language-related problems are encountered by youth; however a greater problem is the lack of relevance that youth, regardless of ethnic background, perceive Christianity to have in their lives.	*Information not available*

Reference	Existence of language-related problems for youth	Opinion of best language to use for youth evangelism
Lutheran Latvian	Some language-related problems are encountered by youth; youth cannot understand Latvian well; however they also find traditional styles of worship, as well as the subject matter, difficult to ascribe relevance to.	English
Lutheran Slovak	Language-related problems are encountered by youth; they do not see the Slovak language as a 'living' language which is useful to them.	English
Orthodox Greek	*Information not available*	English, with some Greek.
Orthodox Russian	Some language-related problems are encountered by youth, however as the congregation is largely made up of first-generation migrants, the problems are not as visible. The priest does not know whether young people would prefer the liturgy in English as he has never asked them.	English
Reformed Chinese (Mandarin)	Language-related problems are encountered by youth; they perceive Chinese as being too difficult to learn.	English
Reformed English (Dutch heritage)	*Information not available*	English
Uniting Indonesian	Language-related problems are encountered by youth; the minister perceives the major problem as being his own lack of English proficiency which he feels is a hindrance to effective communication with Indonesian youth.	English
Uniting Oromo	Language-related problems are encountered by youth; the minister is concerned that Oromo youth will lose their Oromo proficiency in the Australian environment.	Oromo (the minister claims that the youth like it)
Uniting Tamil	*Information not available*	English? *Information not available*

Reference	The future – the church in 50 years	Should the church be 'multicultural' or ethno-specific?
Anglican Chinese (Hakka)	The minister sees the congregation's future as being bright; he has a vision for a 'multicongregational' church, with separate congregations being established to cater for separate needs, for example, a children's congregation, and a university students' congregation.	The minister feels that a 'multicultural' church is preferable to an ethno-specific one, although ethno-specific ministries within a church are appropriate.
Anglican Persian	The minister sees the congregation's future as being dependent upon events in Iran – whether these will give rise to further migration.	*Information not available*
Baptist Arabic	The minister hopes an English-speaking congregation will be established within the context of the Arabic church for the young people; he feels that Arabic-language ministry is necessary as long as Arabic immigration continues.	The church is already multicultural in the sense that its members have come from many Arabic-speaking regions; the pastor welcomes anyone regardless of ethnicity, but feels a continuing need to focus on Arabic ministry.
Baptist Spanish	The minister sees the congregation's future as being bright; while the existence of a Spanish congregation depends to some extent on continued migration, the minister has a vision for establishing a 'multicultural' church, with ministry to a large number of language groups weekly.	The minister feels that a 'multicultural' church is preferable to an ethno-specific one, although ethno-specific ministries within a church are appropriate.
Catholic Croatian	The priest sees the congregation's future as being dependent upon events in Croatia, and whether these will give rise to further migration.	*Information not available*

Reference	The future – the church in 50 years	Should the church be 'multicultural' or ethno-specific?
Catholic Italian	The priest envisages the Italian Catholic community as still being distinctively Italian, for example, through the continuation of traditions; however, he feels the Italian language may no longer be part of the Church.	The priest feels that ethno-specific churches are preferable to a 'multicultural' church; while the priest feels that multicultural celebrations are appropriate on special occasions, their regular implementation is at the cost of parishioners' needs being met ('the purpose of Sunday worship is not to display multicultural diversity or unity, but to worship God'). The priest claims that ethno-specific ministries are vital for first generation migrants.
Lutheran German	The minister does not see the congregation's future as being dependent upon the German community; he feels that as long as it remains a church, the future is bright, irrespective of the community it serves.	The minister does not have a preference, though he suggests that some of his congregation may have strong preferences; the minister sees a need for ethno-specific ministry, but does not see his own call to ministry as being to a specific language or culture.
Lutheran Latvian	As the community cannot rely on immigration for growth, the minister sees the congregation's future as bleak if significant changes are not made (such as the acceptance of English ministry); he has a vision for its revival and renewal. (Even those in the congregation who do oppose the English ministry admit that the future is bleak.)	The minister feels that a 'multicultural' church is preferable to an ethno-specific one, however there is strong opposition by some members of the congregation to having an 'open-door' policy (to the extent that proposed changes to the church's constitution regulate the situations in which a non-Latvian may belong to the church)
Lutheran Slovak	*Information not available*	The minister feels that a 'multicultural' church is preferable to an ethno-specific one, and suggests that both opinions are represented within his congregation.
Orthodox Greek	The priest sees the possibility of language change in the future of the Orthodox Church; but regardless of the language used, people of Greek heritage will always return to the Greek Orthodox church for weddings and baptisms.	The priest considers the Orthodox Church to be 'multicultural' already, as any Orthodox Christian, regardless of ethnic background, may attend any Orthodox church; however, he sees his role as a priest to look after the needs of the Greek community.

Reference	The future – the church in 50 years	Should the church be 'multicultural' or ethno-specific?
Orthodox Russian	The priest sees the church as still catering for the Russian community, but feels that it will also become more of a 'missionary church', catering for the wider English-speaking community.	The priest feels that forcing the church to change is wrong; it will inevitably, with the passing of time, become less Russian.
Reformed Chinese (Mandarin)	*Information not available*	The minister feels that a 'multicultural' church is preferable to an ethno-specific one, although ethno-specific ministries within a church are appropriate.
Reformed English (Dutch heritage)	The minister sees his congregation's future as lying in becoming an 'Australianised' church.	The minister feels that a 'multicultural' church is preferable to an ethno-specific one, although ethno-specific ministries within a church are appropriate.
Uniting Indonesian	The minister sees his congregation's future as bright; he envisages a congregation divided into two groups: (1) one which is integrated into the English-speaking church and is contributing to the development of an 'Australian' spirituality; and (2) one which is Indonesian-speaking and caters specifically for the needs of recent migrants and short-term students.	The minister feels that a 'multicultural' church is preferable to an ethno-specific one, although ethno-specific ministries within a church are appropriate.
Uniting Oromo	*Information not available*	The minister feels that a 'multicultural' church is preferable to an ethno-specific one, although ethno-specific ministries within a church are appropriate; the minister feels that his main ministry is to reach the Oromo people.
Uniting Tamil	The minister sees his congregation's future as bright; he envisages the congregation as being more self-sufficient, with its own church building.	The minister feels that ethno-specific services are valuable: 'anyone wanting to come would need to be happy with Tamil services and style'.

Reference	The goal of the church	Comments
Anglican Chinese (Hakka)	*Information not available*	From 1997, the church will separate into two separate language-based congregations: English and Chinese.
Anglican Persian	The minister's perception of the church's goal is to communicate the Gospel message to Moslems.	–
Baptist Arabic	*Information not available*	The pastor feels that the family is very important in Arabic communities, and seeks to keep families together and within the church by paying careful attention to the language preferences and abilities of youth.
Baptist Spanish	*Information not available*	–
Catholic Croatian	The priest's perception of the church's goal is to look after the spiritual needs of (Croatian) migrants 'who cannot understand the English liturgy'.	The church is part of an extensive Croatian community centre; boundaries between religious activities and other activities are not distinct.
Catholic Italian	The priest's personal goal in ministry is to assist Italian migrants in whatever he is able, when the need arises; the goal of his ministry to ethnic chaplains is to support, encourage and represent them, when the need arises.	The priest is in a number of leadership roles within the Catholic Church, coordinating other ethnic chaplains, as well as being involved in ministry to the Italian community (his primary role as a Scalabrinian Father). He is not attached to any one parish, but is a 'floating priest' and is still the main Italian chaplain in Melbourne.
Lutheran German	The goal of the church is stated on their web page as: 'our main aim is to spread the Good News of Jesus Christ and His salvation . . . in German and English'.	The church's web page states that 'although our members are mostly of European background who speak German, we welcome anyone'.

Reference	The goal of the church	Comments
Lutheran Latvian	*Information not available*	This church is the only one in this study which has its own constitution – containing bylaws governing the use of Latvian and English. Proposed changes to the constitution will define church membership on language/ethnicity-related grounds.
Lutheran Slovak	*Information not available*	This church is very active in the wider community, having established a Christian bookshop in the local area, and a church band which tours throughout Australia; all this, despite heavy opposition to having an English-language ministry and making use of contemporary styles of worship.
Orthodox Greek	The priest's perception of the church's goal is to 'serve those who regard themselves [as Orthodox] and believe in the Greek Orthodox church'.	The priest claims to have not 'felt the need' to provide an English mass; he feels that the presence of God may be experienced regardless of whether a person understands the language of worship. The priest suggests that those who complain about the inaccessibility of a Greek liturgy may simply be too lazy to make the effort to understand it. He says that many within the Greek Orthodox community feel that the church will die if a change to English liturgy is made; it will be seen to have lost its 'spirituality'. In response to suggestions of incorporating English liturgy into the Church, the priest comments that society 'should embrace and accept other languages, rather than having English and only English'.

Reference	The goal of the church	Comments
Orthodox Russian	The goal of the church is to spread the word of Christ, to cater for the spiritual needs of the Russian speaking Orthodox community and lastly to be a 'missionary church' (which is a small but growing goal compared to the preservation of the Russian identity).	The Russian Orthodox church is the physical and spiritual centre of the Russian community in this particular south-eastern Melbourne suburb. Located nearby is the Russian school, the community centre and aged care facilities.
Reformed Chinese (Mandarin)	*Information not available*	–
Reformed English (Dutch heritage)	*Information not available*	The minister commented that he had once considered forming a separate congregation for the Sri Lankan church members but decided against it due to their high level of English proficiency.
Uniting Indonesian	The minister's perception of the church's goal is to become a multicultural church.	The minister emphasised the importance of using one's native language in the religious domain: it 'makes a person feel very close to what they believe'. However, he also remarked that not everyone has the necessary level of fluency in the appropriate speech level, which is needed for religious discourse.
Uniting Oromo	The minister's perception of the church's goal is to reach the Oromo people throughout Australia.	The minister emphasised the importance of using one's native language in the religious domain: '[Oromo is] our heart language . . . you need to use the language you can best express your needs in'.
Uniting Tamil	*Information not available*	The minister commented that the Tamil church exists to fulfil the need to preserve something of the Tamil culture but that they do not wish to isolate themselves from others; they want to have something to offer to 'multicultural Australia'.

References

Aldridge, B.G. (1991) The Reformed Churches in Australian society. In J.W. Deenick (ed.) *A Church En Route: 40 Years of Reformed Churches of Australia.* (pp.149–65). Geelong: Reformed Churches Publishing House.

Alip, F.B. (1993) Social norms and variation in language choice: the case of English-speaking students in Java. PhD thesis, State University of New York.

Anglican Church of Australia (1978) *An Australian Prayer Book.* Canberra: Anglican Church of Australia.

Anglican Church of Australia (1995) *A Prayer Book for Australia.* Canberra: Anglican Church of Australia.

Anglican Diocese of Melbourne (1985) *A Garden of Many Colours: The Report of the Archbishop's Commission on Multicultural Ministry and Mission.* Melbourne: Diocesan Registry, Anglican Diocese of Melbourne.

Anglican General Synod Multicultural Committee (1996) *Disciples of All Nations: Learning to be an International Church within a Multicultural Australia.* Canberra: Anglican Church of Australia.

Ata, A.W. (1988) *Religion and Ethnic Identity* (Vol. 1). Melbourne: Spectrum.

Ata, A.W. (1989) *Religion and Ethnic Identity* (Vol. 2). Melbourne: VICTRACC.

Atta-Bafoe, V.R. and Tovey, P. (1990) What does inculturation mean? In D.R. Holeton (ed.) *Liturgical Inculturation in the Anglican Communion* (p.14). Nottingham: Grove.

Australian Bureau of Statistics (1991) *Census of the Commonwealth of Australia.* Canberra: Australian Bureau of Statistics.

Australian Bureau of Statistics (1996) *Census of the Commonwealth of Australia.* Canberra: Australian Bureau of Statistics.

Australian Bureau of Statistics (2001) *Census of the Commonwealth of Australia*: Canberra; Australian Bureau of Statistics.

Bentley, P. and Hughes, P.J. (1996) *The Uniting Church in Australia.* Canberra: Australian Government Publishing Service.

Bouma, G.D. (1989) Religion and Dutch identity in Australia. In A.W. Ata (ed.) *Religion and Ethnic Identity* (Vol. 2) (pp.34–45). Melbourne: VICTRACC.

Bouma, G.D. (1995) The Dutch in Australia: A case of successful assimilation? In B. Gruter and J. Stracke (eds) *Dutch Australians Taking Stock* (pp. 75–81). Melbourne: Dutch Australian Community Action.

Bouma, G.D. (ed.) (1997) *Many Religions, All Australian: Religious Settlement, Identity and Cultural Diversity.* Melbourne: Christian Research Association.

Boyd, S. (1985) *Language Survival: A Study of Language Contact, Language Shift and Language Choice in Sweden.* (Gothenburg Monographs in Linguistics 6). Göteborg: Department of Linguistics, University of Göteborg.

Buchanan, C. (ed.) (1989) *Lambeth and Liturgy*. Nottingham: Grove.

Church of England (1662) *Book of Common Prayer 1662*.

Clyne, M.G. (1989) Some thoughts on Anglican Church language policy. *Church Scene*, 5–6.

Clyne, M.G. (1991) *Community Languages: The Australian Experience*. Cambridge: Cambridge University Press.

Clyne, M.G. and Kipp, S.J. (1997) Trends and changes in home language use and shift in Australia, 1986–1996. *Journal of Multilingual and Multicultural Development* 18(6), 451–73.

Clyne, M.G. and Kipp, S.J. (1999) *Pluricentric Languages in an Immigrant Context: Spanish, Arabic and Chinese*. Berlin: Mouton de Gruyter.

Crystal, D. (1990) Liturgical language in a sociolinguistic perspective. In D. Jasper and R.C.D. Jasper (eds) *Language and the Worship of the Church* (pp. 120–46). London: Macmillan.

Deenick, J.W. (ed.) (1991) *A Church En Route: 40 Years of Reformed Churches of Australia*. Geelong: Reformed Churches Publishing House.

Dillistone, F.W. (1990) Liturgical forms in word and act. In D. Jasper and R.C.D. Jasper (eds) *Language and the Worship of the Church* (pp. 3–25). London: Macmillan.

Dixon, R.E. (1996) *The Catholics in Australia*. Canberra: Australian Government Publishing Service.

Federal Government (Australia) (1989) *National Agenda for a Multicultural Australia: Sharing Our Future*. Canberra: Australian Government Publishing Service.

Federal Government (Australia) (1999a) *Australian Multiculturalism for a New Century: Towards Inclusiveness*. Canberra: Australian Government Publishing Service.

Federal Government (Australia) (1999b) *A New Agenda for Multicultural Australia*. Canberra: Australian Government Publishing Service.

Ferguson, C.A. (1959) Diglossia. *Word* 15: 325–40.

Fichter, J.H. (1951) *Dynamics of a City Church*. Chicago: University of Chicago Press.

Fishman, J.A. (1991) *Reversing Language Shift*. Clevedon: Multilingual Matters.

Fishman, J.A. (1996) *In Praise of the Beloved Language: A Comparative View of Positive Ethnolinguistic Consciousness*. Berlin: Mouton de Gruyter.

Garner, M. (1988). Church and community: Russians in Melbourne. In A.W. Ata (ed.) *Religion and Ethnic Identity* (Vol. 1) (pp. 51–71). Melbourne: Spectrum.

Godley, S. and Hughes, P.J. (1996) *The Eastern Orthodox in Australia*. Canberra: Australian Government Publishing Service.

Haugen, E. (1953) *The Norwegian Language in America* (2 vols). Philadelphia: University of Pennsylvania Press.

Hofman, J. E. (1966) Mother tongue retentiveness in ethnic parishes. In J.A. Fishman (ed.) *Language Loyalty in the United States* (pp. 127–55). The Hague: Mouton.

Houston, J. (ed.) (1986) *The Cultured Pearl*. Melbourne: Victorian Council of Churches.

Houston, J. (1993) *Seeds Blowing in the Wind: Review of Multicultural Ministry and Mission*. Melbourne: Anglican Diocese of Melbourne.

Hughes, P.J. (1993) *Religion: A View from the Australian Census*. Melbourne: Christian Research Association.

Hughes, P.J. (1996) *The Baptists in Australia*. Canberra: Australian Government Publishing Service.

Imberger, B. (1979) Language use and language maintenance in a small German religious community: a study of trilingualism and triglossia in the Temple Society, with special reference to 'mixed marriages'. BA (Hons) thesis, Monash University.

Jasper, D. and Jasper, R.C.D. (1990) *Language and the Worship of the Church*. London: Macmillan.

Katsikis, M. (1993) Language attitudes, ethnicity and language maintenance: A case study of second generation Greek-Australians. BA (Hons) thesis, Monash University.

Kipp, S.J. (1999) Networks and language use in an historical context. *Monash University Linguistic Papers* 2(1): 25–32.

Kipp, S.J., Clyne, M.G. and Pauwels, A. (1995) *Immigration and Australia's Language Resources*. Canberra: Australian Government Publishing Service.

Lehmann, H. (1981) South Australian German Lutherans in the second half of the nineteenth century: A case of rejected assimilation. *Journal of Intercultural Studies* 2(2), 24–43.

Lewins, F. (1978) *The Myth of the Universal Church*. Canberra: Australian National University Press.

Lloyd-Smith, A.V. (1996) The role of the Saturday School in Latvian language maintenance in Melbourne. BA (Hons) thesis, Monash University.

Luther, Martin (1530) *An Open Letter on Translating*. (Gary Mann trans.). On www at http://www.iclnet.org/pub/resources/text/wittenberg/luther/luther-translate.txt

Lutheran Church of Australia (1998) *Commission on Worship*. Canberra: Lutheran Church of Australia.

Mitchell, A.G. and Delbridge, A. (1965) *The Pronunciation of English in Australia*. Sydney: Angus and Robertson.

Noll, M.A. (1997) *Turning Points. Decisive Moments in the History of Christianity*. Grand Rapids, MI: Baker Books.

Ortiz, M. (1996) *One New People: Models for Developing a Multiethnic Church*. Illinois: Inter Varsity Press.

Overberg, H. (1981) Dutch in Victoria 1947–1980: community and ideology. *Journal of Intercultural Studies* 2(1), 17–36.

Putniņš, A. (1981) *Latvians in Australia: Alienation and Assimilation*. Canberra: Australian National University Press.

Reformed Churches of Australia (1962) *Acts of Synod of the Reformed Churches of Australia*. Canberra: Reformed Churches of Australia.

Silkalns, E. (1988) The role of the Latvian Churches in Australia in the maintenance of the Latvian ethnic identity. In A.W. Ata (ed.) *Religion and Ethnic Identity* (Vol. 1) (pp. 167–76). Melbourne: Spectrum.

Smolicz, J.J. (1976) Ethnic cultures in Australian society: A question of cultural interaction. In S. Murray-Smith (ed.) *Melbourne Studies in Education* (pp. 41–74). Melbourne: Melbourne University Press.

Smolicz, J.J. (1981) Core values and cultural identity. *Ethnic and Racial Studies* 4, 75–90.

Smolicz, J.J. (1994) Multiculturalism, religion and education. *Education and Society* 12(1), 22–47.

Smolicz, J.J. and Lean, R. (1979) Parental attitudes to cultural and linguistic pluralism in Australia: A humanistic sociological approach. *Australian Journal of Education* 23(3), 227–49.

Smolicz, J.J., Lee, L., Murugaian, M. and Secombe, M.J. (1990) Language as a core value of culture among tertiary students of Chinese and Indian origin in Australia. *Journal of Asia Pacific Communication* 1(1), 229–46.

Smolicz, J.J. and Secombe, M.J. (1985) Community languages, core values and cultural maintenance: The Australian experience with special reference to Greek, Latvian and Polish groups. In M.G. Clyne (ed.) *Australia, Meeting Place of Languages* (Pacific Linguistics C92) (pp. 11–38). Canberra: Research School of Pacific Studies, Australian National University.

Smolicz, J.J. and Secombe, M.J. (1989) Types of language activation and evaluation in an ethnically plural society. In U. Ammon (ed.) *Status and Function of Languages and Language Varieties* (pp. 478–511). Berlin: de Gruyter.

Tkalcevic, M. (1988) *Croats in Australia*. Melbourne: VICTRACC.

Uniting Church in Australia (1985) *Minutes and Reports of the Fourth Assembly of the Uniting Church in Australia*. Melbourne: Joint Board of Christian Education.

Van Zetten, R.J. and Deenick, J.W. (1991) The foundational years: 1951–1960. In J.W. Deenick (ed.) *A Church En Route: 40 Years of Reformed Churches of Australia* (pp. 20–51). Geelong: Reformed Churches Publishing House.

Vanderbom, J.F.H. (1991) The faith of our fathers. In J.W. Deenick (ed.) *A Church En Route: 40 Years of Reformed Churches of Australia* (pp. 1–19). Geelong: Reformed Churches Publishing House.

Varcoe, G. (1997) Principles of inculturation in an Australian context. *Australian Journal of Liturgy* 6(2), 63–7.

Waddams, H. (1964) *Meeting the Orthodox Churches*. London: SCM.

Warren, R. (1990) Music and the liturgy. In D. Jasper and R.C.D. Jasper (eds) *Lanuage and the Worship of the Church* (pp. 196–211). London: Macmillan.

Wilcox, C.E. (1994) *Ethnic and Cross Cultural Ministries Handbook*. Melbourne: Baptist Union of Victoria.

Woods, A.V. (1999) Latvian language maintenance in Melbourne: A 'core value' approach. *Monash University Linguistics Papers* 2(1), 33–44.

Wycliffe Bible Translators (1999) *Vision 2025 Resolution*.

Index